"Those who tell our stories show us who we are. Frank Rees's biography of the great Baptist preacher, historian, and educator D. Mervyn Himbury provides the most telling insight into who we are as Victorian Baptists and, even more, who we are still called to be. The life story of this exceptional man is a gift to all of us who remain invested in the Australian church and its mission."

—SIMON CAREY HOLT,
Senior Minister, Collins Street Baptist Church

"Rees succeeds magnificently in his aim of offering a biography which enables the reader to do theology better. In relating the life and thought of Mervyn Himbury, an exceptional preacher and theological educator, the author tells a good story very well indeed, exploring Baptist tradition in both British and Australian cultures, and exposing the theological roots of a radical religious and political freedom."

—PAUL S. FIDDES,
University of Oxford

"This is an excellent theological biography of Mervyn Himbury, a Welsh Baptist preacher and teacher who became a pioneering theological college principal in Australia. In his affectionate, readable, and scholarly account, Frank Rees has not only made an important contribution to Australian religious history but provided a model of how such biographies may have a theological relevance far beyond any provincial interests."

—KEN MANLEY,
Whitley College, University of Melbourne (formerly)

"Here is the story of one of the great nonconformist (unusual) Australian Baptist leaders of the past one hundred years. After reading this book, written by the student of his who perhaps knew him best, I am reminded of the personal debt I owe to Mervyn Himbury as well as the debt all Victorian Baptists owe to him whether they knew him or not, whether they liked him or not."

—ALAN MARR,
former Director of Ministries, Baptist Union of Victoria

"In his finely researched biography, Rees sheds light on a complex character, D. Mervyn Himbury. Rees expertly sketches the diverse forces that shaped Himbury and deals sympathetically but not uncritically with his subject's passions, struggles, and faith. This book is not just for Baptists (that curious breed emerging in tumultuous seventeenth-century Europe) but for anyone who steps into the unknown in response to a persistent 'inner call.'"

—MARITA MUNRO,
Whitley College (formerly)

Mervyn Himbury:
Principal and Preacher

Mervyn Himbury:
Principal and Preacher

Frank D. Rees

WIPF & STOCK · Eugene, Oregon

MERVYN HIMBURY: PRINCIPAL AND PREACHER

Copyright © 2022 Frank D. Rees. All rights reserved. Except for brief quotations in critical publications or reviews, no part of this book may be reproduced in any manner without prior written permission from the publisher. Write: Permissions, Wipf and Stock Publishers, 199 W. 8th Ave., Suite 3, Eugene, OR 97401.

Wipf & Stock
An Imprint of Wipf and Stock Publishers
199 W. 8th Ave., Suite 3
Eugene, OR 97401

www.wipfandstock.com

PAPERBACK ISBN: 978-1-6667-9132-7
HARDCOVER ISBN: 978-1-6667-9131-0
EBOOK ISBN: 978-1-6667-9133-4

MARCH 29, 2022 11:11 AM

Unless noted otherwise, Scripture quotations are from The Authorized (King James) Version. Rights in the Authorized Version in the United Kingdom are vested in the Crown. Reproduced by permission of the Crown's patentee, Cambridge University Press.

Scripture quotations marked NRSV are from New Revised Standard Version Bible, copyright © 1989 National Council of the Churches of Christ in the United States of America. Used by permission. All rights reserved worldwide.

Contents

List of Tables | vii

List of Figures | viii

Acknowledgments | ix

INTRODUCTION | xi

CHAPTER 1   MERVYN HIMBURY | 1

CHAPTER 2   A WELSH BAPTIST | 23

CHAPTER 3   MINISTERIAL EDUCATION | 58

CHAPTER 4   HISTORY PROFESSOR | 101

CHAPTER 5   THEOLOGICAL EDUCATOR | 133

CHAPTER 6   A LONG AND WINDING ROAD | 170

CHAPTER 7   THE WORD IN THE WORLD | 198

CHAPTER 8   PRECIOUS IN THE SIGHT OF GOD | 222

PRAYER OF THANKSGIVING | 236

Appendix A: Minute of Appreciation | 239

Appendix B: Eulogy by Rev. Milton Warn,
    First Registrar of Whitley College | 243

Appendix C: Sermon Preached by Rev. Jim Barr,
   of Canberra Baptist Church | 247

Appendix D: Thanksgiving Prayer Offered by Rev. Alan Marr,
   Director of Ministries, Baptist Union of Victoria | 253

Appendix E: Thanksgiving Service by Rev. Dr. Frank Rees | 255

Bibliography | 261

Index | 265

List of Tables

Table 1: Statistics Published by the Baptist Union of Great Britain | 39

Table 2: Post-war Enrollment by Faculty | 69

Table 3: Student Housing Options in 1948 | 70

Table 4: Records of Himbury's Preaching While Resident at Regent's Park College | 96

List of Figures

Marion and Mervyn Himbury, wedding day, 1951. | 129

The Himbury family soon before leaving for Australia. | 129

Regent's Park College, faculty and students, 1949. Mervyn Himbury is on the far right, middle row. | 130

Cover page of the Order of Service for Mervyn Himbury's ordination, June 1950. | 130

The opening of Whitley College, February 1965. Left to right: Miss Rachel Thomas, Dame Pattie Menzies, Mrs Marion Himbury, Mrs Amelia Lewis, Maelor Himbury, Prime Minister Sir Robert Menzies, Principal Mervyn Himbury. (Miss Thomas and Mrs Lewis are aunts of Mervyn Himbury.) | 131

The Mervyn Himbury Theological Studies Centre, Whitley College. | 131

Ystrad Mynach Stars Rugby Club, 1913–1914. Reginald Himbury is on the far right, back row. | 132

Acknowledgments

It was Ken Manley, successor to Mervyn Himbury as principal of Whitley College, who said to me one day that someone really ought to write this biography and urged me to do so. In the event, I have been greatly assisted by Ken's encouragement and guidance, and his detailed reading of chapters along the way.

I am indebted to colleagues at the South Wales Baptist College for access to the archives and historical sources, and especially to Rev. Dr. Craig Gardiner and his family for their hospitality and local guidance. Similarly, I am grateful for access to the Angus Library and Archive at Regent's Park College, Oxford, and especially for the encouragement of Professor Paul Fiddes.

In Melbourne, special thanks are due to Maelor Himbury for providing me with his father's recorded recollections, which were an invaluable resource; and to Rev. Dr. Marita Munro and Dr. Julie Morsillo who also provided me with copies of recollections they had recorded.

Similarly, the Collins Street Baptist Church has provided me with access to their exceptional collection of recorded sermons by Mervyn Himbury, on which parts of this biography are based.

I am grateful to the Victorian Baptist Historical Society for permission to use parts of an article published in their journal, *Our Yesterdays*.

Special thanks are owed to Whitley College, particularly Ms. Lorraine Mitchell, for access to library and archival materials. During my own time as principal at Whitley College, Rev. Jillian Stewart assisted me in preserving materials from Himbury's funeral, which have also been an exceptional resource. In addition, I thank those colleagues who have allowed me to use their prayers or sermon notes from Himbury's funeral.

I am also grateful for the exceptional skill and patient editorial assistance of Alix Kwan, who helped to make the manuscript much more readable.

Through the time of researching and writing this book, I have been encouraged by colleagues in the University of Divinity, especially the vice chancellor, Professor Peter Sherlock, as well as by many other colleagues within the Baptist community in Victoria.

My deepest thanks go to my wife, Merilyn, and our family, who have lived with this work along the way and encouraged me when I most needed it.

Finally, I wish to give thanks to God for the life of Mervyn Himbury. There is a renewed interest among Baptists in the idea of saints. These are lives which provide inspiration, not by their "perfection" but rather by their genuine humanity, their faith, courage, and dedication to life with God. Here is one such life, for which I am deeply grateful.

Introduction

In 1958 the Baptists of Victoria, Australia, made a courageous decision. They decided to invite a young Welshman, who had never been to Australia, whom none of them had ever met, and who had no experience in leading a college, to be principal of the Baptist College of Victoria. Into his hands they would entrust the training of their pastors; potentially for the next thirty years. What is more, they also envisaged that he would spearhead the development of a new college—not merely a new building to replace their decrepit and cramped facilities, but a different kind of college altogether. The Baptist Union of Victoria had decided also to establish a residential college of the University of Melbourne, as all the larger Christian churches had done almost a hundred years earlier. Now, the Baptists too would take their place within the university. Their future pastors would be educated to a higher standard within the company of other aspiring professionals and community leaders. For this purpose, a young and energetic academic—already making his name as a Baptist historian and teacher, and especially an outstanding preacher and communicator—was chosen.

This is the story of that man, David Mervyn Himbury, and his journey from the coal-mining valleys of South Wales to an academic life in Britain and then Australia. Preacher, historian, pastor, and administrator, Principal Mervyn Himbury was an exceptional figure in both the academic and church communities. He began with a small and impoverished college with twenty-five students and just three faculty members, none of whom had doctoral degrees. Within one generation the new college had more than four hundred students and ten faculty members—most Himbury's own former students, now holding doctoral qualifications. Several generations of students owe so much to his vision and the college he created. Many more, who did not know him at all, have benefited from the advances he led in theological education. Far beyond the building of a college, his contribution remains in the teachers and scholars he inspired, the Baptist heritage of religious freedom he so valued and passed on, and his eloquent challenge to engage with a changing world in caring and creative service.

To write a biography is to tell a story. It is necessarily only part of the story of its subject. For many persons of prominence, whether for their achievements or notoriety, there are often multiple biographies. That is because telling a life story is always a matter of someone's perspective. The sources available and how they are used reflect the writer and their approach, as well as their subject. The decision to write a biography is itself a value judgment, recognizing that a life story is worthy of that much effort, and that the story to be told has value and significance for a wider audience. So it is with this biography of Mervyn Himbury. His life story needs to be told.

James McClendon, a prominent Baptist theologian from the United States of America, proposed the study of biography as a new approach to theology.[1] He contended that the use of life stories could transform Christianity from a religion focused on doctrine or belief into one grounded in values and practices, a living faith. His three-volume work *Systematic Theology* quite distinctively began with ethics, which he proposed should concern the study of character and convictions. For McClendon, convictions characterize a person. Such convictions are deeply held but may not always be explicitly recognized or articulated. A community, such as a local church or a denomination, is similarly characterized by its convictions. In exploring biography as theology, McClendon offered life stories that would exemplify and characterize the Christian faith. The persons whose lives he presents are not saints in the sense of flawless or perfect people (as if there are such people); rather, these are genuinely human persons from whom we can learn, assisting us to affirm our own values and choose wisely our own pathways. They are characters, whose life stories allow us to develop our own theology and faith.

Mervyn Himbury was indeed a character. He used to assert that a college community needed a few characters, by which he meant somewhat unusual and challenging personalities. He was such a person. To his students and to those who heard him preach, he was an impressive person. His physical presence always called for a response. Often, that simply

---

1. McClendon, *Biography as Theology*.

meant listening more intently. His Welsh accent and style of speech were melodious and inviting. His preaching was inspirational and sometimes spellbinding. His prayers could lift one to new heights of hope and call forth depths of faith. Whether in the lecture room or the pulpit, he was at heart a storyteller—from the history of the church or the sacred text—and his invitation was always to become part of this great story.

Himbury was an influential leader—in the Baptist Church, undoubtedly—but also more broadly in theological education in Australia. By the sheer force of his personality he, with the assistance of several other key leaders, pressed the Baptist union to deliver upon its vision of a new college, linked to the University of Melbourne—even when those in denominational leadership doubted its practicability or indeed actively sought to block the project. Himbury's own experience in Cardiff convinced him of the value of the scheme. He was passionate about its vision and drove it forward until the day he stood beside the prime minister of Australia as he opened Whitley College. Himbury's struggle to then develop and defend the college is at the heart of his life story. Moreover, he was continually seeking a relevant and appropriate form of ministerial education for those who would lead the church in a constantly changing society. He had known already the decline of the churches in Wales and saw the same trends developing in Australia. But he knew, too, the passion for justice and peace that gripped the young people of the middle twentieth century and he yearned for a church that would listen to them and respond with a word of hope. His vision for the church and for theological education arose from that concern. Not for him was the focus upon training in the latest "techniques" of ministry, nor a stolid clutching after classical subjects without regard to context and the changing world. Having journeyed to a new country and situation, he wanted a genuinely theological approach to ministry and education, and continually asked how this could be achieved. What kind of leaders could enable the church to respond to a rapidly changing world, and how should those leaders best be educated? Through his entire career, Himbury worked to provide innovative and effective answers to this challenge.

Mervyn Himbury was a historian of some renown. His initial university studies were unimpressive, to the point of failure, except in his chosen field of history. There he found a passion, which also fitted with his faith. Here was a story to be told; a human story but also a story in which we could learn of the wonders of God's presence with people—at least at times. His preaching was enriched by his study of history. His leadership in the church and in the academy were grounded in his Baptist commitment to liberty of conscience for all. In the first half of his academic career, he became widely known for his expert knowledge and analysis of the radical puritan groups that included and shaped the Baptist movement.

To tell the story of Mervyn Himbury's life, then, requires gathering together these many elements. It is the story of a public life. Himbury was at once an impressive public figure and a very shy man. Though he might often have spoken of his own views and convictions, he did not easily disclose himself to others. The sources left to us are mainly publicly available records and official documents. This biography draws upon his publications, some of which include expressions of his personal concerns for his students. It also refers to the official records of Whitley College and the Baptist Union of Victoria, and of the two colleges in Britain where he studied, in Cardiff and Oxford.

In terms of his personal life, however, it is fortunate that three very helpful sources are available. Marita Munro undertook a doctoral study of Baptist life in Victoria during the decades of Himbury's leadership, and as part of this project she recorded interviews with both Mervyn and Marion Himbury. The transcripts of these conversations were a very helpful source, as were a set of recollections recorded by Julie Morsillo, a personal friend of the Himbury family in later years. Most helpful, however, was a set of recollections Himbury himself recorded quite late in his life, particularly relating to his life in Wales. Transcribing these recordings allowed me to hear the man himself once again and to appreciate all the features of his faith, humor, insight, and compassion.

Mervyn Himbury was quintessentially a preacher. This was his calling. Thus, the story of his life begins and ends with consideration of him as a preacher. In a sense, then, the most valuable resources for this study are the recordings and, in some instances, notes (made by others) from sermons he delivered. Himbury famously preached only from a few notes, often on a small piece of paper: the proverbial "back of an envelope." The Collins Street Baptist Church, however, has approximately one hundred cassette recordings of Himbury's sermons and talks given over several decades. My transcription of a number of these has, again, provided foundational material for the later reflections upon his life and ministry. In this process, it was especially helpful to discover an unmarked recording of a thanksgiving service held at the time of his retirement, at which he offered his own reflections upon his ministry at the college.

INTRODUCTION

Clearly an essential element in writing a biography is memory. The nature and function of memory has been the subject of study in many disciplines. Within theology there has been a renewed interest in the character of "re-membering." Here, shared memory enables both individuals and groups to reclaim, or be given afresh, a sense of membership in a common identity. This is surely one of the crucial purposes of preaching; telling the stories of a community so that they remain aware of their history and can participate in their heritage.

Memory, however, is an ambiguous phenomenon. Himbury's recollections recorded late in his life were presumably selective and perhaps even distorted by time. Clearly some of these, such as the story of him preaching his first "sermon" at age three, were derived from other family memories and were given that significance because of his life as a preacher. Studies of memory distinguish various effects, such as the influence of what happened first in a series of events (the primacy effect) as opposed to what happened most recently (the recency effect). Similarly, the impact of events upon the person remembering them, whether at the time or how they are later understood, will also affect memory. The way a story is told, including this one, will reflect some of these aspects of memory.

My personal engagement with Mervyn Himbury's biography is a critical element in the story that follows. I was a resident of Whitley College during my years studying at the University of Melbourne, and then studying theology as an ordination candidate for the Baptist ministry. Himbury was my college principal and my mentor. His direct intervention made it possible for me, a boy from a poor home and resource-deprived country high school, to gain entry to the university. He encouraged my studies and exercised a pastoral concern for me. In due course he conducted my wedding service.

Among my treasured possessions are two handwritten cards from Himbury, sent when I completed my bachelor of divinity and finally left Whitley College. He had more than once publicly lauded my examination results, to my great embarrassment—but here drew attention to my degree being awarded with first class honors (something he had achieved in his own university studies) and drew a link between such achievements and his own vision for the college. In the first of these cards, sent immediately the results were announced, he wrote:

> This is an amazing achievement and opens up many possibilities for your future. The gifts which God has given you put a great burden on your shoulders for much is expected of those to

whom much has been given. May your future realize all of your present potential.

Those words of challenge have remained with me all my life. In the other card, sent both to my wife and me, he congratulated us both on examination results, saying that it had been a good year for us. He then added these poignant words:

> Your future has almost unlimited potential and were I not so content with what Providence has done for me, I would envy you.
>
> Naturally, I am particularly delighted with Frank's "first"...
>
> This is one of those times when all the work that we did in building up Whitley and changing our system of theological education is very worthwhile. You now have a key to open many doors and I am certain you will not allow it to rust.

After my doctoral studies in Manchester, UK, where he also visited me to see how I was going and to ask what I intended to do next, I accepted a call to be minister of the Hobart Baptist Church, where Himbury preached for my induction service. One of his ambitions for me was fulfilled when I was appointed as professor of systematic theology at Whitley College and, perhaps even more so, as principal. It was my honor to conduct his funeral service in the college chapel.

This biography arises from a personal relationship and while it recounts some of the critical personal events in Himbury's life and family, these are not the primary focus. Rather, the biography is focused on Himbury's public life, his academic career, and ministry. For this reason, it does not follow a chronological path, but begins with a portrait of Himbury as a preacher before delving into specific aspects of his early life, his education, and his time as principal of the Baptist college.

Himbury was a Welsh Baptist and each of those descriptors was important to him, as was his education as a Baptist pastor, and all of these topics are explored in this retelling of his life's story. The biography recounts his time as a history professor, the story of building and defending the Baptist college over which he presided, as well as looking in depth at Himbury as a preacher. After his death in 2008, it was clear that Himbury had made an immense contribution in many spheres. Some of the items from services celebrating his life are provided at the conclusion of this book. It is my belief that Himbury's life was devoted to the biblical conviction that God's word will not turn out to be empty or worthless but will achieve the purpose for which God has sent it forth. Of this word, Mervyn Himbury remained a faithful servant.

CHAPTER 1

Mervyn Himbury
Principal Preacher

IN FEBRUARY 1959 TWO great Baptist preachers came to Melbourne. One stayed for four weeks and conducted a highly successful evangelistic crusade that in some ways changed the life of the city and its churches for decades to come. The other came and stayed for the remainder of his days, forty-nine years. He also had a profound influence on the life of the churches, but particularly the education of ministers in a rapidly changing world.

When Billy Graham (1918–2017) came to Melbourne, he was already well-known in evangelical and Baptist circles for his crusade ministry in other parts of the world. What happened in Melbourne, however, was at that time unprecedented. Such large numbers of people attended that the organizing committee had to keep changing the venue: from the West Melbourne Stadium to the Sidney Myer Music Bowl, where as many as seventy thousand people attended. The culmination event on March 15 saw more than 143,000 attend the largest-ever gathering in Melbourne Cricket Ground. Innovative use of technology was a feature as well, including television programs, with telephone counseling offered to respondents. As many as ten thousand phoned and overwhelmed the telephone exchanges. There was landline transmission of video and audio to country regions. Graham had a powerful influence on a generation of local church ministers and preachers.

David Mervyn Himbury (1922–2008) came to Melbourne at the invitation of the Baptist Union of Victoria. He, too, had a reputation for his preaching ministry, and for his theological teaching and scholarship as a Baptist historian. Himbury was to become the founding principal of a new Baptist college, already planned as the centenary project of the Baptist union. He would lead the Baptists of Victoria during a period of immense social and educational change, growth, and more than a little tension. He would push the boundaries of church life toward a more international vision, while affirming deeply the essential mission of the church within the world. For Himbury, this was the fundamental role of the preacher; to provide a vision of the world in which God is both present and active, and a vision of the church as a participant in that world. This understanding of church and world was precisely what was needed in this time and Himbury's imaginative and evocative preaching became a model for many who came under his influence and example. His mission was not only to preach but to produce preachers.

It is helpful to begin with Himbury's formation and approach as a preacher. His understanding of the purpose of preaching, and his approach to it, were shaped by his early experience. I describe here Himbury's own preaching, and some of the contexts in which he preached, before reflecting upon his understanding of the importance of preaching and its purpose in the life and mission of the church. Finally, his contribution as a teacher of preaching is considered.

The Making of a Preacher

In many ways, Mervyn Himbury was born to preach. The story was told within the family that he preached his first sermon when three years old. He placed a book on the back of a chair, stood behind it and declared, "Salvation." In an important sense, this was the message he would deliver all his life.

There were several crucial influences in Himbury's formation and development as a preacher. The first of these was his home church environment, which placed a great premium on preaching and encouraged young Christians to try it and to develop their skills in this form of ministry. In addition, the minister in his church conducted classes for young people to learn to pray in public. After each child had prayed, they would be encouraged with helpful suggestions. Here we note the beginnings of one of the most important dimensions of Himbury's public ministry.

At age fourteen he preached his first sermon in the local church (Hengoed Welsh Baptist Church) and when he was fifteen he was quite often preaching twice on a Sunday, for which he was paid ten shillings. This was a significant contribution to the family finances. What is noteworthy here is the willingness of local churches to allow and to nurture this ministry. The context of the local church as the place where future leaders are identified and equipped is a vital dimension of healthy Baptist church life.

Himbury's uncle Idris Thomas, his mother's brother, was another important influence on his formation both as a preacher and a pastor. Thomas was an ordained Baptist minister, considered a very accomplished preacher, who delivered his sermons in fluent, refined Welsh. From 1937 until his death in 1962 he served the Tabernacle at Cefn Mawr, near Wrexham. For a short time early in his career Mervyn lived with his uncle, during his own pastorate at Chester Road, Wrexham.

There are several vital aspects to his uncle's influence upon Mervyn. First is his commitment to preparation. Mervyn told a story about the day after his first Sunday evening sermon at Wrexham. His uncle asked him for his text for the next Sunday. The young preacher was shocked by the question: he had not had time to prepare a sermon for next week! His uncle explained that he was not asking for the sermon, just the text. The preacher needed to be reflecting on the text all through the week and the sermon would emerge from that process of reflection. Two things are critical here: the centrality of the biblical text and the importance of "living with" the text as the process of preparing a sermon.

Mervyn also recalled that his uncle would ask him on a Saturday night, "What have you for the saints tomorrow?" When Mervyn outlined his sermon plan, his uncle would make comments such as, "You have two sermons there," or, "You have the climax at the beginning, it should be at the end." Here, too, a commitment to structure and the form of the sermon, and the process and experience of the hearers and not just the "argument" of the sermon, was of vital importance.

Voice production was another feature of the Welsh preacher's preparation. I recall Himbury describing how, in earlier days, preachers would work on their voice production by climbing opposing hills, in the one of the Welsh valleys, and calling to one another. Some of the Welsh chapels were large auditoriums, seating many hundreds of people, and in the days before microphones they needed strong voices to be heard by all. I also remember Himbury explaining the importance of relaxing the stomach muscles to avoid attempting to produce one's voice from the throat muscles only. Mervyn recalled also his uncle engaging in voice exercises, warming up his voice by singing scales in the car on the way to a service. These practical activities were part of the preparation and commitment of the preacher.

Another anecdote concerning his uncle indicated a different aspect of Mervyn's formation as a preacher. This has to do with the crucial relationship between preaching and pastoral care. While he personally was in demand as an occasional preacher, his understanding of preaching was primarily that it belongs in the local church and is an expression of, and foundational to, pastoral ministry. On one occasion Mervyn visited an older member of his congregation, who related to him her deep regret that the person she had loved dearly long ago had married someone else, while she had remained a spinster. When he went home, he told his uncle that he had spent the afternoon listening to an old lady "ramble on," while there were many important things he could have been doing. His uncle's response shocked him: "Don't you dare speak like that. You probably did more good today than you'll do for the rest of the week. . . . You listened. You didn't have to do any more." But, he went on, there is an extra benefit: "If you have your text in mind, you can be working on how it relates to this person. You are not wasting your time at all."

The fact that Himbury recalled this event late in his life, reflecting on himself at several levels, shows not only its importance in his early formation but also the commitment he made (perhaps despite his nature and inclinations) to focus on people, listening to what was important to them, and bringing this perspective into his sermon preparation and prayers. Despite appearances at times, he was, in fact, a very good listener when needed and many were helped by his pastoral attention.

The final element to note here is the significance of example. Himbury's essential approach to learning to preach was not instruction but example. He learned from others. In the context of his youth and his early ministry, preachers talked with each other about their sermons, shared their preparations, and contributed to each other's preaching in practical ways. This was to remain a feature of Himbury's life. For example, for some years he played golf on Monday mornings with several other ministers and their conversation included discussion of their sermons.

What and Where

Until his very last years, in declining health, he was in demand as an occasional preacher; but he was also committed to the task of regular preaching with a single congregation. He had continued regular Sunday preaching at Croes-y-Parc Baptist Church, in the Vale of Glamorgan, during his years at the college in Cardiff (1951–1958). During his years at the college in Melbourne he undertook interim minister appointments at various suburban Baptist churches for some months on end. He served the Ivanhoe Baptist Church from late 1973 until June 1975. The church records show that he preached most Sundays, led the mid-week meetings and "involved himself in the life of the church far beyond what we have any right to expect from a man already so heavily committed."[1] When not otherwise committed, he preached very often at evening services at Collins Street Baptist Church. After he retired from Whitley College, he took up a role as associate minister at Collins Street. This is the one context in which there are some minimal records of his preaching activity. Himbury himself did not keep such records.

Nonetheless, it is possible to gain some indication of the breadth of his contribution as a visiting or occasional preacher from other records and various personal anecdotes.

The recently published history of the Ashburton Baptist Church records that Mervyn Himbury was the occasional preacher for the opening of their new building on July 26, 1959.[2] Later that same year, he preached at the annual assembly of the Baptist Union of Tasmania in Hobart. In 1962 he preached to a gathering of more than two thousand people for the opening of the new campus of the Baptist College of New South Wales, later known as Morling College.

In personal reflections recorded by family friend Julie Morsillo, it is noted that he preached at a "Pleasant Sunday Afternoon" in the Essendon Town Hall—on this occasion as a stand-in for the Anglican Archbishop of Melbourne. Another time he preached at an ecumenical Good Friday service held at a drive-in theater.[3] Still another time, he preached for a

---

1. Ivanhoe Baptist Church, *1974 Annual Report*, kindly supplied by Mr. Brian Sherry.

2. Otzen, *So Great a Cloud of Witnesses*, 94.

3. I recall there was some criticism from more traditionally minded Baptists of this, to which Himbury responded that he would preach the Gospel whenever and wherever he was invited.

Baptist youth rally, as part of the annual "Country to City Weekend." All these events were early in his time in Melbourne, but the pattern of these commitments continued throughout the next decades.

In addition, he accepted invitations to preach at services for other Christian churches, as well as ecumenical events, and made television presentations for the Christian Television Association. He preached one time for one of the Catholic churches in Brunswick. After the service, the parish priest invited him for a cup of tea and said how much he had enjoyed the sermon. Nonetheless, he would not be inviting Himbury to preach there again. Surprised, Himbury asked why. The priest explained that if they heard him again the congregation would begin to expect a superb sermon like that every Sunday.

It is something of an insight into Himbury's sense of the importance of preaching, and his own need to be seen as a good preacher (if not the best!), that he retained and recounted many of these stories. A further insight into that aspect of his self was his public reference to Rev. Dr. Graeme Garrett, at that time a member of his college staff, as the only man who could make him sin. By this, he explained, he meant that when he heard Garrett preach, he sinned the sin of envy. He wanted to be that good a preacher!

Several personal anecdotes depict something of Himbury's enigmatic presence as the visiting preacher. Rev. Dr. Geoffrey Blackburn recalled the time when he was pastor of the Heathmont Baptist Church and had asked Himbury to preach for the Palm Sunday service. Mervyn arrived with one piece of paper with just a few notes on it. When he informed Blackburn that he was going to preach on an Old Testament text, Blackburn was quite dismayed, but he later said that Himbury preached a very fine Palm Sunday sermon. This sense of surprise, working from an unusual text, sometimes with a quite peculiar image, was characteristic of Himbury's preaching. To try to address the story of Palm Sunday without its Old Testament context and significance would surely be a significant failing.

Rev. Ian Carmichael offered this recollection of his induction to the Paisley Street Baptist Church, Footscray, at the conclusion of his college training:

> It was, I think, November 1985. When we were planning the service, I asked my pastor, Alan May of Brunswick Baptist Church, to pray the induction prayer and Mervyn Himbury, principal of the college, to preach. So I thought! Come Sunday morning,

we'd all gathered in the vestry and Mervyn said something like, "I'll be looking forward to hearing Alan preach, if he arrives." (Alan had been delayed a little.)

I said, "Oh no, I've asked Alan to pray; I'd asked you to preach, I thought."

"Ooh, well," said Mervyn. "I think I'll go for a little walk and gather some thoughts!"

Which he did, and came back; we settled and went on with the service. I don't really remember the text (I think it was in Isaiah.) I do remember the illustration. "The job of the prophet, the job of the preacher, is rather like a postman delivering parcels which have the address tags missing. He has to go to all the people and say, 'I have a package. Is it for you? Is it for you?'"

What a brilliant man, whom I counted as a good friend! To be surprised with a preaching task within a few minutes of the service time, and to draw out something entirely appropriate—as far as I was concerned. He said later, "Well, I haven't preached that since 1956 back in Wales." He had a parcel. That one was for me!

In a similar vein, at Himbury's funeral Milton Warn (who was registrar of Whitley College for many years) told of a day when the students gathered in the chapel for the weekly service, but no one had turned up to preach. With only a few minutes' notice, Himbury preached. Afterward he said to Warn, "I'd rather die than say I'm not ready to preach."[4]

There were many other special occasions for which Himbury preached, including my own induction as minister of the Hobart Baptist Church on November 11, 1983. After this service, a colleague made the observation that Himbury really was "a preacher's preacher," who not only provided an excellent example of preaching but also powerfully stressed the importance and value of this form of ministry. The sermon was based on the story found in Jeremiah 36, where a scroll of Jeremiah's prophecy is presented to the king, who orders it to be cut to pieces and burned. Subsequently Jeremiah dictates the message all over again. Himbury suggested in this sermon that the question for the church is "what will become of the message that is preached?" It is the congregation who must take the message to the people for whom it is intended; but again, they may rip it up or burn it. So the pastor must preach it all again and the people must carry the message again, and again. In this sermon, which

---

4. Elements of this tribute are included in chapter 8, "Precious in the Sight of God," and the full text is provided at Appendix B.

Himbury preached in a number of places, we see his fundamental idea of the role of preaching—that it serves the people of the church in their witness in the wider community.

Himbury's habit of working from a small piece of paper as his only notes was often remarked upon. Once he was invited to preach at the two morning services of the Blackburn Baptist Church. He took as his text the stories in Luke 15 of the two sons, the prodigal and his brother. At one service he preached on the prodigal. For the other service, he turned over the envelope on which he had written his notes and preached about the elder son.

There is one story of his work as a visiting preacher that Himbury himself loved to tell. Rev. Gardiner C. Taylor was minister of the Concord Baptist Church of Christ in Brooklyn, New York (a position he held for forty-two years). It happened that Taylor was in Melbourne once, when he heard Mervyn Himbury pray, and the prayer so impressed him that he invited Himbury to come to New York to preach for anniversary services in May 1967. In the event, the local church leadership was not impressed with the idea of them paying to bring a white man to preach in their church. Other African American pastors warned Taylor this was not a good idea as well. At the first service, the most senior deacon of the church sat in the very front row and Himbury noticed that as he began preaching the congregation was silent. No one said "Amen" or any of the characteristic responses—until, some minutes into the sermon, the senior deacon turned in his place and said to the congregation, "He's all right!" and from then on the amens and other responses flowed. Himbury spoke later of the impact upon a preacher of this responsiveness, which drew something extra from the preacher as well. Indeed, another time when he was preaching at the Concord church in Brooklyn one of the officers from Whitley College was present and noticed a difference in Himbury's preaching there. He asked why Himbury did not preach like that at home in Melbourne, and Himbury replied that congregations did not listen like that in Melbourne.

There are very few records of the specific content of Himbury's sermons, though there are many recollections of his themes. A small exercise book lists the preachers and sermon titles at the Sunday services of the Collins Street Baptist Church from January 1994 till July 1999. These were the years after Himbury had concluded his period as associate pastor at Collins Street. The following entries indicate sermons preached by Mervyn Himbury, with titles or themes indicating the breadth of his teaching and challenge:

January 2, 1994; "A Light to the Gentiles"
January 9, 1994; "Who Carries Whom?"
July 30, 1995; "The Holy and the Horses"
September 9, 1995; "Three Days"
January 7, 1996; "God's New-Year Gift"
January 14, 1996; "Water and Spirit"
January 21, 1996; "The Rainbow"
September 15, 1996; "The Open Door"
April 6, 1997; "God's Worthiness and Our Unworthiness"
August 23, 1998; "Tangled in the Land"
December 6, 1998; "Who is Coming?"

It is not possible from these titles alone to infer the precise Scriptures on which they were based, but undoubtedly they were. Always, Himbury's approach to preaching was to present the word of God from a scriptural text, which was to be seen not only in relation to a historical context but also the context of his hearers and the world in which they lived. That, in essence, is the function of the sermon: to enable the people to sense the word of God for them, for their lives and their church at that time and place.

An incident which took place during my own time as a ministry student illustrates this perspective. The weekly chapel service was an event where, on most weeks during term, a student was allotted the task of leading the worship and preaching a sermon. On this day, the student leader was a fellow known for his very casual style in public presentation and dress. (It was, at that time, considered "cool.") The student read the Scripture passage on which he would later preach and then said, "Righty-o, we'll leave it there for now." In the "crit" session that followed the service, Himbury picked up on this remark. He was not concerned with the informality of the statement so much as the idea that we would "leave it there." "Whatever else we do with the Bible," he said, "we cannot just leave it there." His lesson to us was that our task is to engage with the Bible and work to help our people also to engage with it.

This response clearly indicated Himbury's concern for preaching and worship that is both biblically-based and focused upon the life of the people. The task of the sermon is to lead the people to encounter with God. Commonly this meant into prayer, and Himbury would very often pray in direct continuation of his sermon. There would be no, "Let us pray"; simply he would close his eyes and begin speaking to God. There could be no "leaving it there" for now. What becomes of the word of God—not merely in the worship service, but in the life of the people, the church in the world—that is the critical issue and concern of the preacher. The Bible reading and the sermon must go somewhere. That is the purpose to which Himbury devoted his life and work as a preacher—and yet the preacher cannot determine this outcome. That is why the sermon so often must end in prayer; for it is an offering to God, who will guide and direct the people in what they now must do and be, in light of that word.

The Need and Promise of Christian Preaching

In the year that Mervyn Himbury was born (1922), a young Swiss theologian, who had created quite an impression with his recently published commentary *Romans* and was becoming known for his "dialectical theology," presented a series of lectures to conferences of pastors around Germany. Karl Barth (1886–1968) had spent eleven years as the reformed pastor at Safenwil in his native Switzerland and was now in his first teaching appointment, at Göttingen, Germany. These lectures and conference presentations introduced Barth's theology and developed some of the themes of his *Romerbrief*. They were published as *The Word of God and the Word of Man*, and they provide a very helpful basis for theological reflection upon Himbury's approach to preaching. There is a common foundation in a broadly Calvinist theology and a common conviction of the need of Christian preaching. I titled my commemoration of this particular work of Barth "The Need and Promise of Christian Preaching" because inherent in this theology is a conviction that the Holy Spirit will enable the offering of the preacher to become the word of God for its hearers.[5] Speaking the word of God, Barth wrote, is the *promise* of Christian preaching—a promise that we can only reach out for and only God can fulfill.

Barth's approach is famously indicated early in the chapter "The Task of the Ministry": "As ministers we ought to speak of God. We are human, however, and so cannot speak of God. We ought therefore to

---

5. Barth, *Word of God*, 124. A commemoration of Barth's view of preaching can be found in Rees, "The Need and Promise," 107–21.

recognize both our obligation and our inability and, by that very recognition, give God the glory."[6]

The sense of radical dependence upon God is again firmly expressed in the lecture on "The Problem of Ethics Today." Human life is thrown into profound, even shattering, questioning by the reality of God, which may seem to be a thundering "No," but is in fact the "Yes" of God's love: "love, forgiveness, life, mercy, *grace* . . . awaits us."[7]

Barth's theology of preaching centers upon this encounter of the questioning, self-doubting people and the affirming and life-giving word of God. In his lecture on "The Need of Christian Preaching," he pictures the Sunday morning congregation gathering in expectation, waiting for something to *happen*. The building, the people, the reading of the Bible all evoke the idea that God is present. But what, in reality, does this mean? It is clearly a different kind of presence to the reality of the world around, the cherry blossom tree, Beethoven's ninth, or the people's daily work. Barth then suggests that the reality which grips the people here is, in fact, a question. But this question has two sides, as it were—another expression of the dialectical theology. The entire situation, good and bad, the riddle of existence, draws out from the people their own question: *Is it true?* "Is it true, this talk of a good and loving God, who is more than one of the friendly idols whose rise is so easy to account for, and whose dominion is so brief? What the people want to find out and thoroughly understand is, *Is it true?*"[8]

Barth goes on to argue, however, that the situation is only partially understood in terms of the questioning people. The event, the happening of the word of God, takes place only when they discover that their own questions, and their lives, are challenged by even more radical questioning.

Here Barth has some salutary words for the church and the pastor concerned to be "relevant" and topical, addressing what he describes as "secondary utterances." So many turn from the church including, he notes, the preacher's own children, because they are disappointed. Their own questions are given voice, but are not confronted with that more radical questioning, in which the word of God asks: Are you serious? Do you really want to know? The word of God seeks a questioning people

---

6. Barth, *Word of God*, 169.
7. Barth, *Word of God*, 186. Emphasis in the original.
8. Barth, *Word of God*, 106.

who are prepared to have their questions answered by another question. As Barth puts it, a question that questions them: Are they, are we, really and seriously seeking after God?

As such, then, the preaching event is in Barth's view eschatological in character: the miraculous inbreaking of God's presence and grace into our human situation. It is for this word and this event that we should all pray, especially those who seek to preach.

This theology of preaching expresses well the ethos and perspective of Himbury's own formation and his ministry. It is not possible to say whether Barth's theology was directly taught in the courses Himbury undertook as a student. It is nonetheless clear that the themes just summarized resonate well with Himbury's approach and objectives.[9]

The Purpose: Building up the Church in the World

For Himbury there was nothing accidental or incidental about the churchly context of preaching. Even when he served as an occasional preacher, his concern was always the life of the local church and, as a Baptist, that meant the lives of its people. Preaching is about building up the church and its witness to the Gospel in lives of faith.

The decline of traditional forms of church life throughout the wider society was a feature of the decades of Himbury's ministry both in Wales and in Australia. His own history of the Collins Street Baptist Church, where he was a member, documents this decline. It also indicates the strategies adopted to build new forms of ministry under the leadership of Rev. Ron Ham. The development of a "mission unit" would enable the church to engage in fresh ways with the life of the city, "learning from it and making a distinctively Christian contribution to it."[10] Concurrently, the growth of the church would be the task of "the traditional ministry of Word and Sacrament which involves pastoral care." In this simple clause we see Himbury's understanding of the central purpose of what he called "the ministry": it was all to build up the life of the people as the church.

---

9. Certainly, Himbury's colleague J. Ithel Jones, who came to South Wales Baptist College as principal just before Himbury moved to Melbourne, and later came to Collins Street as minister, was an advocate for Barth's theology, along with several other Welsh preachers at this time. It seems reasonable to presume that Barth's "Theology of the Word" was at least a subject of discussion at pastors' conferences during the years of Himbury's ministry in Wales.

10. Himbury, *Theatre of the Word*, 53.

During these decades there was much writing about the life of the church "in the world." It was the mission of the church to be the church in the world and for the world. Himbury's own view was that the people were the church, and his historical study and publications indicate that position. In that historical perspective, the local congregation exists to support and enable the members to live as Christians within their local communities, often with a somewhat harsh focus on the "discipline" aspects of discipleship. In his own time, Himbury did not focus on that discipline but rather encouraged and inspired the diverse responses of people to practice their faith in all aspects of their lives, in their local and professional contexts, as well as within the life of the gathered church.

The phrase "which involves pastoral care" is really quite interesting. At the time, there was a strong focus upon pastoral care as a discipline in theological studies, and many pastors claimed a distinctive focus on pastoral counseling. Himbury was not sympathetic to these trends and clearly indicates here his view that the traditional forms of ministry as Word and Sacraments *include* pastoral care. They provide the basis and context for pastoral care, "the cure of souls." This should not be taken to mean that he did not value pastoral conversations, nor the many programs that churches maintain for the nurture of children, youth, and adults. His history of Collins Street makes very clear his appreciation of these activities. Here we recall his early lesson in the value of biblical reflection during the week of pastoral ministry, each contributing to his preparation for the Sunday sermon. What Himbury did not accept was the developing idea of "specialist" ministries, often separating pastoral care, counseling, and education from the "traditional" activities of preaching and worship. On the contrary, for Himbury these were integral to pastoral care. He saw an interdependence of pastoral care and preaching. For him, then, the pastor must be a preacher and the preacher a pastor. These convictions deeply shaped his approach to ministerial education and led to some tensions within the developing life of Whitley College and its relations with Baptist union leaders.

The concurrent arrival in Melbourne of Mervyn Himbury and Billy Graham, two Baptist preachers who each had a significant influence on both church and society, was mentioned earlier. Perhaps the most significant influence upon many of the churches at the time was the Graham style of evangelistic preaching. Billy Graham's influence produced evangelistic preachers and churches keen to exercise various forms of evangelism.

During the 1960s and '70s, however, this approach also faced a very significant challenge. Graham himself recognized this difficulty in 1971, in an article in *Christianity Today*, "The Marks of the Jesus Movement":

> I have four points that I give after asking people to make a commitment to Christ. I tell them to read the Bible, to pray, to witness, and to get into a church. I see them nodding their heads and often smiling when I give the first three, but when I give the fourth, I can sense that I have lost many of them. They just don't want to be identified with the established church. In our crusades we are increasingly trying to bridge the gap between young people and the church.[11]

For his part, Mervyn Himbury saw the role of the preacher set clearly within the life of the local church, seeking to build up the church. For him, that was a matter of engaging with the questions and concerns of those people, not as "topics" for preaching, but in the light of the biblical text. Karl Barth before him had famously said the preacher must prepare with the Bible in one hand and the newspaper in the other; so, too, Himbury envisaged the task of preaching as for the church in the world. It is the life of the people when *not* gathered in the church building that is the ultimate destination of the sermon. They are to be the church, a Christian presence and witness, in their homes and places of work, study, and recreation.

Very clearly, Himbury was aware of the tenuous and ambiguous place of the church in the modern, secular world. This is evident, for example, in an article he wrote for the British Baptist ministers' journal, "Preaching in an Age of Uncertainty" and published in a year of much social upheaval, 1968.[12] Without offering specific analysis of the times, Himbury identified three ways in which contemporary preachers sought to meet "the feeling of uncertainty which the [modern] period has engendered."[13] The first of these is called *expository preaching*, which can be a style of preaching so engrossed in the history of words and texts that this becomes an end in itself, a means of disengagement from the world around us. A similar temptation is seen in what Himbury called *social preaching*. Himbury sees the great danger that the social emphasis of the church is largely negative, and the churches are known for what

---

11. Graham, "The Marks of the Jesus Movement," 5.
12. Himbury, "Preaching in an Age of Uncertainty," 7–13.
13. Himbury, "Preaching in an Age of Uncertainty," 9.

they oppose. Finally, Himbury notes the response to the uncertainties of the age which concentrates on *literary style*. Here the assumption is that people will respond positively to the Gospel if it is attractively presented. The upshot of this analysis is that the period and its uncertainties demand from the preacher a genuinely theological engagement:

> Most of the questions asked by our contemporaries are basically theological. Two world wars have shown the evil of which man is capable and have destroyed our optimism concerning the future. Our scientific advances have been phenomenal but have brought with them a sense of frustration that arises from man's incapacity to control the devices he creates. These and other factors compel men and women to ask questions which concern the very nature of human personality and destiny.[14]

Thus, Himbury calls for preaching that is both theological and contemporary, moving from the jargon of the theological classroom into the lived experience and thought forms of the contemporary world. In this movement, Himbury sees great hope in a renewed concern for biblical theology: "We are re-discovering the simple fact that the Word of God is contemporary. In the Bible, historian, prophet, poet, evangelist, and apostle spoke words which are of our age. The work of the preacher is that they shall be heard."[15]

The conclusion of this short but powerful article offers its own evangelical appeal to preachers of his time. Preaching is more than any of these arts or techniques: It is "a means whereby God confronts His Church with His Word, that Jesus Christ may be glorified and His saints sent into the world to conquer in His name."[16]

None of this should suggest, however, that Himbury was uninterested in the genuine struggles and pains of ordinary people and their daily lives. His call for a "theological" perspective meant precisely that the word of God could and should be addressed to the reality of the contemporary situation of individuals, their local churches, and the wider society. Julie Morsillo has recorded notes taken from a sermon Himbury preached in 2004 on the subject of doubt. He spoke of the many frustrations of age and his own ill-health. He still wanted to be healthy and noted that for many people life can be full of frustrations. Julie notes him saying that

---

14. Himbury, "Preaching in an Age of Uncertainty," 12.
15. Himbury, "Preaching in an Age of Uncertainty," 13.
16. Himbury, "Preaching in an Age of Uncertainty," 13.

"life feels hopeless for some people. Everything has gone wrong." While necessarily these notes reflect Julie Morsillo's own hearing and interest, they clearly indicate the pastoral insight of the aged and infirm preacher, establishing empathy and rapport with the congregation and still urging them to receive the word of God as the basis for their life and healing in a troubled and uncertain world.

Himbury the Preacher

It is clear that Himbury was an *enthusiastic* preacher. He preached with passion, and he was passionate about preaching. For him it was a calling, a profession in the best sense of the word. He used to say, rather oddly, that the Almighty took two minutes off from running the universe to call him to the ministry. The statement reflects his genuine conviction that preaching was his raison d'être. Furthermore, his enthusiasm for preaching expressed itself in a readiness to preach wherever he was invited. He was more than willing to preach in small and seemingly unpromising church situations as much as in prominent places or on important occasions.

Several features of Himbury's actual preaching also need to be noted. First, it was *erudite* preaching, in that it arose from his scholarship into Baptist history and principles, along with his wider knowledge of the history of the church. Himbury could place contemporary issues and trends within a broader context. Rarely would he actually provide a detailed history lesson as such, for he did not confuse preaching with teaching. He was very happy to provide classes and short lessons for church groups, but this was a different function from preaching. Nonetheless, those who listened to his preaching would learn much about the character and purposes of God, the character of the church, and, most of all, the impact of God's grace upon human life—that is to say, the Gospel.

It is also important to add that Himbury's preaching was *empathetic*. For him, pastoral care was intertwined with the ministry of Word and Sacraments, evident in his willingness to speak personally about matters of struggle, frustration, doubt, and despair. While he would openly engage with views he did not find helpful, and was often ironic and humorous in representing some such elements, he generally did so with a sensitivity to his listeners. His purpose was to challenge, help, and guide, not to condemn. Perhaps the most poignant expression of this empathy was in his prayers, often at the conclusion of the sermon. These frequently used the term "we," thus gathering the congregation into a collective sense of confession, challenge, and commitment.

The elements we have mentioned so far all indicate that Mervyn Himbury was an *evangelical* preacher. Here there is value in distinguishing that term from the word "evangelistic." This latter form of preaching is often shaped by a specific focus on a concept of sin and salvation, based on particular understandings of atonement. While all of this has its place, to imagine that this ethos and style of preaching is all that is meant by "evangelical" is to rob the term of its rich biblical and theological meaning. In recent decades, especially within the United States of America, the term "evangelical" has developed various connotations relating to particular theological emphases, and lately a distinctive position in regard to social-ethical matters. In its much broader sense, however, the Evangelical movement in the church has been characterized by a passion for presenting the Gospel of Jesus Christ, in word and deed, with a strong focus upon the Bible as the guiding authority for the life and teaching of the church. Himbury was too much a Baptist to allow his theology to be corralled into the ongoing doctrinal debates of the more recent Evangelical movements. But his commitment always to preach the Gospel, as a positive message of hope and calling, and to challenge and build up churches shaped by and witnessing to this Gospel in daily life, surely merits the label evangelical.

Another unfortunate development in relation to the term evangelical has been the sense of contrast many have seen between Evangelical groups and the modern ecumenical movement. Himbury was an important counter-instance to this separation. Indeed, his preaching must rightly be termed *ecumenical*. Here I am not only referring to his willingness to preach in churches of other Christian denominations. More importantly, his preaching reflected an ecumenical vision of the church, within which he held to a strong sense of Baptist identity. In his teaching and preaching, he maintained the importance of the sacraments of baptism and the eucharist as fundamental to the life of the church and, as we have seen, as part of its care of the people and their care of each other. Thus, Himbury's preaching did not encourage Baptists to keep apart from other Christians, as if somehow this was necessary for the integrity of their faith. Rather, it was in the context of the whole church that Baptist identity arises, both through all that is shared with the whole church and in the distinctive perspective that Baptists have to offer on these realities.

Along with all that has been said, however, it is also worth adding that Himbury was in some ways an *eccentric* preacher. This is not to say that the content of his preaching was unorthodox, in an inappropriate sense. On the contrary, his was a thoroughly orthodox Christian theology and teaching which, if anything, hoped to help Baptists to remember and maintain such a faith. But the manner of his style and presentation was often somewhat eccentric and this was intentional. Here I am thinking of his deliberate action in growing his hair long, at a time when he perceived all Baptist ministers to be like "peas out a pod," with "short back and sides" military-style haircuts and very traditional attire. Himbury would constantly flick his long hair back as he preached. Few Baptist ministers wore a clerical collar compared with their British counterparts of the time. Himbury would often appear wearing a clerical collar in those early days and preached wearing his academic gown. Very often, he would move to the back of a church at the end of a service, dramatically removing his gown and flinging it into an empty pew. All of this was to address what he considered was a situation where pastors enjoyed very little personal freedom. As he preached and taught the Baptist ideals of freedom of conscience and faith, he modeled it in his personal presentation.

Similarly, he might occasionally present his theme in somewhat surprising ways. In urging the Baptist young people of Victoria to relate their faith to the changing local context, Himbury preached a sermon asking, is not the Yarra as good as the Euphrates? Himbury's Palm Sunday sermon on "borrowing" is another example of a distinctive take on a very familiar story. On another occasion, as the guest preacher for the annual bankers' service at St. Paul's Cathedral, Melbourne, he began, "My text is from Acts 8, verse 20, 'To hell with you and your money, because you thought you could buy the gift of God with money.'"[17]

None of this was trivial or self-indulgent. Rather, through all of these aspects Mervyn Himbury sought to be an *exemplary* preacher. His commitment to excellence in preaching was not for himself as a performer but arose from his passion for preaching as the ministry of the Gospel. It asked nothing but his best and he sought to challenge and encourage others to their best. For this reason, Himbury was not only a preacher but one who also taught preaching.

---

17. Phillips, *The New Testament in Modern English*.

The Teacher of Preaching

Graeme Garrett has written of Mervyn Himbury's approach as a teacher of preaching:

> Mervyn Himbury was a great preacher. And the best homiletics critic I ever knew. As principal of the Baptist College of Victoria, he used to hold what he called "preaching class" in Collins Street Baptist Church on Tuesday nights during term. We students took it in turns to conduct a worship service, complete with Bible readings, hymns, prayers, and sermon. Our fellow students, with Himbury in the midst, formed a ramshackle congregation scattered in ones and twos around the dark and cavernous belly of the church. At the conclusion of the ordeal, we trooped into the vestry. There, as we sat in a circle of close-knit chairs, Himbury would lead a conversation "of appreciation and criticism" in response to what had just taken place. The luckless leader endured whatever gleeful or outrageous remarks his—and in the early 1960s it always was *his*—colleagues might care to heap upon him. At the close Himbury summed up. He spoke uninterrupted for ten or fifteen minutes, occasionally glancing at notes scribbled on a scrap of paper. His critique could be devastating, and often was. But for those who had ears to hear it was inevitably instructive. It went to the heart of the challenge which speaking the word of God in the church presents to any would-be preacher. Limping from the scorched earth of such exchanges I frequently felt dazed and bewildered. Out of my depth. In time, however, I discovered there was more to be learned about theology, hermeneutics, biblical exegesis, pastoral care, and prayer—in short, about preaching—in those terrifying Tuesday evenings than in most other classes put together.[18]

What Garrett describes here was known as the preaching class in many Baptist colleges throughout the world. It indicates what I will call Himbury's formal approach to teaching preaching.

In his own history of the South Wales Baptist College, Himbury described the preaching class in which students were expected to preach a sermon and then college staff would offer a critique. The sermon class was a feature of the precursor college as well, the Baptist college at Abergavenny, and had the following stated aims: "To furnish an opportunity for detecting false grammar, promoting a natural and just arrangement,

---

18. Garrett, "Where is '. . . and earth'?" 110.

and pointing out any erroneous construction that might be laid upon divine truth."[19] Other Baptist colleges adopted similar approaches.

Himbury's records of various developments in the college curriculum during the nineteenth and twentieth centuries show that homiletics, together with a concern for elocution and reading in public, remained consistent features, while such elements as euclidian geometry dropped out. Nonetheless, in his final discussion of the curriculum and the college's relationship with the University of Cardiff, he observes that the academic development, of which the college may justly be proud, "has also so filled the timetable that intensive study of pastoral and homiletical matters has been crowded out, though a course in these subjects as well as the sermon class is still regarded as a sine qua non of theological education."[20] Written in 1957, those words signaled where Himbury's emphasis would be placed as principal of the Baptist College of Victoria. He was concerned to produce preachers who were pastors, and pastors who could preach.

Not everyone recalls the preaching class with quite the same sense of terror described by Graeme Garrett. Rev. Bob Edmonds provided me with a paper offering some of his own experiences and recollections. He described the "crit session," where Himbury would nominate two students to lead off the discussion, without notice, and observed that this could be hard on the preacher but also on those asked to lead the critique. Then, "principal Himbury always ended the crit sessions with a summing up and thanked the preacher, then prayer and a blessing." Further, Edmonds said he and his fellow students valued these opportunities and the supportive and encouraging words of the principal.

Very helpfully, Edmonds also offered his own commentary upon the role and purposes of the preaching class in the college and the training program:

1. It was part of the spiritual life of the college.
2. For students to learn how to prepare a sermon.
3. For students to learn how to deliver a sermon, including techniques such as to know how to throw your voice and fill a space without damaging your vocal cords.

---

19. Himbury, *South Wales Baptist College*, 26.
20. Himbury, *South Wales Baptist College*, 125.

4. How to take criticism. The crit sessions enabled us to receive criticism of our work from fellow learners who were sympathetic and supportive.
5. That preaching is an art form that must be learned, and sermon class fulfilled that role.
6. You needed to find your personal style and method of working and sermon class did this by practice and feedback.
7. Building a form of collegiality.

These observations were supported by the recollections of Rev. Barrie Sutton and Rev. Barry Watson, students also in Himbury's first decade in Melbourne. Watson commented that Himbury would always work the critical discussion toward the biblical text: What is it actually saying? On one occasion when Watson was the preacher, on the text Matthew 5:13, "Ye are the salt of the earth," Himbury observed that Watson had enjoined people that they ought to become salt for the earth, whereas the text uses the indicative "you *are* the salt of the earth."

In my own experience of this process, I recall that the critique was often initially provided by other faculty members. One would commonly critique the logic of the sermon and another challenge the exegesis. Not uncommonly, Himbury would comment upon and moderate those criticisms, moving the conversation more toward what the sermon itself was hoping to achieve and how it might best have done that.

The sermon class was but one of the ways Himbury taught preaching. A more informal, but nonetheless immensely influential, element was his teaching by example. This was a vital part of his own formation. In the life of the college, he would remark upon the fact that a certain international guest was preaching at some prominent city church and urge students to make sure that they went to hear this person while they had such an opportunity. In addition, his own regular preaching in college provided the opportunity to learn from his example.

Students who lived in the Errol Street college remarked upon an exceptional contribution Himbury made to their training as preachers. On Saturday mornings, for college devotions, Himbury would preach a sermon that he said he would not preach anywhere else. This was offered to the students then as something they could take and develop in their own ministry contexts and according to their style. Knowing that student pastors were often stretched for time, this was a real gift to them, and many recalled and remarked on how much they learned from these sessions.

In October 1959, Mervyn Himbury was the guest preacher for the annual assembly of the Baptist Union of Tasmania, held at the Hobart Tabernacle. Several months later, in January 1960, he preached at the Burnie Baptist Church on the text "he took me out of the miry clay and set my feet upon a rock" (based on Psalm 40:2), a sermon that had a powerful impact upon a young man who was at the time sensing a call to ministry. A deacon of that church, Mr. Ivan Bewsher, had noted that the various Baptist colleges from the mainland states produced distinctive styles of pastors. He predicted then that "Himbury will produce preachers."[21]

He was the principal preacher.

---

21. This remark was recorded in personal conversation with Rev. Barry Watson, who was the young man mentioned in this paragraph.

CHAPTER 2

A Welsh Baptist

THOUGH HE LIVED MORE than half his life in Australia, Mervyn Himbury remained a Welsh Baptist. In order to understand better his life and approach to ministry, I found it helpful to identify each of these aspects of his personal and family background: the Welsh nation and its heritage, the Baptist community and its identity, and the Baptist Church in Wales.

Wales and the Welsh People

Through almost a thousand years of subjugation to the Norman and English powers, the Welsh people have struggled to maintain their identity, particularly evident in cultural forms, language, and religion.

Geraint Jenkins has described four crucial elements in what he called the Heroic Age in Welsh history, from 383 to 1063: "the emergence of multiple political kingdoms, the codification of the native laws, the vigorous missions of the Welsh saints, and the genesis of the Welsh language and the vernacular literature." These elements provided a "recognizable territorial and cultural identity."[1] The language developed in quite specific forms, one of which was poetry, passed on from generation to generation and only later taking written form. By the time of the Norman conquest, Wales was a widely recognized distinctive area of Britain with its own language, culture, and spiritual traditions.

Wales was not, however, a single political entity. Rather, as J. Graham Jones puts it, Wales was "a miniature chess-board of small, independent kingdoms, each ruled by its own dynasty which passed on kingship

1. Jenkins, *Concise History of Wales*, 33.

from father to son."² Similarly, the Norman invasion did not conquer the whole territory of Wales. Rather, as Jones explains, "what occurred were isolated invasions by Norman lords who seized lands for themselves."³ Thus began the long period of engagement and gradual domination of English politics and language, leading to the legal assimilation and "union" of England and Wales through Acts of Union in 1536 and 1543, "the culmination of a drive to extend the authority of the English Crown over Wales."⁴

With time the measures of English domination led to the effective destruction of many aspects of Welsh culture. The Welsh language was proscribed. English law replaced local law and a growing London-centered culture gradually overcame Welsh cultural life. The landed gentry became increasingly anglicized, which in turn led to the emergence of a widening gap between them and the "lower orders" of Welsh society.

Nonetheless, the local society and economy remained, largely rural and agriculturally based, until the Industrial Revolution in the eighteenth and nineteenth centuries, when parts of Wales developed a new significance as the source of coal—fuel for factories in the growing cities and towns near and far. The Protestant Reformation, particularly the creation of the Church of England by Queen Elizabeth I, was welcomed in Wales. As Richard Allen and David Ceri Jones put it, "the Welsh transferred their allegiance to the new Church of England, becoming Protestants at least on paper."⁵

Another important religious development in the period post union with England was the emergence of the very distinctive form of Protestantism known as Nonconformity, the most powerful religious movement in Wales for many centuries. The growth of Nonconformity led to a movement for the "disestablishment" of the Church of England in Wales through the nineteenth century, though it was not effected until the 1920s.⁶ In the intervening centuries, various streams of Independent and Nonconformist churches developed, the strongest being Methodist

  2. Jones, *History of Wales*, 12.
  3. Jones, *History of Wales*, 19.
  4. Jones, *History of Wales*, 55.
  5. Allen and Jones, *Religious History of Wales*, 4.
  6. The Welsh Church (Temporalities) Act, 1919 was brought into effect in 1920, as the movement for disestablishment had been suspended during the years of the First World War. It has been argued, however, that it was some decades before leadership of the Church of Wales really took imaginative advantage of this change.

churches in several groups: Calvinist Methodism—"the first version of the Protestant faith which could be said to be indigenous to Wales,"—and Wesleyan Methodism.[7] Baptist churches were another strong Nonconformist group.

One of the most significant developments in this time was the labor movement, strongly supported by the Nonconformist churches for some decades. Geraint Jenkins observes that many aspects of Welsh society that contributed to the growth of the labor movement can also be seen in the Nonconformist communities. These aspects include deep collective loyalties and "a rich associational culture," together with adult education activities and a sense of heritage that encouraged "the growth of greater consensus and harmony."[8] It is no coincidence, Jenkins asserts, that three of the most influential figures in the creation of the British welfare state were Welsh—Lloyd George, Aneurin Bevin, and James Griffiths.

The Welsh industrial economy was hit very hard by unemployment during the Great Depression and, apart from the years of the Second World War, there was steady decline through the whole of the twentieth century. While there was significant expansion in government sponsored education, including the University of Wales, other activities such as Workers' Education declined. "Even more striking was the decline in the influence and membership of the chapels, manifested above all in the decay of the Nonconformist ethos, once all-powerful in Welsh life," observes Graham Jones.[9] At the conclusion of the century, Geraint Jenkins suggested a "three-Wales model" for understanding the national situation, based on a combination of linguistic patterns and perceptions of identity: the Welsh-speaking heartland in the North-West, "Welsh Wales" in the industrial valleys of the South, and "British Wales"—perhaps better considered "English Wales"—mostly in the northeast and south coast.[10]

In common with the wider British population, life expectancy for the Welsh people improved greatly during the twentieth century, from fifty-seven years for a male in 1922, when Himbury was born, to eighty-one years in 2010, just after his death. These advances, together with a declining birth rate, led to a gradual aging of the population.

7. White, "Calvinist Methodism," 79.
8. Jenkins, *Concise History of Wales*, 291.
9. Jones, *History of Wales*, 179.
10. Jenkins, *Concise History of Wales*, 282. It has been noted in the wider discussion of recent "Brexit" voting patterns that the "Welsh-Welsh" voted differently to the "British Welsh."

Statistics on the use of the Welsh language reflect a period of decline, then a resurgence, and more recently a tailing off from that peak.[11] Interestingly, reports were formulated in 1920 in terms of those who "could now speak English": 90 percent of the population compared with 69 percent in 1891 and 85 percent in 1901. The "disuse of Welsh" is recorded in these same census reports. In 1921, homes where only Welsh was spoken were reported as 6–7 percent. Homes where both English and Welsh was spoken were 31 percent in 1921, down from 35 percent in 1901. A century later the terminology used in these reports has changed. The 2001 census recorded that 20.5 percent of the population could speak Welsh, with a further 7.9 percent with some understanding of the language. In some areas, however, Welsh was spoken by as many as 87 percent of the people. Changes in the population have not only included "in-migration" of English people and the emigration of many Welsh people, but also the development of a multicultural society in more recent decades.

Who Are the Baptists?

It is notable that Baptists constantly feel called upon to answer for their identity. This challenge involves responding to their heritage and indeed the wider history and tradition of the church, but even more so responding to their present situation in the light of the Gospel and what they understand to be the promised future with God. Every time and situation is one in which the meaning of Baptist church life is to be worked out afresh.

There continues to be historical debate about the precise origins of the Baptist movement. One critical element in this debate is the question of the relationship between Baptists in a broad sense and Anabaptists. This debate relates quite specifically to the emergence of Baptist groups in England and the Netherlands in the very early years of the seventeenth century. In his history of British Baptists, Himbury observes (perhaps with some exaggeration) that "the determination of the relationship between the Baptists and the Anabaptists is one of the greatest problems that confront modern church historians."[12] In that work he notes various approaches, including an ongoing debate at that time in the pages of the *Baptist Quarterly*. There, in 1956, Winthrop S. Hudson published a

---

11. Jenkins, Concise History of Wales, 261–62.
12. Himbury, *British Baptists*, 16.

sustained argument seeking to distinguish the two movements, beginning, "if the early Baptists were clear about any one thing, they were clear in their insistence that they were not to be confused with the Anabaptists."[13] Hudson argued that the Baptists emerged from Congregationalist groups but then, in distinguishing themselves from that group, divided over questions of baptism. So fundamental were these differences that John Smyth who, with Thomas Helwys, had led the first group of Baptists to Amsterdam, was "excommunicated" from Helwys's group when they had returned to London, on the basis that he had "denied the Lord's truth" and fallen from grace. Hudson shows that various English critics of these groups were aware of the differences between Anabaptists and the more moderate Baptists in England.

Positively, Hudson asserts that the importance of this distinction is in recognizing the true origins of the Baptists: "the identification of the Baptists with the Continental Anabaptists has obscured the fact that the Baptists constituted the left-wing of the Puritan movement."[14] The Baptists and their theology, arising from Congregationalism, held an essentially Calvinist or Puritan understanding of the Christian faith. This contrasted in several significant ways with the "university-trained humanist" origins of some of the Anabaptist leaders, which represented the ethos of the Northern Renaissance. Critical to these differences was the Baptist (and more broadly English) conception of the human condition and original sin, which led to an inherent suspicion of institutional power, both in ecclesial and political contexts.

On the other hand, David Bebbington's careful evaluation of these issues concludes that there are "several dimensions" to the possible relationship of Baptists and Anabaptists. While he remains unconvinced by the arguments for direct historical linkage between the two groups, he asserts that "the argument in favor of the Anabaptists being the source for John Smyth's revival of believer's baptism has much more to recommend it."[15]

Hudson's contentions are further supported by the more recent work of Ian Birch, who has undertaken a very detailed examination of the theology and polity of the Particular Baptists from the first decades of the seventeenth century. "The emergence of English Particular Baptists

---

13. Hudson, "Who Were the Baptists?" 308.
14. Hudson, "Who Were the Baptists?" 310.
15. Bebbington, *Baptists Through the Centuries*, 40.

may be traced back to the congregation of Independent Puritans founded by Henry Jacob in Southwark, London, in 1616."[16] It is recorded that Jacob and a group of a dozen or so others, after prayer and fasting, stood and joined hands and each made a profession of faith and "covenanted together to walk in Gods ways [sic] as he had revealed or should make known to them." Here Birch draws attention to the covenantal nature of the group. I would note further the commitment to discipleship, with an openness to further revelation of God's ways.

Himbury's own account of this early period in Baptist history gives significance to the influence of Calvinist and Separatist ideas in *both* Anabaptist and Baptist streams, and then turns to the period of political turmoil in which Nonconformity became the dominant concern. When the Parliament sought to reform the religious life of the country, it passed the Corporation Act in 1661, which limited public office to those who received Communion only according to the Church of England, while the Conventicle Act of 1664 prohibited any form or gathering for worship other than those specified by the established church. In this context, Baptists and many other groups experienced persecution, their meetings invaded and dispersed by clergy and magistrates.[17] Leading Baptists spent time in prison, most famously John Bunyan. In 1672, Charles II issued a Declaration of Indulgence which provided significant relief to Nonconformists who were, at least for a time, allowed to license their places of worship. There were further waves of persecution, however. James II, who succeeded in 1685, sought to continue the policy of toleration but was mostly concerned for the freedom of his fellow Catholics rather than the Nonconformists. Nonetheless, in the following century, the Baptist movement spread throughout the United Kingdom and to the "new world," where a number of groups sought refuge.

Two vital elements emerge from this sketch of Baptist origins. First, it is clear that Baptist identity is fundamentally concerned with the nature of the church. Thus Brian Haymes, Ruth Gouldbourne, and Anthony Cross say in their introduction to *On Being the Church: Revisioning Baptist Identity*: "When Baptists have written about their convictions and principles, in explanation of themselves to other Christians or to each other, they have usually started straight in with their doctrine of the church."[18]

---

16. Birch, *To Follow the Lambe*, 2.
17. Himbury, *British Baptists*, 59–60.
18. Haymes et al, *On Being the Church*, 3.

In his study of Particular Baptists, Ian Birch helpfully sets out the vision of this movement for "a true visible church of Christ." His contention is that Christology was the guiding principle of this ecclesiology: the rule of Christ.[19] The idea was that Christians are called to follow Christ wherever his purposes may lead and thus to become a visible gathering of believers. The true visible church will be a believer's church, consisting of those "gathered out of the World by the preaching of the Gospel, by the powerful ministry of the Spirit."[20] This church, then, would be a gathered church, a visible church, and a separate church. Importantly, while believers' baptism was a defining practice of this group, it was not baptism as such that was the essential element—so much so that a variety of practices were allowed within different groups. Rather, the essential concern was voluntary or responsible profession of faith in Jesus Christ, which was contrasted both with circumcision in the period before Christ and pedobaptism in the national church.[21] Crucial to this vision of the church, then, was the idea of being responsive to the Gospel in faith and obedience, and only those who had made such a personal commitment to faith and obedience were admitted to membership of the church.

Nigel Wright has further explained that this vision of a believers' church centers not only upon freedom in matters of belief but on a wider vision of freedom. It concerns a free church but also a free state. Wright quotes Ian Randall as arguing that Thomas Helwys "was not only seeking to establish a new model of church, but also a new model of society, one free from the oppression which he saw in a national, state church."[22] This vision of a free society would be built on "the consensus of the people rather than the command of the ruler."[23] Thus, Baptist identity understood as a form of "free church" is not to be concerned only with the freedom to worship, to baptize, and conduct the Lord's Supper in ways different from other groups—and especially the state church. What was at the heart of this movement was a concern to be free in thought and belief, *in response to the call of Christ, as mediated through the preaching of the Gospel, itself attested through Scripture.* It is this distinctive vision of

---

19. Birch, *To Follow the Lambe*, 48.
20. Birch, *To Follow the Lambe*, 37.
21. Birch, *To Follow the Lambe*, 43.
22. Wright, "Baptist Christians," 5. Here Wright is quoting Randall, *Communities of Conviction*, 23. Wright has considered these themes in much more detail in Wright, *Free Church, Free State*.
23. Wright, "Baptist Christians," 5–6.

Christian discipleship, within church and society, which best characterizes Baptist identity.

In drawing together the preceding discussion of Baptist identity, there are three crucial elements in this Baptist vision of a free church. Fundamental to this vision is the idea that the freedom affirmed here is not merely freedom *from* restraints or other traditions which may claim to be normative. Here we are speaking of a positive freedom, which may be characterized as "freedom for."

The first of these is the notion of *freedom for the God of the Bible*. Baptists envisaged a community called "out of the world" by the power of the Gospel, made known through the witness of Scripture. The God of the Bible is the champion of the people's liberty, for Israel and for all nations. Jesus of Nazareth sets people free from the burdens of guilt and fear, hunger and disease, discrimination and rejection. In the teachings of the Apostle Paul, the God of the Bible calls people to live in freedom from "the law of sin and death" and to walk in a new life (for example, Romans 8:1–4).

A second critical dimension of Baptist identity as a free church is a *freedom for the God of the church*. Here it is vital to assert that Baptist identity is never adequately summarized by individualist ideas of personal salvation. The call of Christ is to participation in his body, a living community of people on earth. While there is a strong independent spirit in Baptist life, Brian Haymes sees also "a Catholic spirit," by which he means "a readiness to seek the fellowship of other Baptists, in association, in partnerships, in societies," and extending also to fruitful relationship with other Christian communities.[24] There is a vital balancing of the local, independent ethos of Baptist church life (commonly referred to as the principle of autonomy of the local church), and the call to fellowship with the whole church (the principle of association). Baptist confessions of faith draw upon the historic, credal forms of Christian faith and, at least in principle, are committed to the unity of the whole church in Christ.

The freedom Baptists claim is thus not freedom *from* association with other Christian groups but rather a freedom *for* the God of the church, and thus for whatever forms of shared witness and worship are possible, as expressions of that discipleship to which they are called. In recent times, some Baptists have called for a stronger expression of this commitment, calling themselves "Catholic Baptists" in contrast with

---

24. Haymes, "One Church," 29.

those in their own context who have come to stress a much stronger separatism.²⁵ Brian Haymes observes that Baptists' twentyfirst century inheritance includes both this independent spirit and forms of associating in local districts, wider associations, national unions or conventions, and internationally through the Baptist World Alliance (BWA).²⁶ The weakness of this inheritance, however, is that Baptists find it so difficult to hold these two principles or spirits together. Thus, Curtis Freeman has remarked, reflecting his own situation in contemporary USA:

> The Baptist vision emerged within a movement of radical protest intent on reforming the one, holy, catholic, and apostolic church. It resulted in the founding of a sect committed to maintaining its place at the top of the hierarchy of denominations. It is in danger of becoming, if it has not already become, a set of principles maintained by an affinity group of mystic individuals, determined by personal choice.²⁷

The movement for a renewed "catholicity" among Baptists seeks to reaffirm the freedom for the whole church as a principle of fellowship within the Gospel.

A third critical principle in Baptist life and history arises from the missionary ethos of the movement, and this is a *freedom for the God of the world*. Baptists have never accepted a retreat into monasticism or disengagement from the life of the world. Rather, Baptists have envisaged the whole world as God's, and have sought to live in the world as witnesses to God's presence and purposes. Not the least expression of this conviction was the development of missions to convert people of other nations and faiths, exemplified by William Carey going to India in 1792 and Adoniram Judson going to Burma in 1812. More broadly, however, Baptists have participated in local community life, politics, and commerce, as a form of discipleship. Their faith is not only concerned with an inward spirituality, nor only with the life of the gathered church. Rather, the whole of life is the arena of faith and witness, and all Christians are "priests" in offering the collective worship of their daily lives.

---

25. Among others, Curtis Freeman has advocated for this view, using the term "other Baptists" to contrast with the dominant position of Baptist separatism in the USA. See for example, Freeman, "A Confession for Catholic Baptists", 83–97. Steven Harmon has similarly proposed a recovery of "Baptist Catholicity," in Harmon, *Towards a Baptist Catholicity*.

26. Haymes, "One Church," 30.

27. Freeman, *Contesting Catholicity*, 9.

Furthermore, at least some Baptists have developed a conviction that the primary focus of their witness and service is not merely the activities of the gathered church, as if God's purposes in the world are limited to the church and its members. Rather, there has been a significant move in missional thought toward the idea of the *missio dei*, the mission of God in the world. The focus of Christian discipleship, then, is to engage with what God is doing in the world, both within and beyond the gathered church. To be free for the God of the world is to seek to discern God's presence and to become part of God's mission in the world. To this end, Southern Baptist theologian Findley Edge wrote, "It is imperative that we become a people who understand who we are, who God is, what God is about in the world and what God is calling us to be about in the world."[28]

Taken together, these freedoms form the ethos of Baptist identity and provide for a rich and sometimes confusing diversity across the many groups of Baptists around the world. David Bebbington's study of the history of Baptists includes a detailed consideration of the bitter divisions among Baptists in the United States during recent decades, especially among those associated or previously associated with the Southern Baptist Convention. He observes seven strands of identity and church life which had already existed but have been accentuated by these decades of struggle. These are:

1. Liberals. There were very few of these in the Southern Baptist Convention, but nonetheless there were some who welcomed God's presence in secular life.
2. Classic Evangelicals, endorsing the emphases on the Bible, the cross, conversion, and missionary activism.
3. The premillennial point of view, characterized by common emphases on "the book, the blood, and the blessed hope."
4. Charismatic renewal.
5. The Calvinist strand.
6. An affinity for the Anabaptists.
7. A high church orientation: Baptist sacramentalists or "Catholic Baptists."[29]

---

28. Edge, *Greening of the Church*, 37.
29. Bebbington, *Baptists Through the Centuries*, 271–72.

As something of an understatement, Bebbington concludes, "so Baptist identity in the early twenty-first century was diverse."[30]

The BWA today embraces approximately forty-eight million Baptist church members, with 239 member bodies (state or national associations) across 125 countries. The Southern Baptist Convention, which withdrew from the BWA in 2003, incorporates another fourteen million Baptists. Among this worldwide community of Baptists are the Welsh Baptists.

Welsh Baptists

It is not exactly clear when the first Baptist church was formed in Wales. Himbury's own history of British Baptists notes a gathering of Welsh Baptists at Olchon, in Herefordshire, England in 1663.[31] There were people holding "opinions similar to Baptists" in Wales for some time prior to this date. At Llanfaches in Monmouthshire, William Wroth led members of his congregation of the Church of Wales in resistance to James I's injunctions on how people should spend their time following the divine service. James had issued the *Book of Sports* in 1618, encouraging various Sunday recreations including dancing, vaulting, may-pole dancing, and the like. Wroth was ejected from his living and, together with many others of a Puritan mind, formed a congregation in that town. Several other Church of Wales ministers joined this group as well, some eventually joining the Baptist church at Broadmead in Bristol, with others moving to Wrexham as early as 1634, forming a community that comprised both Baptists and Independents.[32] In southwest Wales a Particular Baptist congregation formed at Ilston in 1649. This and other missionary work in Wales was greatly assisted by the passage of the Act for the Better Propagation and Preaching of the Gospel in Wales in 1650.

Up to that time the established church had not made significant inroads into Wales, where only a small proportion of the people spoke English. Much evangelistic effort ensued the passage of the Act, giving rise to many Nonconformist groups in Wales. While the Act itself expired in 1653, its provisions were continued in the payment of preachers for each parish in Wales, many of whom were, in fact, Baptists. Hugh Matthews

30. Bebbington, *Baptists Through the Centuries*, 273.
31. Himbury, *British Baptists*, 45.
32. Himbury, *British Baptists*, 46. Himbury himself was to be ordained in this same Baptist church, three centuries later.

observes that "it was not unusual for the incumbent in a parish church at this time to be a Baptist without formal theological training, but a person 'sent forth' by one of the Particular Baptist churches in South Wales."[33] Already, then, we see the collective action of a group of churches: the beginnings of associations of Baptist congregations. In following decades this became the pattern of Baptist church life in Wales—local congregations formed into regional associations. This principle has continued into the present century. The Baptist union is not, as it has been in many other places, a union of local churches directly formed into that union but is rather a union of associations. The local groupings thus continue to have significance for the life and support of each congregation.

It goes without saying that these groups of Christians were Nonconformist, though exactly what this meant was often in debate. As Matthews observed, it was possible for some time to hold to Baptist ideals and remain within the established church. The broad ethos of these emerging Baptist communities was defined by a focus upon preaching and singing in their gathered worship and a strong sense of responsibility in Christian lifestyle, puritanical in many respects, and devoted to industriousness in their working lives. There were differences, however, over several matters, particularly open or closed Communion—that is, whether those who had not been baptized by immersion may partake of the Lord's Supper.

Matthews describes the life and ministry of these congregations by identifying a "six-point key pattern" which had been set out during the general meeting of the churches in Llantrisant in 1654. First, a pastor presided over each of the larger churches. This minister was assisted by "teaching" elders who, like the pastor, were set aside by "the laying on of hands." "Ruling" elders contributed through the discipline or guidance of the smaller, scattered groups. A fourth tier of ministry were the deacons, while widows and "ordinary prophets"—lay preachers—provided the remaining forms of ministry. In effect, this pattern provided something akin to the pattern established in the Acts of the Apostles, where some focused upon the ministry of the Word while others attended to the nurture and discipling of the people in everyday life. Matthews noted that traces of these various levels of ministry continued into the nineteenth

33. Matthews, "Baptists," 42.

century, eventually to be replaced by the two-tiered pattern of pastors and deacons.[34]

It is impossible to discuss the life of Welsh Baptists without some consideration of Christmas Evans, who might be called the archetypical Welsh Baptist pastor. Densil Morgan asserts, "Christmas Evans embodied the profound religious, cultural and social transformation which created 'Nonconformist Wales.'"[35]

Born on December 25, 1766, Evans's family of origin included Calvinist and Arminian influences, the two contesting theological elements in Welsh Baptist theology of the time. His father died when Christmas was just nine years old and the boy was sent to live with a "cruel, drunken, and selfish uncle," but soon after went to work on the farm of a Presbyterian man, David Davis, who pastored a congregation and ran a small grammar school. Christmas Evans experienced conversion to faith and Davis encouraged him both to study and to preach.[36] Evans very soon gained a reputation in the region for his preaching and was invited to preach in many local Independent and Baptist churches. Morgan notes here the "inter-Dissenting solidarity," notwithstanding doctrinal differences, of such churches.[37] Evans's study of Scripture led him to reject pedobaptism and affirm the Baptist position. He was baptized by immersion in 1788 at twenty-two years of age and soon after attended the annual meetings of the Baptist Association, where he met representatives of what was to be his first pastoral setting, at Lleyn in Caernarfonshire. There he was ordained in 1789.

During this time, Morgan explains, a profound transformation occurred in the style—and indeed the purpose—of preaching in Wales. From a focus on content, ideas, cerebral reception, and belief, the new ethos of evangelical awakening offered an *experience* of those ideas as realities transforming personal life. Christmas Evans became a very powerful evangelist. Mervyn Himbury wrote of him that "he brought to preaching a sanctified imagination and could move a congregation

---

34. Matthews, "Baptists," 44–45.

35. Morgan, *Wales and the Word*, 28. Though there are numerous biographies of Christmas Evans, I will in this section draw only from Morgan's essay and Himbury's comments.

36. Morgan, Wales and the Word, 19.

37. Morgan, *Wales and the Word*, 20.

to tears of joy or sorrow. The actor and the poet who inhabit the Welsh character responded to his oratory."[38]

Similarly, Morgan records that "great powers accompanied his ministry in those days," as hearers would respond with weeping or physically jumping and leaping "as if the world were igniting round about."[39]

Two years later Evans moved to Anglesey where he served for thirty-five years. The Baptist church grew from 150 members to more than one thousand. During this time, he traveled to many other places to preach, including South Wales. Morgan makes two significant comments here. Christmas Evans's name "became synonymous with peripatetic preaching in the dramatic revivalist style." But this activity was in part a means of augmenting his inadequate salary, and here Morgan quotes D. M. Evans's biography as noting one of the anomalies of Welsh religious life, "that it combines an insatiable appetite for sermons with a marvelous disregard for the temporal comforts of the preachers."[40] In 1826 Evans moved to Caerphilly in Glamorgan, where again his ministry met with considerable success. Within one year, 140 new members were added to the church and the revivalist experiences of his earlier ministry were also evident. In 1828 he accepted an invitation to Cardiff where he spent his last decade writing, preaching, and publishing.

Morgan describes Christmas Evans's life and ministry as exemplifying "the nature of the newborn Nonconformist Wales." It was "a religious impulse," rather than cultural and political factors, that was of primary significance for the nation's life. While basically Calvinist in its theology, this revivalist ethos was warm and emotional, and more effective in transforming the lives of the people for many decades to come.[41]

The broader themes in this brief sketch of Christmas Evans's life and ministry indicate the character of Welsh Baptist life. It is the story of a people of the Word, whose gathered life was shaped by preaching, singing, and the inevitable tensions arising from their Nonconformist stance. All too easily, a people shaped by opposition and resistance find the lines of division as much within as between themselves and others. Differences between Calvinist and Arminian theology, open or closed Communion, and various other aspects of church life generated both a lively awareness

38. Himbury, *British Baptists*, 136.

39. Morgan, *Wales and the Word*, 21.

40. Morgan, *Wales and the Word*, 23. The source quoted is D. M. Evans, *Christmas Evans: A Memoir*, London, 1863, 147.

41. Morgan, *Wales and the Word*, 26.

of Baptist identity and, at times, divisions and schism. Hugh Matthews's succinct account of Baptists within the religious history of Wales frankly identifies "schism" as one of the themes.[42] To focus on these tensions, however, would be to present much too negative a picture. The nineteenth and early twentieth centuries were periods of significant growth and developing cooperation for Baptists in Wales. In Mervyn Himbury's own local church, the Sunday school was a vital aspect of local ministry, not only for children. Bible teaching, training for praying in public, and choral singing were some of the riches of Baptist experience.

A commitment to education was a feature of Welsh culture in general and Baptists certainly shared this commitment. Mervyn Himbury began his own history of the South Wales Baptist College with the affirmation that "the story of the development of ministerial education among the Baptists of Wales is one of the most significant chapters in their history."[43] That story was not just a Baptist story. The emerging Nonconformist groups of the seventeenth century were not permitted entry to English universities. Only confirmed Anglicans were so admitted. Scottish universities did allow Nonconformists to enroll, but distance was a great disincentive. The solution was to begin their own academies in Wales. Thus, for example, the Presbyterian Academy in Carmarthen, which opened in 1703, provided training for more than one hundred Baptist pastors during its first century, while many others went to Bristol Baptist Academy.[44] From 1732–1770 there was a small Baptist academy at Trosnant, though its role was more as a preparatory school for those seeking to enter the Bristol Baptist College.

It may seem ironic today, but it was the missionary concern of Welsh Baptists for the English-speaking populations of Glamorganshire and Pembrokeshire that led to the foundation of the Baptist college at Abergavenny. These places were deemed as "dark" as regions of Africa "for want of English preachers."[45] The new academy was established by Rev. Micah Thomas, in his own home originally, with just three students. It was supported by Baptists from all around Wales. Thomas taught English and provided reading materials and sermon classes and, with time, an entry requirement was set: the ability to read English. Welsh grammar

---

42. Matthews, "Baptists," 49–50.
43. Himbury, *South Wales Baptist College*, 11.
44. Matthews, *From Abergavenny to Cardiff*, 12.
45. Matthews, *From Abergavenny to Cardiff*, 15.

was soon added to the curriculum, along with philosophy and science. The college soon moved to a suitable building in Pontypool and by the middle of the century classics and mathematics were also parts of the curriculum. Particularly capable students now also proceeded to study at Regent's Park College (at that time in London).

Two other Baptist academies were created in the mid-nineteenth century, at Haverfordwest (1839) and Llangollen (1862). By this time, however, there were calls for the creation of a single college, for more efficient use of the support donated by the churches—but instead each of the institutions moved to other locations, to serve their constituencies more effectively. Llangollen moved to Bangor (1892), Pontypool to Cardiff (1893) and Haverfordwest to Aberystwyth (1894). By the turn of the century, just two colleges remained, at Bangor and Cardiff. The Cardiff College was later renamed the South Wales Baptist College and became the premier institution for training Welsh Baptist ministers.

So we come to the time of Mervyn Himbury's life as a Welsh Baptist. Local Baptist churches were strong in the nurture of children and young people but, as the century proceeded, many factors contributed to a decline in attendances and membership, not least two world wars and the closure of the coal mines. Densil Morgan has detailed many aspects of this decline from the 1930s onwards. The standard of preaching is a particular focus of interest. While it was widely affirmed that the preaching in many places was of higher quality than ever before, the chapels were in fact "becoming moribund . . . The day of the popular preacher and his vast and expectant congregation seemed to be numbered."[46] Morgan notes what he calls a cleft between the profession of Christian faith and the discipleship that would evidence that faith. Rather, worshippers "come to listen to the preacher not because he is sent by God, but because he is an able man or talented or he is entertaining to listen to."[47] Similarly, the singing may become "mere self-indulgence" rather than a means of profound worship.

These comments reflect, too, the influence of a Barthian theology of the word of God and its sense of the deep confrontation of human religious feeling with the Gospel as God's call to discipleship and faith. Later, Morgan notes a number of significant Baptist preachers who were to take up the Barthian theology in the period after the Second World

---

46. Morgan, *Span of the Cross*, 164.

47. Morgan, *Span of the Cross*, 165–66.

War, including J. Ithel Jones, who was to be a colleague of Himbury's both in Cardiff and Melbourne.

While the theology and quality of preaching were advancing, however, Welsh society was moving in quite different directions. The coming of television and the growing secularism of Western societies took their toll. At the same time a growing interest in Welsh identity took a new direction. The youth section of the Welsh Council of Churches reported in 1973 that "the whole question of what it means to be Welsh is of more concern to young people than what it means to be a church member."[48] Movements for ecumenical and evangelical renewal both developed, though the former did not advance very far.

Official statistics published by the Baptist Union of Great Britain indicate the effective decline, particularly relative to the growing population of the country. Most noticeable in Table 1 are three aspects: the membership relative to the seating capacity of the chapels, the rapid decline in Sunday school scholars in the 1940s, and the steady decline in the numbers of pastors and preachers.

Table 1 Statistics Published by the Baptist Union of Great Britain

Year	No. of churches	Total seating capacity	Members	Sunday school scholars	Local preachers	Pastors in charge
1920	938	404,000	124,888	131,342	516	633
1940	957	409,759	116,813	97,945	504	530
1950	958	404,771	107,817	75,058	416	470
1960	952	Not recorded	94,548	64,263	379	470

Statistics held by the Baptist Union of Wales provide some further detail, indicating the number of Welsh-speaking churches in 1950 and 1960 was 556 and 544 respectively. English-speaking churches numbered 190 and 189 for the same years.[49]

Collectively, then, the life of the Baptist churches in Wales in the middle of the twentieth century can be seen to reflect the overall decline in participation in Nonconformist Christianity. Some other denominations experienced earlier and even more rapid decline. Nonetheless, the

---

48. Morgan, *Span of the Cross*, 257.

49. These statistics vary from the Baptist Union of Great Britain figures, as they do not include Monmouthshire.

Baptists in Wales continued with their commitment to local communities of worshipping believers, a focus upon preaching and teaching, music, and corporate fellowship. It was within this community that Mervyn Himbury was nurtured and found his own calling and career.

Mervyn Himbury, a Welsh Baptist

Mervyn Himbury was born on July 22, 1922, in Ystrad Mynach, a mining village in South Wales.[50] His first name was David, but by Welsh custom he was known by his second name. His parents were Reginald Harry Himbury and Olwen (or in some records Oliven) Thomas.

Reginald Himbury was born on August 20, 1894, though some records also indicate 1895. He moved as a young man from his native Dorset in England to Wales, where he worked as a coal miner. Like many hundreds of other English men, he came to this region when mines were opened up and there was strong demand for workers. Ystrad Mynach was a small village but the mine there was one of the largest coal mines in South Wales.

Reginald Himbury's war service records may well include several inaccuracies. The record indicates that he volunteered for the services in November 1911, when he was seventeen years of age, though his date of birth is there given as 1887 and his age on enlistment as twenty-four. One possible reason to question the accuracy of his enlistment date is his involvement in 1914 with a local football team. A photograph survives of Reginald Himbury with the Ystrad Mynach Stars Football Club from 1913–14. He is one of several men who appear to be officials rather than players. He is not in military uniform but wears a suit and tie, with his watch chain evident as well.

The service record refers to him belonging to the Third Regiment, First Battalion of the South Wales Borderers, a historic unit which had been formed as the First Monmouthshire Regiment in 1859.[51] As a stand-

---

50. The origin of the name of the village is debated. Some hold that it derives from a Latin phrase meaning "monks' walk." "Ystrad" is a wide, flat valley and "mynach" is the Welsh word for monk. Others, however, deny this translation, considering mynach a corruption of Man–Ach. It was a junction town for the railway as early as 1857.

51. This expression, "Third Regiment, First Battalion" is somewhat unusual military language and most likely means the third time the regiment was formed. The South Wales Borderers' website seems to indicate a process of such reforming. http://www.regiments.org/regiments/uk/volmil-wales/vinf/mm-1.htm

ing section of the British army, the South Wales Borderers enlisted men into Reserves, and this may well be the explanation of the 1911 date. If Reginald Himbury did enlist as a reservist, he would have continued at his work and community engagement, including the football team, then proceeding to full-time service after the outbreak of the First World War in August 1914.

Reginald Himbury saw service overseas during the First World War and rose to the rank of sergeant. He was awarded the Silver War Badge 1914–1920. He was discharged on January 8, 1919, and returned to Cardiff. He had been injured when a piece of shrapnel entered one of his lungs. Quite dangerous surgery followed to remove the lung. Though he survived, he was no longer fit to work down the mines, and was employed as a colliery timekeeper.

Olwen Thomas was born on December 12, 1898. She was from Aberystwyth, North Wales, but later moved to Merthyr Tydfil, a large industrial town in South Wales, where she lived and worked with her aunt in a hotel. Mervyn had frequent contact with his maternal grandmother in his childhood and early adolescence. The family were strongly committed Baptists. Mervyn had two cousins who were Baptist preachers and his mother's brother Idris Thomas (1889–1962) was one of the most well-known Baptist ministers in the country.

Reginald and Olwen had decided that when they were married, they would not have a divided home, so Olwen was confirmed and became an Anglican, in the Church of Wales. Mervyn was sent to the Anglican Sunday school. On Sunday evenings, however, he would sometimes go with his grandmother to a service at a Baptist church.

Reginald Himbury is described in the *Dictionary of Welsh Biography* as an ardent Anglican all his life. Nonetheless, there do not appear to be any records of his children being baptized at the parish church he attended, Holy Trinity, Ystrad Mynach. Mervyn did mention in his recollections a "gracious old man," Vicar Williams, who had "christened" him. The family burials also took place at Holy Trinity. Olwen Himbury died on March 6, 1956, and Reginald Himbury on May 2, 1970.

From the little information we do have, we can see that the family comprised some significant differences. Mervyn's mother was from North Wales; his father was from England but had lived most of his life in South Wales. His mother was a Baptist and his father an Anglican. For the first ten years of his life, Mervyn was an only child, probably rather unusual at the time. His precociousness, evident in the story of him preaching his first "sermon" at age three, is at least in part related to being, at the time, the only child. The entry in the *Dictionary of Welsh Biography* is incorrect, however, in stating that he was the only child, as John Hywel Himbury was born on July 17, 1932.

Himbury's own recollections offer some helpful insights into his early life. He was born at home, in 42 Station Street, Ystrad Mynach, but a year later the family moved to 13 Duffryn Street, a two-storied house, rather more substantial than the homes of many of the coal miners. From this house the pit could be seen on one side and the roof of the Hengoed Welsh Baptist Church on the other. Nearby were vegetable allotments, where Reginald Himbury had a plot. Mervyn would have attended the small Tir-y-Berth primary school not far away.

One fundamental feature of Welsh community life at this time was that people walked almost everywhere they went. There were very few motor cars. Mervyn walked three to four miles to school.[52] The year of his birth was the beginning of the Great Depression. In 1921 a "summer strike" at the mines had failed. Reginald Himbury's wage was cut in half just before Mervyn was born. Many people "lived rough." Himbury remembered one such man, a street character who described himself as "an unlucky fool" but who urged the young lad to learn the Bible as he had, too. Himbury recalled youth squatting in the street, passing a single cigarette between them. Cigarettes dominated society—Himbury recalled the prices of Woodbines, five for threepence, or ten for sixpence. He too got into the smoking habit. The school tuckshop sold Players cigarettes individually.

Himbury's recollections also offer some insight into local ecumenical relations. From the beginning, his Christian experience was ecumenical. Mervyn described "the church" (the Anglican Church) as for the elite, while the Nonconformist churches were middle-class. Although he began church life attending the Church of Wales, he became fed up with it by his early teens. As noted earlier, he sometimes attended a Baptist chapel with his grandmother. Now, with several teenage friends, he joined the youth meetings at Hengoed Welsh Baptist Church and soon after decided for himself to become a Baptist. His mother joined him in attending services there.

The wider ecumenical situation is worthy of some comment. In the background was the ongoing debate about disestablishment of the

---

52. This and the following information is derived from Himbury's recollections, recorded in approximately 1997 and made available to me by Maelor Himbury.

Church of Wales (which had officially taken place about the time Mervyn was born, but there remained much discussion of whether, in fact, anything had changed). For some time at least, there appears to have been no noticeable change due, as some have suggested, to a lack of imagination on the part of the church leadership. With this lack of change, the ongoing post-war depression, and the growth in socialist ideas, the Church of Wales was rapidly losing support among the general population. There was also the continuing matter of the Welsh language versus the "anglicizing" of Wales. Reginald Himbury refused to allow Welsh to be spoken in his home, whereas at school Mervyn was learning Welsh language, literature, and history, and it is possible that this, too, was a factor in his teenage decision to move to a Welsh-speaking chapel and become a Baptist. He was baptized at the Hengoed Welsh Baptist Church in October 1937.

While there were many cooperative activities between the Nonconformist churches, generally the Anglican churches did not participate. One vicar of Holy Trinity would have nothing to do with the Nonconformist churches. The Whit-Monday procession each year was led by an Anglican band and moved toward a park where the people joined in games. This vicar refused to allow the Holy Trinity Sunday school to join in, which created real tension in the community. Prize money for these games was collected by Reginald Himbury (through his office at the mine), the men contributing one penny per week. Eighty percent of the men canceled their "subscription" to this community project. Reflecting on this experience, Himbury observed that there was never any real relationship between the Anglican and Nonconformist churches, and it was a joy for him to see warm ecumenical relationships in Australia, including Catholics.

Himbury observed that for their part the Nonconformists' attitudes toward the Anglican Church were "not all grace and harmony" either. Hengoed Baptist Church could be very narrow and uncooperative. They practiced a closed Communion, which meant that the table was "fenced." It was not open to Presbyterians or Anglicans, those not baptized by immersion. Literally (and ironically) the words were spoken, "We will divide for the Communion." Strangers visiting the service would be asked whether they qualified to take Communion.

The Baptists did not hold a service on Good Friday, an old Puritan view that recognized only the days commended in Scripture. Similarly, there was no Ascension Day service, which had the effect that Anglican boys at Himbury's school had a half day off while the Nonconformist boys did not. An ecumenical Good Friday service was organized, though not with the Anglicans. There was not a large gathering, since it was a working day for all the men. The service culminated in Communion, but the Hengoed Baptists did not partake.

Funerals were another distinctive feature of local community life. These were often shared, when more than one person had died within close proximity. When someone died, window blinds went down in the entire street as a mark of respect and everyone related, as family or neighbor, visited the home. Funeral ceremonies began at the house, though not everyone could be inside. Someone would announce a hymn, which was sung as the coffin was brought outside. Then everyone walked as the coffin was carried to the church. (The community walked together in this way for wedding services as well.) At the church there was a long service. Any minister present in the congregation was asked to take some part, such as a reading, prayer, or eulogy. There would be two or three hymns. Then the funeral moved to the grave where another service was held, culminating in singing. The community was united in death, with a sense of belonging to each other regardless of status or role. Much of this changed after the Second World War, however, with increased use of cars and higher incomes. The walking processions ended, substituted by cars and hearses required to move at a minimal speed. Something of essential community value was lost.

Hengoed Welsh Baptist Chapel was one of the earliest Baptist churches in the region. Hugh Matthews asserted that its history goes back to 1650.[53] The original chapel building was on the top of a hill.[54] Hengoed Baptist Church, as it is now, is further down the valley. The records of this church make for fascinating examination. One volume, the church membership register, dating from 1861 onwards, has not only a list of members' names but also whether or not they participated in the Sabbath school, whether they could read, if and when they were removed from the membership—whether by death, or because they were "suspended" or "excluded" for reasons such as "neglect," "drunk," "adultery," or "fighting." The minutes of the church and deacon's meetings from 1940 to 1978 are handwritten in Welsh until 1961; thereafter in English.

53. In personal conversation with me, June 2018.

54. There continues to be a Baptist Church on that original site. The building was closed for many years, but in 2010 it was reopened as the base for a new form of ministry seeking to serve the community.

Two other sets of records are the grave records and Sunday school register. The grave records include handwritten volumes dating back through the nineteenth and twentieth centuries. Most of these have since been typed up and indexed. These typed records indicate the names of those buried, location of graves, a description of the headstones, and quote, where possible, the wording on those memorials. One striking instance, which illustrates something of the context of the community, is the grave of David Davies of Powell's Cottage, "who died from an accident received at the Ocean Colliery, Treharris, February 6, 1901, aged 29 years." This example indicates the not uncommon experience of accidents and deaths affecting very young men and their families. The predominance of common Welsh names is very striking also: Davies, Morgan, Jones, Rees, Thomas, and Roberts. There are no records of any Himbury graves.

It is unclear when exactly Mervyn Himbury began attending the Hengoed Welsh Baptist Chapel. What is definite is that from January 1937, when he was fourteen years old, he attended the Sunday school at Hengoed. The Sunday school register is a remarkable book detailing the names of scholars and teachers, with a tick for attendance and a dot or cross for absence, through every Sunday of the years 1937 to 1949. In the absence of any register for earlier years, we do not know if this was the beginning or the continuation of Mervyn's involvement in the Sunday school.

The register is arranged with what appears to be an adult class first for each year. For at least some years, the teacher of this class was the minister, whose name, title, and qualifications are stated: Rev. Haydn Morgan, BA. It is presumably this minister who encouraged Mervyn to begin preaching, and who also baptized him. In 1937, the name of Mrs. R. Himbury (always known with her husband's initial) appears as the teacher of what was most likely a junior class, from January to April, but then from August 29 she was regular in attendance at the adult class for the duration of this entire record. In the list for 1940, the word "Sup't" appears in brackets after her name: perhaps indicating that she was a supplementary teacher. It could be that she was the superintendent, but this seems unlikely as that term is not used of any other person in the record. In 1947, Mrs. Himbury is listed as the teacher of a class of fifteen children.

Mervyn Himbury attended from the beginning of January 1937 and was consistent in his attendance through the next six years, into the first years of his university education. It is interesting that his name remains on this roll even into those years when, as a college student for the ministry, he was preaching regularly at other churches. In the final years of his studies at South Wales Baptist College he attended infrequently. Thus in 1944 and 1945, Mrs. Himbury attended almost every week while Mervyn was with her only five times for the year. At this stage, both Mervyn and his mother were members of the "adult" class. It is not named as such, but I infer from the list itself that this is what it was. Some of those listed in this class were also listed as teachers, at the head of other class rolls. John Himbury also attended regularly through these years.

Two other features of this record are noteworthy. During the years of the Second World War, there are names of men against which there are long strings of dots, indicating that the Sunday school continues to hold them as members of the class, even though presumably they were absent on military service. Also during these years, the Sunday school shrank to just over half its strength in 1937. Many factors would have contributed to this, one of them being the widely noted general disillusionment in the community with matters of faith and the traditional institutions of society.

In addition to the Sunday school classes, young people attended meetings on Friday evenings or, when a little older, Monday evenings. Himbury recalled that in these gatherings the young people were schooled in public prayer. "We learned to pray with fluency." As he was in fact the only boy exactly his age, Himbury joined with a group a little older and "just tagged along," he said. It is clear that, in addition to school, the church and its activities took up a significant proportion of these young people's lives.

A final feature of Baptist church life is worthy of mention: the place of alcohol. There is a mistaken view of the Nonconformists as being anti-alcohol, Himbury observed. Actually, there was not a great tradition of abstinence. Ale had been a part of the life of the church in the eighteenth century, when a cupboard was installed to one side of the pulpit to store an amount of ale so that the preacher could soothe his throat after the service. At Croes-y-Parc, where Himbury served during his years at South Wales Baptist College, an elderly lady related to him that, as a girl, she was responsible for going to the pub to get a pail of ale, which was then to be mulled by the stove for the minister. From some time in the mid-nineteenth century, American influences led to a changed view of alcohol as a social evil, and many of the churches no longer used alcoholic wine at Communion services after that time.

Several other brief comments in Himbury's recollections provide insight into the nature of the Hengoed church and his own family. One of the deacons changed his shifts at the mine so that he could travel to Wrexham to attend Himbury's ordination in 1950. Another suffered so greatly from silicosis that his wheezing could be heard as one walked past his house.

Rev. Haydn Morgan, who was the minister at Hengoed Baptist Church during the time Himbury was there, had a difficult time, in some measure due to problems caused by his wife, who was a very competent Welsh scholar. The church was increasingly divided over language. There was a concern to preserve the language, but there was also a desire to involve the young people who did not speak Welsh. Himbury believed that the divisions between his loyalty to his wife and her career as a linguist and the needs of the church ruined Morgan's ministry. There were also many financial problems, including times when the bank could not honor the church's checks. Only once the war came was there new prosperity.

Another problem was that Morgan was an ardent pacifist (as were very many Baptists at this time). Himbury recalled that the church set up a wireless in the building, so that the 10.30 a.m. Sunday service could stop to listen to the 11.00 a.m. announcement when the prime minister declared the nation at war with Germany. "Absolute horror came over the whole congregation."

Haydn Morgan and Reginald Himbury would often discuss the former's commitment to pacifism, most likely during pastoral visits to the home. Himbury's mother would struggle to maintain peace within the home at these times. Matters came to a head when Morgan accepted appointment as a military chaplain. For him, this solved a problem as he could support the war effort without becoming a combatant, but Reginald Himbury criticized Morgan, as "he did not like chaplains." The basis for this dislike was an appalling incident in Reginald Himbury's own experience during the First World War. At Mons, in France, on a day the battalion was to go into battle, the chaplain administered Holy Communion to the officers but not to the men, claiming not to have time for that. As an Anglican, Reginald Himbury resented that all his life. On the other hand, he had also known and made tea for the famous chaplain "Woodbine Willy" (Rev. Studdert Kennedy). Although some acrimony is evident in these recollections, it is also clear that Reginald Himbury continued an active concern for and interest in Mervyn's career and was often present to hear him preach in Baptist churches. He did not go back on his original commitment that he would not have a divided home.

School

Mervyn and John Himbury attended the local primary school and then went on to attend Lewis' Grammar School, Pengam, which was not far from their home. They would have walked or ridden a bicycle the three to four miles to school. The school buildings, other than the original headmaster's house, have all been replaced since that time. The original rugby field does remain, however! Lewis' School provided an excellent academic foundation. Until recent decades, it was a school for boys only. There was a partner school for girls at Hengoed. Ewart Smith's history of Lewis' School provides much helpful detail of the life of the school in the years between the two world wars, including the period when Mervyn Himbury was a student.[55] Established in 1729, the school has a long and proud academic strength, including a focus on its Welsh heritage. For example, in 1929–30, of the eighty-three students who left the school, fourteen went on to university studies (a very high proportion for that time). Only one of these went to an English university—Oxford. All the others studied at the tertiary institutions in Cardiff: University College, Technical College, or Medical School. In 1936 the school psalter was published, with 136 psalms. Of these, forty-three were in Welsh and all but six of the psalms and tunes were composed by staff or pupils. The new psalter was used for the first time in a service to celebrate the coronation of George VI in May 1937. Undoubtedly, Mervyn Himbury would have attended this service.

In this period also the school rugby colors were light and dark blue. Smith comments that perhaps these colors were chosen with Oxbridge in mind.[56] It is noteworthy that when Whitley College was founded, these same colors were chosen for the new college. Another feature of the school's life in this period was the reclamation of what had, for a time, been known as the school hall for its intended purpose as a chapel, with pews installed to seat 260 boys.

---

55. Smith, *Lewis' School, Pengam*.
56. Smith, *Lewis' School, Pengam*, 86.

A significant feature in the life of the school were red-letter days, particularly the school eisteddfod. Smith comments, "the School Eisteddfod produced more items in English as the years rolled by, but back in 1931 even the program, which listed the prizes and scholarships awarded in the previous year, was in Welsh."[57] The eisteddfod was always held on St. David's Day, March 1. Speech Day and Founder's Day were other red-letter events.

Entrance to the school was competitive. There was a common entrance examination to the grammar schools in the area. Roughly one thousand applied for the one hundred places in Lewis' School. This examination was generally known as "the scholarship" or the "elevenplus."

Himbury's parents would have been required to pay fees of up to £7.10 per year (plus a games fee) but this could be reduced on examination of the return of income. A maintenance grant could also be received for parents on low incomes. It seems likely that the Himbury family would have received assistance of this nature. That both sons completed their secondary schooling and went on to university is evidence of the family's commitment to education. The strong Welsh cultural value placed on education was expressed in the fact of lower university fees than in England, for those who could gain entry: £20 a year for arts, £25 for science degrees. The 1944 Education Act further extended these provisions, including Local Authority Grants which greatly assisted students over many decades.

Mervyn was a student at the Lewis' School from 1933 to 1941. During that time, the school curriculum was very broad, involving many academic subjects as well as several "practical" subjects. Students would take a range of subjects during the first three years: English, Welsh, mathematics, history, geography, physics, chemistry, biology, botany, zoology, French, German, Latin, woodwork, metalwork, technical drawing, physical education, art, music, religious instruction. By the end of the third year a boy would have selected his subjects to be studied up to O level. Success at this level allowed further selection of normally three subjects for the A level.[58]

We do not know which subjects Mervyn chose, except that they were in the humanities, and definitely included history. As became even

---

57. Smith, *Lewis' School, Pengam*, 76.

58. This information was provided by some former students who were members of the Gelligaer Historical Society in July 2018 and forwarded by the chairperson, Ms. Annie Owen.

more evident at university, and in his own words, he "never had any linguistic ability." He took Welsh for his higher school certificate, called the O levels, drilled by a teacher named H. G. Jones; but Latin was his bête noire. Clearly other boys knew of his struggle, as when the results came out the boys were all told, "Himbury's got his Latin!"

John Himbury studied and passed pure and applied mathematics, physics, and chemistry. In 1951 the examination run by the Central Welsh Board was changed to A—Advanced Level and S—Scholarship Level. John Himbury was one of the first pupils in the country to sit and pass examinations in science at A Level.

There is only limited information about Mervyn's years at school. We do know that he was a keen rugby player, as were his father and brother, and his preferences in study led him more toward history than the sciences. John Himbury took the opposite direction. He was a member of the editorial committee of the school magazine for 1949–50, was a prefect from 1950–51, and was the hooker in the First XV.

The school year 1950–51 was the commencement of a "purple period" in the school's academic and athletic history. The school First XV became a dominant force in school rugby and produced a number of schoolboy caps as well as full internationals, even one for England. Academically it was outstanding, with four state scholarships in 1951, seven in 1952, seven in 1953, two in 1954, and three in 1955. The observation was made that John Himbury combined athletic with academic ability.[59] There can be little doubt that Mervyn Himbury celebrated his brother's success in all these areas.

During his years of secondary schooling Mervyn was regularly engaged in preaching at various local churches, which provided supplementary income for the family. It is also recorded in some of his recollections that teenage boys were employed to attend at the head of the coal pit and to have lighted cigarettes ready for the men as they emerged from the lift cage. Mervyn attributed his addiction to smoking cigarettes to this activity during his teens.

From these few details we can perhaps gain a little insight into the family home. It was a Christian home, where education was valued and participation in church life was a priority. The few photographs which remain from his years at college indicate a person always well presented, neatly shaven, and well-dressed. Clearly, too, value was placed on working

---

59. Further information from the Gelligaer Historical Society.

hard. Mervyn did not always engage strongly with his studies. For at least his first two years at university he wanted more to have a good time than to study. This stands in contrast to other years when he gained strong grades and was awarded scholarships to enable him to go further than most of his peers, eventually to Oxford University.

Another feature of the family home which we can assume likely was an active interest in the world around them, through the reading of newspapers. A fascinating study of the history of journalism in Wales details the large number of local newspapers published during the years between the two world wars, and the growing readership, including the increasing numbers of women reporting that they read the papers. This study indicates the importance placed upon the publication of the papers during the Second World War, in the face of censorship, shortages of newsprint and the trebling of costs. The stories of interruptions to the printing during Luftwaffe bombing raids on Cardiff are extraordinary, including the incident on March 31, 1941, when an unexploded bomb was noticed on the print floor of the Western Mail, which led not to cessation of printing but merely to running the presses slowly to reduce vibration![60] Before the era of television, newspapers and the radio would have been a vital feature of home and student life.

Marriage and Family

Mervyn proceeded from Lewis' Grammar School to the South Wales Baptist College and Cardiff University. He undertook studies toward a bachelor of arts and then a bachelor of divinity between 1942 and 1948. He graduated BA with first class honors in history in 1945 and completed the BD in 1948. He was then accepted into Oxford University to undertake research toward a BLitt, which at that time was the highest earned degree offered at Oxford. He went to Regent's Park College, then a small Baptist college, where he lived and studied until early in 1950 when he was appointed to Chester Street Baptist Church, Wrexham, where he was ordained. This was the oldest of the Dissenting churches in Wales, fitting for a man who had just spent several years researching the period of its foundation. The church has a very old Dissenters' graveyard. During his time at Wrexham, he lived with Rev. Idris Thomas.

---

60. Jones, *Press, Politics and Society*, 218.

Later that same year, however, he was called to the staff of the South Wales Baptist College as tutor in church history. Mervyn asked the church deacons to assist him in discerning whether he should accept this call, as it was so soon after he had been appointed their pastor.

At the same time as his transition from Wrexham to Cardiff, from pastoral ministry to teaching and training ministers, Mervyn became engaged to be married to Gwladys Marion Phillips, who was from Llanelly, in Carmarthenshire.

Marion's parents were Blodwen Bevan and William Phillips, who were married in 1920 in Llanelly. Marion was born in July 1921. Late in her life Marion offered the following recollections of her early life and church involvement:

> When I was young there was no time like Easter. We were confident that the snows had ended and the darkness of the long winter nights were being swallowed up in longer days. We always had our new summer outfits for Easter and warmer days: usually a dress and coat outfit.
>
> In many parts of Wales, Good Friday was not a holiday and we had no special services on that day. The New Testament did not specify that festival, it only commends us to observe the Sabbath.
>
> Easter was a time of song. Preaching had priority in our churches, but at Easter we knew we could sing our praises in full and show our love for our Lord. For weeks we had practiced for the festival, learning new hymns, anthems and more.
>
> The English population called the festival Easter after the pagan goddess of spring. For us it was the passe, after the Greek word for God's redemptive act on our behalf. No wonder we sang so lustily at Easter.[61]

After her school years, Marion moved to Cardiff to take up a scholarship to study public health nursing, at the School of Medicine at Cardiff University. She and Mervyn were friends for some five years before they married and had, in fact, often traveled together to the university in Mervyn's time there also.

There is a story that suggests Marion had long hoped that Mervyn would ask her to marry him, but he seemed either too shy or preoccupied with his studies. When, however, another young lady seemed to take a

---

61. Extract from the magazine of the Moreland Baptist Church, provided by Maelor Himbury. The extract has no date.

strong interest in him, Marion decided she needed to encourage him a little more directly. They were married early in 1951 and their first son, Philip Maelor, was born on June 23, 1952.

John Himbury

John Himbury was born ten years after Mervyn. Though they went to the same grammar school, the significant gap in ages meant they did not move in the same social circles. John's son Simon shared with me the following helpful notes regarding his father's schooling and career:

> John was a bright student who enjoyed the sciences more than history and literature, and who enjoyed playing rugby for his school. At the age of seventeen, John went to Urdd Welsh Language Camp in Llangranog, Wales, where he met my mother and his wife to be, Eleni Stephanakis, who was born in 1934 and was fifteen at the time. She had learned Welsh after being evacuated from Cardiff from 1939–1945. Prior to that Eleni had spoken Greek at home to her parents who had emigrated from Thessaloniki, Greece, to Cardiff in 1920 and used English at school.

John stayed in contact with Eleni and visited her in Cardiff from time to time. After finishing school, John went on to study metallurgy at Cardiff University. He later completed his national service at Royal Air Force (RAF) St. Athan. John and Eleni were married on March 25, 1955, at Y Tabernacl, a historic Baptist chapel in Cardiff, and they also had a Greek wedding service at the Greek Orthodox Church, Cardiff. Mervyn, Marion, and a very young Maelor were guests at the wedding. John later worked for British Zeon in Sully for a few years and then moved to London and Hildenborough, Kent, where he worked for Bowater PLC. John and Eleni then returned to live and work in Cardiff.

Eleni and John wanted to have a large family but were unable to conceive children of their own. They adopted Simon John Himbury, born December 24, 1962; Thomas Stephen Himbury, born December 16, 1964, and Rachel Sophia Himbury, born December 12, 1969. Although each had different birth parents, the loving nurture of John and Eleni formed a rich family life. Close contact with Rachel Thomas, one of John's Welsh aunts, was an important feature of their life, perhaps especially after John's death. It was at Rachel Thomas's home that Simon, Thomas, and Rachel Himbury met Mervyn on one occasion and Maelor on at least two occasions.

John had been self-employed for a number of years and was returning home from work on November 19, 1970, when he was involved in a car accident. He was fatally injured in the crash. His funeral was held in Ystrad Mynach.

Eleni was left with three very young children, the youngest not yet one year old. In 1972, Eleni took in her nephew and niece, Charles and Soula Stephanakis, after their mother (her sister-in-law) was overcome by smoke and passed away in a fire at The Belfry Hotel and Golf Club. Simon Himbury remarked that his mother "brought us all up as siblings, so I often refer to them as an extra brother and sister."[62] At the time of writing, Eleni continues to live in Cardiff.

Simon Himbury offered the following tribute to each of his parents:

> Eleni is a wonderful mother and brought us all up with a healthy combination of good food, love, and affection. Thanks to her we did well in our studies, played rugby and hockey for the school and county, attended Albany Road Baptist Church, and were active Cubs, Scouts, Brownies, and Guides.
>
> My memories of Daddy (John) are of a kind, softly spoken man with a big smile. We often watched him play rugby for Dinas Powis where he played hooker. John had previously played for Ystrad Mynach and Tonbridge. We had some lovely family holidays staying in our caravan near Llangranog, where my parents had met many years before, and playing on the beach. In 1970 we drove to Greece to stay with my mother's extended family. Her mother was one of eleven children and there was a very large and welcoming family living in and around Thessaloniki to for us to meet. That was the last holiday we had with Daddy.

Simon Himbury also remembers Mervyn, whom he met two or three times when he was a child: "I remember him as a substantial, confident, talkative man with a large smile like my father, John." After studying law for his first degree, Simon went to work in Japan, learning the language and teaching English in a variety of settings. This allowed him to visit Mervyn, Marion, Maelor, and Michael in 1987 when he traveled around Australia for the summer, then again in 1995 when he and his

---

62. This information of John Himbury's life and family was offered in personal messages to me.

wife, Sita, met Mervyn, Marion, and Maelor. This was a valuable time of reunion for family members who lived such a long way from each other.

The year 1970 was clearly a very difficult year for all the Himbury family. On May 2 of that year Reginald Himbury died at the age of seventy-five. He was buried at Holy Trinity church, Ystred Mynach. Then in November, John Himbury was killed, leaving Eleni with her very young children and the only remaining members of the Himbury family on the other side of the world. No doubt they too felt this profound loss, made all the more acute by distance. Communications and the means of travel were not what they are today and there was no question of going there at short notice.[63]

Beginning a Career

During the years he was teaching at South Wales Baptist College, Mervyn also provided pastoral oversight for the Croes-y-Parc Baptist Church. This involved him in regular preaching there, although it is likely he was also invited to preach in other places as well, as a representative of the college. Croes-y-Parc Baptist Church is located in Chapel Lane, Peterston-super-Ely. It is set in a semirural location, on the outskirts of Cardiff. The *British Almanac* for 1956 lists David Mervyn Himbury as resident at Bayleigh, Peterston-super-Ely.

When he began at South Wales Baptist College, his salary was £9 a week, but with no house. For the first month there (before his marriage), he lived at home and traveled to Cardiff every day. For a short while after they were married, the couple had a small flat off Cathedral Walk. Then Professor Aubrey Johnson, who was a great friend and encouragement to Mervyn, said that if only he had a car there was a manse available at Croes-y-Parc: Mervyn could preach there regularly, and the house would be provided. He and Marion discussed this possibility. They decided it was much cheaper to buy a car than a house!

Mervyn taught at the South Wales Baptist College and the University of Cardiff until the end of 1958 when he accepted the call to be principal of the Baptist College of Victoria, in Melbourne.

The idea of a move to Australia arose through the coincidence of two things. Marion had seen an advertisement for a position at the

---

63. In addition, Mervyn Himbury was struggling with some serious difficulties in the life of Whitley College at that time and would not have absented himself.

Queensland Baptist College and then Ernest Payne, who had recently visited New Zealand and Australia, told Mervyn that the Baptist Union of Victoria was looking for someone to be principal of their college. Payne knew that Mervyn was not happy at the South Wales Baptist College. They knew so little about Australia, however. In their recollections, as recorded by Marita Munro, Mervyn says that the only thing they had heard really had to do with cricket and that was hardly complimentary from either side.

Then came an invitation for Mervyn to deliver some lectures at the Ecumenical Institute in Geneva. Marion traveled with him and, while they were there, they began to wonder what it would be like to be head of a place such as the Institute, or the college in Melbourne. They had begun to feel that they and their family would have a much better future somewhere beyond Wales. It did not take them long to decide. It was a joint decision: they would accept the invitation to go to Melbourne.

Marion has described how difficult it was for them to leave. In the period leading up to their departure, Marion was quite unwell. She had hoped to have another child and had more than once miscarried. Now, her health was seriously endangered. Again, we quote some of her recollections:

> We left Wales for Australia in January 1959. The northern winter was extremely cold with snow and ice, so there was no fun in packing the crates in an empty house ready for transport to our new world. It was just like Abraham going out not knowing whither he went. The cold matched the chill in our hearts.
>
> As Mervyn was preaching in Sutton, Surrey, the weekend before we left, Maelor and I spent the weekend with our doctor, who was also our friend. We were to travel by train to London from Cardiff. I was extremely unwell with deep jaundice and our doctor ordered me to hospital where I was told not to travel as I would not survive the journey. There was no doubt in our minds that God had called us, and we were going. A pharmacist at the hospital and a nursing colleague provided treatment for me, which might help. As it was a weekend, he was to meet the London train and provide enough medication for the journey. As if to test our faith further, he missed the train and had to send the medication on to each port of call.
>
> It was not very easy to leave my family on the platform. The snow continued on our way into Cardiff platform.

Marion then explained that the principal of the college, Dr. Ithel Jones, and his wife, Nana, "cared for Mr. Himbury Senior, for which we have always been grateful." What an emotional wrench it must have been for them, Welsh Baptists now about to travel to the other side of the world.

CHAPTER 3

Ministerial Education

IN SEPTEMBER 1941, DAVID Mervyn Himbury began studying at the Cardiff College of the University of Wales and began an informal association with the South Wales Baptist College. He had, in fact, applied to become a ministerial student of the Baptist college and had sat the entrance exam for that purpose. He was not at that point accepted. The college had interviewed thirty-four applicants but had funds for only four students. In his recollections, Himbury said that it didn't matter that much that he was not accepted at that stage. Having passed the matriculation, he gained entrance to the university, for which he was also awarded a County Scholarship which covered his fees and provided £40 a year for living. He would live at home and travel to the university each day. Nonetheless, Himbury was close to many of the students at the Baptist college, as they also studied at the university and in some instances were in the same classes.

Thus began a pattern which continued throughout his career, participating in two colleges or institutions, first as a student in Cardiff, then again at Oxford, and again when he returned to Cardiff as a teacher.[1] It is of benefit to consider some of the history and character of each of these colleges to gain some insight into his somewhat checkered career as a student in Cardiff. Since it was Himbury's desire to train for the Baptist ministry and it was also the context for the first part of his teaching career, we begin with the Baptist college.

---

1. These patterns were also, in slightly different ways, part of his life in Melbourne.

The South Wales Baptist College

In the introduction to his history of the South Wales Baptist College, written for its ter-jubilee in 1957, Himbury asserted that "the story of the development of ministerial education among the Baptists of Wales is one of the most significant chapters in their history."[2] It is noteworthy that Himbury used the term "ministerial education." There was a strong desire that preachers within the Baptist churches in Wales should be *educated* as well as *trained*. In an article published much later in his career, Himbury explained that this desire was firmly rooted in the Puritan traditions of the Baptist communities.

> The Puritan tradition which did so much to mould many of the forms of English preaching was founded on the belief that the preaching ministry was so great and holy that those who were called to exercise it needed the best training that could be offered them. . . . All pastors must have an adequate education and should have those skills in ancient languages which alone can unlock the door to the truths of the Scriptures. They should be trained "in such arts and sciences as are handmarks unto divinity."[3]

It was the missionary concern of Welsh Baptists for the English-speaking populations of Glamorganshire and Pembrokeshire that led to the foundation of a Baptist college at Abergavenny. These areas were deemed as "dark" as regions of Africa "for want of English preachers."[4] The new academy (as it was termed, despite its size) was established by Rev. Micah Thomas, in his own home originally and with just three students. It was supported by Baptists from all around Wales. Thomas taught English, provided reading materials and sermon classes and, with time, an entry requirement was set: the ability to read English. Himbury's short article on "Academic Life at Abergavenny" notes "the 1814 Report tells us that hardly any students, when they entered the college, were acquainted with the meaning, orthography or pronunciation of English words."[5] Welsh grammar was soon added to the curriculum, along with philosophy and science. The college soon moved to a suitable building

---

2. Himbury, *South Wales Baptist College*, 11.

3. Himbury, "Training Baptist Ministers," 337. Quotation is from *Directory of Public Worship*, 1644.

4. Matthews, *From Abergavenny to Cardiff*, 15.

5. Himbury, "Academic Life at Abergavenny," 13.

in Pontypool, and by the middle of the century classics and mathematics were also parts of the curriculum. At this time particularly capable students also proceeded to study at Regent's Park College, London.

The vision for an educated pastoral leadership gained such support that two more Baptist academies were created in the mid-nineteenth century, at Haverfordwest (1839) and Llangollen (1862). On the one hand, it was considered desirable that ministry training should be more local—especially given the differences between North and South Wales. On the other hand, maintaining three colleges was expensive, so there were calls for the creation of a single college, for more efficient use of the support donated by the churches. Instead, each of the institutions moved to other locations, to serve their constituencies more effectively. Llangollen moved to Bangor (1892), Pontypool to Cardiff (1893), and Haverfordwest to Aberystwyth (1894).

Mervyn Himbury wrote an article celebrating the life of Thomas Thomas (1805–1881), who had studied at the college in Abergavenny and in due course was the first principal of the Baptist college in Pontypool. He was also the first Welsh-speaking person to be elected president of the Baptist Union of Great Britain and Ireland and gained recognition for his public declarations on social matters and on Christian unity. When Thomas retired as principal of the college in 1876, Himbury states, "that institution was one of the largest centres of ministerial training among Baptists; it was also a centre of social and spiritual influence that helped to make the Baptists of Monmouthshire not only strong, numerically, but influential in every aspect of the life of the Principality."[6]

By the turn of the century just two colleges remained, at Bangor and Cardiff. The Cardiff college was later renamed the South Wales Baptist College and became the premier institution for training Welsh Baptist ministers.

The education provided in these institutions developed also with the changing social context and closely followed changes within the universities in Wales. The Baptist colleges each formed a partnership with the University of Wales.

In 1896 the University of Wales established a graduate theology degree, the bachelor of divinity, but in order to do this the university drew upon the teaching staff of various theological colleges. Thus was born the pattern which continues to this day, an interlaced relationship whereby

---

6. Himbury, "Thomas Thomas," 156.

small denominational colleges can draw upon the strengths of adjacent universities, while the universities gain the contribution of scholars and teachers who are not immediately on their payroll. In Bangor, the Congregationalist college and the Baptist college combined to form the School of Theology within the university there. In Cardiff, there was no other theological college with whom the Baptist college might join, so no School of Theology was formed within the university at that time. Rather, the university established a direct link with the Baptist college, in effect recognizing its teaching program as part of the university. Since the college did not have the requisite four members of staff, however, the university itself provided one member of staff to join the existing three "tutors," as they were called, from the Baptist college.

This arrangement worked well enough until 1927, when Theodore Robinson, tutor in Old Testament at the Baptist college and already a highly distinguished Hebrew language scholar, was appointed a professor at the university. Technically, this meant that the Baptist college was no longer contributing its full quotient to the joint program, but the situation was permitted for some years. In 1930 the new principal of the university college at Cardiff, J. Frederick Rees, worked to resolve this difficulty by promoting the creation of the Cardiff School of Theology, formally beginning in 1936.[7] Rees's ecumenical vision was not fully realized until 1958, when St. Michael's College, Llandaff, joined, and was further enhanced in 1962 when a Presbyterian center was created in Cardiff. Interestingly, this center was established by Baptist scholar George Davies, and his successor, Paul Ballard—another Baptist—led the center from 1968 till 1973 when it was incorporated into the university's department of biblical studies. The commitment of Welsh Baptists to quality education is evident in their participation in these relationships.

In 1934 it was recognized that not all those seeking education for ministry were eligible to enter the bachelor of divinity course and the University of Wales created a diploma of theology, something the Baptist college had been seeking for almost three decades.

The education provided to students of the Baptist college was remarkably broad. This reflected the needs of students, many of whom would not have completed their secondary education. Mervyn Himbury noted that the relationship with, and physical proximity to, the university

---

7. The full title of the college was the University College of South Wales and Monmouthshire, though it was generally referred to as the university college at Cardiff, and in 1972 was renamed University College Cardiff.

led to "a general rise in the standards demanded of students" prior to entry to the college. Even from 1893 it was hoped that all candidates would matriculate, either into the University of Wales or the University of London. Should students gain such entry, the college's own entrance examination was waived. Himbury described the requirements of this examination (in 1893):

> Of the following list of ten subjects, candidates were to choose eight, of which 1, 2, 9, and 10 were compulsory:
>
> 1. General biblical knowledge
> 2. English grammar
> 3. Welsh grammar
> 4. English history from Henry VII to Charles II
> 5. Greek, the elements of Greek grammar, together with chosen texts in Classical and Hellenistic Greek
> 6. Latin, the elements, and a text from Caesar
> 7. Arithmetic and algebra
> 8. Geometry, Euclid, Book 1
> 9. A sketch of a sermon in either English or Welsh on a specified text
> 10. Reading and delivery.[8]

What is evident from this entry requirement is a focus upon those skills mentioned in the quotation from Mervyn Himbury's paper on the training of Baptist ministers: language ability, along with biblical and historical knowledge. These elements also clearly reflect Welsh culture and suggest the desire of the churches for preachers who could provide edification and understanding on both a broad and deeper level for their congregations. Interestingly, however, there was no direct focus upon literature or music, although the subject on reading and delivery perhaps alludes to those elements in Welsh culture.

The relationship with the university and the advent of the BD led to the formulation of a clear course plan for all students, whether undertaking a degree or not. The pattern was devised in 1905 and followed for many decades, as is evident in Mervyn Himbury's own studies. Students taking an arts degree would in their first year study Latin, Greek, Hebrew or philosophy, plus one other subject chosen from English, Welsh, history or political science. In the second year they were to take Hebrew, Greek, and philosophy; then in the third year they would focus on two

---

8. Himbury, *South Wales Baptist College*, 79.

of these subjects, or an honors course in one of them. The arts degree thus provided a firm foundation for biblical and theological subjects to be taken in the bachelor of divinity.

The college itself provided subjects for the non-degree students, though from as early as 1908 it had urged the university to create a diploma course for this cohort. The diploma pathway incorporated many of the same disciplines required of the degree-enrolled students and we may surmise that, given the very small numbers in each group, many of these classes were combined.[9] The "college course," as it was commonly called, involved the following:

1. First year: Greek, Hebrew, English, and one of Welsh, philosophy or history

2. Second year: Hebrew, philosophy, and other theological subjects as prescribed by the college senate

3. Third year: Hebrew, plus Old Testament literature, canon and exegesis; Greek, plus New Testament literature, canon and exegesis; philosophy of religion, including theism; apologetics; the history of Christian doctrine; and church history, involving the first five centuries and the Reformation.

In addition to these subjects, students attended classes in pastoral theology, homiletics, Welsh, and "such other subjects as the principal and staff felt necessary."[10] These subjects would have been taken by all Baptist college students during their years in training.

The college itself was generally staffed by three teachers, known as "tutors" but in this period honored with the title Professor. One was appointed as principal, and for much of the history of the college the principal lived on site. Often it was the principal's wife who managed the physical conditions of the college as a kind of matron, overseeing the housekeeping and meals for the college community. Other tutors lived elsewhere and usually engaged in some form of ministry with one of the local Baptist churches. They also maintained close links with the various Baptist associations, including conducting the annual drive for donations to support the costs of educating students for the ministry.

---

9. This was also the pattern of studies at the Baptist College of Victoria during the early years when Himbury was principal, with some students taking the BD and others the Dip Theol.

10. Himbury, *South Wales Baptist College*, 80.

With this brief outline of the history of the South Wales Baptist College, it is worth considering the ideals of ministry and of education inherent in its operations. Here it is helpful to apply the contemporary idea of "graduate attributes": What skills or competencies did the college hope to engender and develop through the years of study and ministry training?

To begin with, the fundamental vision of ministry centered upon the roles of preacher and pastor. Almost everything that was included in the college courses was directed toward these aspects of ministry. The preaching class was a central and continuing element for every generation of students. Graduates were expected to have skills for preaching, including languages (Welsh and English), elocution, and competence in reading in public. A related skill was praying in public. Biblical and theological studies were another essential element, which in turn provided exegesis for preaching, and doctrinal guidance for the people. The educated pastor was to be an educator of the people. An understanding of Baptist identity and polity was also critical to the role of pastors as leaders of a local church.

Several other elements were inherent in this vision of ministry. One was a broad understanding of the society within which the local church would exercise its witness. Such understanding would contribute relevance to the preaching and teaching offered by a pastor.

The factors already mentioned indicate that the focus of ministry envisaged by the college education was on the lives of Baptist church members *as Christians*. This was the pastoral focus: to enable, support, and challenge local church members toward Christian faith and witness. Bible studies, prayer meetings, pastoral visitation, preparation for baptism, and the general life of the local fellowship were all means of nurturing Christian living. It is interesting to note the presence of an adult Bible class in the Hengoed Welsh Baptist Church where Himbury was baptized and nurtured as a Christian disciple and preacher. Later in his career, while in Melbourne, he became an admirer of the Southern Baptist Convention's Sunday School Board which had these same objectives and focus.

Reflecting upon this vision of education for ministry, it is also interesting to note what is not immediately to the fore. Some elements were more assumed rather than omitted. For example, whereas today there might be a strong focus on spirituality, in the training of pastors and in their work as spiritual guides, the personal prayer life of a pastor was more or less presumed through well-established norms and daily routines. On the other hand, there was virtually nothing focused upon the health and self-care of ministers, nor upon counseling as a pastoral activity. These aspects were developed in later decades. Relationship skills and "management" were assumed, rather than taught or nurtured. Administration was shared within a local church with the deacons and was not of itself taken as part of the pastor's role. Another later area of focus was upon community engagement, sometimes with a prophetic edge to it and at other times primarily seen in terms of service of the needy. These aspects were so much a part of local church life that, again, they were not separated as distinct activities or areas of pastoral training.

What then of the life of the students in the college? For a substantial part of its history, the college expected students to live in, though the facilities for doing so were very limited. As a result, some may have lived close by in "digs," while others commuted from their homes. The situation improved for a time when, in 1953, a new residential wing was opened, following a concerted effort to raise funds from both local and international Baptist sources. The presumption that ministerial candidates were unmarried men was not to last. At the end of the Second World War the college had several older students who had returned from war service. Most of these students were married and would not live in; neither could they rely on their family of origin for housing and support as most of the single men did. This development foreshadowed the changes of later decades, and today the college does not have any students in residence.

Himbury's "retrospect," the conclusion of his history of the college, notes that "student life through the 150 years has changed only in superficial ways." Among the candidates for ministerial education he observed "the same mixture of piety and fun, of diligence and rebellion, of irresponsibility and anxiety for the work of the ministry."[11] At times there were few organized student activities, while at other times there was a more formal community life, with rules, student meetings, and organized sports, and even a system of seniority by which men chose their bedrooms and studies.

Baptist college students were provided with a grant to support their living costs. These grants drew upon the annual contributions from the churches: £18 for a first-year student and £36 for each subsequent year. Himbury records that in 1939–40 the college had very good numbers of applicants and the buildings as they were then could accommodate

---

11. Himbury, *South Wales Baptist College*, 130.

thirty-five students; but there were only funds to support twenty-eight students. In 1940 it was decided to change the allocation of grants to provide £30 per year to all students, which meant that the college could afford to support thirty students.[12]

Both Mervyn Himbury and Hugh Matthews, in their respective histories of the college, recount several times when there was significant tension over staff appointments. One such controversy surrounded the appointment of a principal, another for a professor of church history, yet another of a professor of New Testament.[13] The details of these matters are not relevant here, except to note that they indicate the active interest, and sometimes covert exercise of power, on the part of the local churches toward what continued to be "their" college. Himbury observes that in several instances controversy might have been avoided if the applicant had been more fluent in the Welsh language or at least been seen to be so.

It is also significant that the relationship between the Baptist College of South Wales and the Cardiff University College meant that Baptist students could be actively involved in the life of the university itself. In fact, two Baptist college students were elected as presidents of the University Students' Union—Mervyn Himbury while a student at Cardiff, and Dafydd Davies, who was president while a student at Bangor University College and later treasurer of the Central Students' Representative Council for Wales. Davies served as professor of New Testament at South Wales Baptist College at the same time as Himbury was professor of church history. The two men remained lifelong friends.

Himbury's personal recollections also observe that, at the time he was there, the university college was "dominated by the Semitics department" and particularly Theodore Robinson—also a faculty member of the Baptist college. Robinson was "a very dominant character" who would urge any Baptist students who went to the university to do honors in Hebrew. A similarly-strong linkage existed when Aubrey Johnson, another Baptist, succeeded Robinson as head of that department.

---

12. Himbury, *South Wales Baptist College*, 98.

13. Himbury, *South Wales Baptist College*, 89–90, 100–105; Matthews, *From Abergavenny to Cardiff*, 27–28.

Going to University in the 1940s

It is worth contemplating the situation of the University of Wales in particular, and universities more generally, when Mervyn Himbury was a student.

The University of Wales was a multi-campus university for some time, with university colleges in Aberystwyth, Bangor, and Cardiff. The college at Cardiff began as the University College of South Wales and Monmouthshire in 1883, then became the Cardiff College of the University of Wales in 1893, generally called Cardiff University College. In 1999 it achieved its own identity as Cardiff University.

Unlike the later third of the twentieth century, when British students commonly left home and went to university in another part of the country, the Welsh university colleges were local. Proximity to a college was the primary determinant of where people studied. Up to the Second World War, 87 percent of those who went to university from the Cardiff County borough went to Cardiff University College, including those who attended its medical school. Similarly, 87 percent of students from Swansea went to Swansea College.

As the twentieth century progressed, the student body was overwhelmingly Welsh. In 1896 the proportion of students from beyond "Offa's Dyke," as the border was called, was as high as 39 percent, and these were mostly women. There was no danger that English students would overwhelm the Welsh or Celtic ethos: rather, a college council minute from March 1896 stated: "English students were brought into touch with Welsh ideals and in turn contributed a social breadth . . . of unquestionable advantage." The Welsh ethos was strongly emphasized at Cardiff. There was some contention among students whether the Welsh language should be so dominant. Others saw it as an obligation, especially to those beyond the colleges, to maintain the language.[14] T. M. Bassett, who later wrote a history of Welsh Baptists, recorded in the university publication *Cap and Gown* (May 1935–January 1936) that he did not fully comprehend what it was to be Welsh until he became a student at Cardiff.

From very early in the new century, the number of students from England and abroad declined, at least in part as a result of the growth of the universities in Manchester, Liverpool, Leeds, Bradford, and Sheffield, falling from 31 percent in 1903 to just 16 percent in 1914. These are figures for the entire University of Wales. For its part, the Cardiff University

---

14. Williams, *University of Wales, Volume 2*, 296.

College never attracted many students from outside Wales before World War Two—in 1938, only 3 percent. Larger numbers of students from beyond Wales, and indeed from other countries, was a new phenomenon in the 1950s and later decades. A more recent history of Cardiff University describes many aspects of the close relationship between the college, as it was, and its community.[15]

The number of students also changed significantly during the first half of the century, reflecting the radical changes in the local communities. University students made up only a very small proportion of the population. In the 1920s (the time of Himbury's birth), only nine or ten per ten thousand were students in Glamorganshire. The numbers increased during the inter-war period, reaching a peak of sixteen per ten thousand in 1934. There were several critical factors at play here, which led both to the increase and following decline. Even before the turn of the century, coal mining in some of the Welsh valleys was in decline, but by the 1920s there was widespread unemployment. In South Wales, unemployment averaged 36.5 percent during the 1920s. Merthyr Tydfil (where Marion Himbury lived as a young person) reached 61.9 percent unemployment, while the Dowlais area nearby recorded 73.4 percent. More than a quarter of a million people left the region at this time, while many others were drawn to various educational offerings, including newly-created community colleges in addition to the existing university college. Only the onset of war brought a significant change in these employment conditions and in university enrollments.

The aggregate enrollments for the University of Wales during these decades provide a clear indication of these trends. In 1938–39, there were 2779 students. By the end of the war, 1944–5, enrollments fell to 2009. Of these, 1684 were from Wales itself, with the remainder from England, some of whom had evacuated to Wales. Some university departments from elsewhere in the country also evacuated to Wales during these years. Notably, in that same year there were 415 diploma students. It is also significant that during the war years, science students were exempted from military service. In the years immediately after the war there was a sharp increase in the numbers of arts students.

Student numbers rose very significantly as the war ended. In 1945–6, when Mervyn Himbury was president of the students' union, there were 2921 students in the entire university: 2190 from Wales, 262 from

---

15. Smith and Stephens, *Community and Its University*.

England, and fifty-four from other countries. The rapid increase continued so that by 1947–48 the university had 4762 students, of whom 3609 were from Wales. In all, 1856 men and seventy-eight women had seen war service. In October 1946, the principal of the university college at Cardiff reported to the Court of Governors the enrollment at the college, reflecting these changes.

Table 2   Post-war Enrollment by Faculty

Faculty	1945–1946	1946–1947
Arts & music	273	436
Science	367	469
Medicine	132	159
Theology	20	22
Training	252	334
Law	5	5
Total	1049	1425

Attitudes to the growth in student numbers varied. A critical interchange between several leaders of the time reveals differing views of the purpose of university education. Williams records that a pro-chancellor of the University of Wales in an address referred to the "over-production" of this period of high enrollments. The statement met with strong disapproval among the teaching community, with J. Morgan Jones asserting that the university and its colleges were not out to produce articles on demand nor to satisfy a demand like a business house. Rather, their purpose was "to create an educated community."[16] This statement of purpose fits well with the vision of those who established the Baptist colleges, seeking not only training as preachers but an education for those who would lead the communities into a changing world. Mervyn Himbury's own educational philosophy reflected the same vision and values.

Student living conditions during these decades were often quite appalling. There was much debate about the advantages of residential student accommodation, but in reality only a very small proportion ever lived in formal student housing. A report to the university council in 1948 on student welfare indicates the following housing options:

16. Williams, *University of Wales, Volume 2*, 275.

Table 3 Student Housing Options in 1948

Accommodation Type	Male Students	Female Students
Home	1051	258
College	646	236
Lodgings[17]	1608	
Total	3305	494

Roy Jenkins, noted Welsh member of Parliament, born just two years before Mervyn Himbury, is an example of how students lived during this time. He attended University College Cardiff for a year before going on to Oxford. As a student at Cardiff, he traveled by bus two and a half hours daily, from his home in Pontypool and back. The university council report found that most who lived at home traveled long distances by bus or train. They often did not eat until the evening when they returned to their parents' home.

The situation in Cardiff was especially difficult, as the refectory was bombed in 1941. A student was killed and the building so badly damaged it had to be demolished. It was not until 1951 that building work began on a replacement. Students did not have a place where normally cheaper meals might have been provided. The 1948 report to the university council found that in the years of austerity after the Second World War, students generally ate badly (as they had done before the war) and some even starved themselves by sending their ration books home to help their families. These conditions were to have a significant impact upon Mervyn Himbury's attitude later in his life as head of a university residential college.

There was much emphasis in the university upon sport, as in the Welsh community as a whole.[18] One reason that sport was encouraged was because there was such alarm about the health of students. Intercollege sporting events were also seen as one way of developing the sense of being one federated university. Participation in university teams in hockey or rugby often led to playing for Wales. Here the influx of ex-servicemen in the student body had an interesting effect. These men were a little older and often of stronger physique than younger undergraduates and tended to dominate the college teams.

---

17. No figure was provided for women students living in lodgings.
18. Williams, *University of Wales, Volume 2*, 286.

It is also important to recognize the ways in which class influenced the participation in university life in Wales. An insightful essay by David Adamson describes patterns of inclusion and exclusion among the working and middle classes in the valleys of South Wales, primarily the impact of class upon expectations. "The middle and working classes each in turn recognize social boundaries," a "self-regulating system" which Adamson calls a social apartheid.[19] Even today, despite more recent social advances, some parts of the community do not imagine attending a university as a prospect for them or their children.

Two implications of Adamson's work are relevant to the post-war era. The first is the broader potential for universities to have created opportunities, seeking to invite people to consider university education as within their possibilities. The second is the personal implications for those who crossed social boundaries to enter universities. Profound emotional as well as intellectual changes were implied, which no doubt added to the challenges faced by students, including poverty, hunger, and the burdens of travel—not to mention the bombing raids and other immediate effects of war. These factors were part of the experience of Mervyn Himbury: son of a coal miner, student of the University College Cardiff.

In reality a university education continued to be well beyond the reach of most people in the working classes. In 1930, at an honorary degree ceremony, the claim was made that now university training was "within reach of nearly every capable Welsh boy or girl." Historian J. Gwynn Williams commented on this incident in 1997 that "there are many still alive who know that this was not the case."[20]

Religion also continued to play a role within the student community. Williams observed that "genuine religious convictions and expressions persisted despite the advancing skepticism of the age." In the early years of the century, the Student Christian Movement [SCM] was wary of the revival ethos prevalent in 1904–5. Later, in what was now a questioning context, the SCM encouraged a more thoughtful conviction through publications and conferences, influenced by men such as William Temple, C. E. Raven and C. H. Dodd. It is also noteworthy that at the Cardiff University College there was what Williams calls "a wholesome habit" of sending the president of the student union to various conferences, such

---

19. Adamson, "The University of Glamorgan," 135.
20. Williams, *University of Wales*, 271.

as those of the International Student Service or the World Christian Student Federation.[21]

A final element worth noting in the life of the university when Mervyn Himbury was a student was the sense of anticipation that surrounded the 1944 Education Act. Already, in 1943, the university had begun planning for its life after the war ended. There was strong recognition of the importance of research. In July 1944, Cardiff academic leaders met with the University Grants Commission. From these processes, the Academic Board proposed that the university colleges should teach more social studies and languages, including Russian and Portuguese. The Butler Commission Report of 1944 also recommended bringing education and teacher training together.

Interestingly, while most commentators regard the expansion of tertiary education arising from the Education Act of 1944 in very positive terms, Hugh Matthews notes what he considers "dire consequences" for Nonconformist ministry in Wales. The Act provided for the teaching of religious education in the secondary school curriculum. Many suitably qualified ministers saw this as an opportunity for ministry to the broader community, while Matthews refers to this move as "serious hemorrhaging" from the ministry of the Nonconformist churches, leading inevitably to the decline of the churches themselves.[22]

Such, then, was something of the life of the university in which Mervyn Himbury participated, not merely as a student but also a significant student leader, from 1941 to 1948.

Mervyn Himbury: Student of History and Theology

Himbury was not especially disappointed that he had not been accepted as a student of the Baptist college in 1941. His immediate interest was in study at the university. At the same time, given his longer-term goal of entering the Baptist ministry, he accepted the advice of the college staff when choosing his university subjects. He was told he would need to do Hebrew and Greek if he wanted to go into the ministry. So he started on

---

21. Williams, *University of Wales*, 291–94. Mervyn Himbury benefited from this opportunity and attended the second International Conference of the World Christian Student Federation in Oslo in 1947.

22. Matthews, *From Abergavenny to Cardiff*, 29–30.

the pathway that would involve both a bachelor of arts and a bachelor of divinity.

Himbury's academic record shows that in 1941 he enrolled in mostly language classes, as was the standard course: Greek, Hebrew, English, and history. These subjects were all taken toward the bachelor of arts. He failed Greek and Hebrew and passed English and history. His second-year results show him failing in English as well but doing well enough in history to enter the honors course the following year. The English class included a lot of Anglo-Saxon, which presented him with its own problems. Though he was a native English speaker, this course effectively involved study of another language.

In recollections recorded by Marita Munro in 2006, Himbury claimed that he failed English in his first year as well, but that is not what the record shows. He said to Munro that he should have been thrown out of the university, but the history department "went in to bat for him," saying that he could get a first class honors degree. Consequently, Himbury's progress through the arts degree was highly non-standard and, he noted, was actually made "illegal" after he had completed. In his own words:

> Some of the other heads of departments didn't like it. But I actually failed a first-year subject the year after I was granted a first in history! So I was stupid—it was sheer stupidity. It was also partly that the Baptist college insisted on my doing Greek and Hebrew, in which at that time I had no interest. I had no problems with the subject when I came into my third year. But nobody bothered to spend any time telling me why I should do this, that, and the other one.[23]

Himbury said that many times later he castigated himself mentally for that "stupidity." Undoubtedly this experience deeply shaped his way of dealing with students who struggled. On reflection, he contrasted his own experience and approach with that of a colleague in Melbourne who had never failed anything.[24] He continued to stress the value of biblical languages but sought always to help people to "see the point" rather than merely do what they were told to do.

---

23. The quotation is from the personal recollections of Mervyn and Marion Himbury, recorded by Rev. Marita Munro in her doctoral research. I am grateful to her for making these notes available to me.

24. Here he referred to his colleague Professor Basil Brown, professor of New Testament at the Baptist College of Victoria and then Whitley College, from 1952 to 1978.

For the present, however, he was having a good time. He said that he did not study; rather, he was having the time of his life. He had become very interested in the social life of the university and had determined from the first day (he claimed) to become president of the student union. That was where he put his efforts. Having done well at school and satisfied the entry requirements for the Baptist college, it is clear that he had the ability to undertake entry level studies at university. He had completed the higher school certificate in July 1941 with English, Welsh, and history as his subjects. He simply was not interested—as he said, he could not see the point. When required to do these subjects in later years, he did pass them.

In light of these factors, we may surmise that the principal and staff of the Baptist college saw it as wise to challenge Himbury with the obligations implied in the college's support of his education. Was he seriously intending to become a Baptist pastor? Would he commit to his studies and complete his side of the agreement? We can imagine these questions being asked when he applied again to become a student of the Baptist college for the academic year 1942–43.

In November 1942, Mervyn Himbury was asked to sign an agreement. The document was printed on parchment quality paper and indicates that the college would provide him with training to become a Baptist minister, while he agreed to undertake that training. It also provides that if he completed that training but withdrew from Baptist ministry within ten years, he would be obliged to pay the college £300—a very substantial sum at the time. This agreement reveals the seriousness with which the college and its students viewed the responsibility of education for ministry.[25] There is here a sense of mutual accountability within which the student would not only be educated but also trained and, in due course, participate in the leadership and growth of Baptist community life.

Was this a standard agreement, signed by all students? It appears that it was, though it is not mentioned in any of the histories of the college, where costs and student life are discussed. Perhaps it was an innovation, given the financial difficulties the college faced and a concern to ensure the best use of its limited resources. It seems that the agreement was presented to Himbury at this time to make a clear point to

---

25. The agreement was signed in November 1942. Interestingly, this document is held in the National Library of Wales Archives, together with other SWBC reports—while a folder of similar documents is held among many uncatalogued historical items within the college library annex.

him: Simply put, he had not done well in his first year of studies and may well have contemplated another pathway. Whether this was a standard procedure for ministry candidates entering their second year or not, in Himbury's case this more formal commitment to Baptist ministerial education would have provided a strong sense of both expectation and obligation as he continued with his studies.

Himbury's lack of passion for biblical languages can be contrasted with his enthusiasm for the study of history. In his personal recollections he referred to the history department as a home: they had adopted him. He recalled two of his teachers with special warmth—to them, he said, he was eternally grateful. They showed him "the world of learning." One was Dr. Dorothy Marshall, modern historian, the other Dr. Gwen Whale, medieval historian.[26]

> They made me some kind of historian. I found it so exciting, I had no idea how much work I was doing. My work was so tremendous I had no time to bother with these little things [like languages] that petty-fogging people wanted me to do.[27]

Again he said that he had been stupid: he could have done the language work, but did not want to. Himbury also mentioned William Rees, professor of Welsh history and head of department, who was "extremely good" to him. That goodness included his defending Himbury's place in the university despite his poor results and his specific encouragement to work toward a first in history. Clearly Rees saw Himbury's potential and actually allowed him to do his honors in history before he had completed other parts of the standard degree. The regulations were changed soon after so that "no one else could do that sort of thing again," Himbury said. For his part, in gratitude, "I worked, and got my first."

After his honors year, he continued in close contact with the history department, including participating in two groups which met at the flats of his teachers Dr. Dorothy Marshall and Dr. Gwen Whale. One group focused on medieval history and the other a more general history seminar.

---

26. Dr. Dorothy Marshall (1900–1994) was an English social historian, who concluded her career teaching at Cardiff. Dr. Gwen Whale (1896–1983) was senior lecturer in history at the University College of South Wales, Cardiff and who, interestingly, had followed a similar pathway to Himbury: BA (Cardiff), BLitt (Oxon).

27. These comments, and those following, are drawn from personal recollections recorded by Mervyn Himbury approximately in 1997. I am grateful to Maelor Himbury for making these recordings available to me.

These added important aspects to his life, intellectually and socially, he said.

These recollections provide further insight into Himbury's years as a university student. He relished both the study of history and the wider student life, clearly involving many contrasts with his previous life comprised mainly of school and church. "I discovered this wonderful world of ideas, romance, social changes. I grew to love the society of the university itself."[28]

He determined to become involved in the life of the student union, in such things as the Debating Society, the SCM and other groups; but all this contributed to his "lack of success in handling my language studies," as he put it. He formed some close friendships with other students, including several fellow Baptist students, some of whom were also students at the college. Henry Loyn was a fellow student in history, who was subsequently appointed to a personal chair in medieval history at Cardiff University and remained a lifelong friend.

In these first years he was only minimally involved in the life of the Baptist college. "My life was the university and I loved it." He spent much of his time in the student lounge (such as it was, a temporary structure following the bombing of the union building in 1941), "talking widely about all sorts of things." He did, however, go to the Baptist college at least once a week, on Thursdays. He explained that this was necessary to see if he had been assigned a preaching appointment for the coming weekend. He welcomed these opportunities, but if he had some other engagement there was still time to change the arrangements. At that time the Baptist college provided most of South Wales with preachers for all the small, pastor-less churches. As a result of this regular contact, he knew all the students. Once he was formally accepted into the college, after again sitting the entrance examination, he attended house meetings, worship services, went to the ordination services of graduating students, and came to appreciate what he called "a real fellowship." Some of these students he also saw at the university, though it was about this time that the number who did the double degree (arts then divinity) began to decrease.

The bachelor of divinity course, following on from the BA, provided Himbury with the opportunity to focus more specifically on the things he could see were pertinent to his sense of calling to be a Baptist pastor. Still, he had to complete the required language studies. The standard form of

---

28. Personal recollections of Mervyn Himbury.

the degree required seven subjects in the first year, internally examined in the Baptist college. Four of these subjects, including one biblical language, were then to be taken in the second year and examined externally, by the university. In addition, a further class in holy Scripture was taught within the college but not examined. Other "pastoralia" subjects, as they were called, were taught within the college all through these years as well. The final year of the BD provided for more focused study on just two subjects. While this was the standard pathway, many students who were taking other degrees might follow a different program. Students might take more than the expected five or six years to complete all these requirements. Mervyn Himbury was not one for the "standard" pathway.

The 1943–44 annual report for the college includes a paragraph on student results "at the University College": two students completed BA, with third class honors, "and Mr. D. M. Himbury has been awarded first class honors in history, a notable achievement."[29]

The records show that in 1944–45 Himbury undertook Greek, English, and Hebrew and passed them all, except for the final term in Greek, which he failed. Then in 1945–46 he took Old Testament, New Testament, church history, Christian doctrine, philosophy of religion, and Greek—this time gaining a pass. For such a heavy year, his results were remarkable, gaining three As, in history, doctrine, and philosophy of religion, and B in his biblical subjects as well. This is all the more remarkable considering that this was the year he served as president of the University Students' Union and had some period of illness as well.

From this point his focus had clearly shifted, for in 1946–47 he completed New Testament, church history, and Christian doctrine for two terms, all with grades of B+ or A, and gaining a B for a single term in history of religions. Then in 1947–48 he finished his degree with two subjects, church history and Christian doctrine, earning an A for each. Clearly, when motivated toward the study of his faith and the subjects upon which he might preach and teach, Himbury applied himself well and earned very good grades.

Study, however, was only a part of his life. He was regularly preaching in local churches all through these years. It was expected of students for the Baptist ministry that they would undertake such responsibilities and the churches were keen to have their students serve them in this way.

---

29. South Wales Baptist College, *Annual Report 1943–44*, 6.

Himbury also continued to attend the adult class in the Hengoed Baptist Church, though as his university years progressed this was less frequent.

Himbury recalled that most students would ride their bicycles to small village churches for these preaching assignments. They "went everywhere by bike," including a holiday trip to Carmarthen. Riding to the village churches at times involved long distances over many hills. Often the student would get wet and would need to be provided with replacement clothing for the services. The students would be provided with overnight accommodation and food. Sometimes the meals were very meager, or eccentric, during the times of rationing. One hostess told him that she had prayed for the provision of food and a black marketeer had provided! In another context, a local leader told him he could preach from the Hebrew, Greek, Welsh, or English Bibles; it would not matter as the people would not know any difference. From all of this, however, Himbury concluded that it was very good to get to know and understand people.

Student life within the Baptist college involved some critical differences. There were those who were considered liberal and those of a more evangelical leaning. These perspectives were broadly identified with the SCM and the Evangelical Union groups on the university campus. At the college, the two groups would meet informally in different locations: the liberals in the common room, where they smoked, and the evangelicals in the library. At one point, the SCM proposed a "mission" on the university campus and invited the Evangelical Union to join with them. The response was to decline participation but with an assurance to pray for them. One thing that did bring the two groups together at the Baptist college, however, was fire watch during the heavy bombing periods of the war. On a rostered system, three students per night were to sleep at the college, on camp beds set up in the common room. Himbury recalled how some of the students insisted on opening the windows to alleviate the smoking smells. Students were paid three shillings per night for this duty.

During his years at the South Wales Baptist College, Himbury was taught by some quite remarkable people. There were, in fact, three principals of the college in the time Himbury was there. Himbury's own history of the college provides a significant portrait of his first principal, T. W. Chance. Born in 1872, Chance had a very limited school education as his father had died when he was just four months old. He worked on a farm in his teenage years, but continued active involvement in a Baptist church, walking sixteen miles each way to attend Sunday services.[30] He was given the opportunity to attend a grammar school at Glaston-on Wye and from there went to the Baptist college in Cardiff. In his BA, he gained first class honors in Hebrew, went on to do an MA, and then took up a local Baptist pastorate. When called to teach at the college in 1908, he also undertook several outstanding subjects to complete his BD. Himbury remarked:

> He will always be remembered for the way in which he reorganized the finances of the College, and invested its resources in such a way that, when it was decided to make a residential hostel for the students in Richmond Road, the property and the money were available.[31]

Himbury's admiration for that administrative skill and stewardship reflect important values for his own career, but he goes on to say that this assessment is not entirely fair to Chance, for his fundamental passion was the proclamation of the Gospel and "winning souls for the Master."

Himbury notes that Chance was doubtless disappointed not to be made principal in 1928 and many had expected him to leave the college. But he did not, serving faithfully while Rev. Thomas Phillips held that position. Phillips died suddenly in 1936 and Chance was this time made principal until he retired in 1943. Though suffering from ill-health, he carried the college forward during the early years of the Second World War, in what was a period of growth and academic strength.

Chance was the first principal of the college who was not a Welsh-speaker. He was principal in the first years of Himbury's studies at the university and the Baptist college. Other members of the staff were John Griffiths, tutor in Christian doctrine, and Edward Roberts, tutor in church history. Each of these men would serve as principal during Himbury's time.

When Chance retired in 1943, Professor Griffiths was elected principal. Himbury observed, "the period of Principal Griffith's principalship was one that had to face the changed conditions created by the war, and the return of service men to college life."[32]

In his first year as principal, Griffiths also served as president of the Welsh Baptist union. Himbury recalled that John Griffiths was "a

---

30. Himbury, *South Wales Baptist College*, 95–96.
31. Himbury, *South Wales Baptist College*, 96.
32. Himbury, *South Wales Baptist College*, 100.

wonderful preacher-pastor," whom he felt was a little out of his place as principal of a college. He carried the responsibility with conscientiousness, but much preferred to be engaging with the Scripture text, always seeking to exegete it in such a way as to "discover truth that would enable him to live."[33] His approach was more homiletical than purely academic. He exuded a sense of devotion and was a man to whom prayer was very important. Himbury knew him only as an old man, already unwell, and wished that he had heard him preach at the best of his powers. A son of John Griffiths, named Maelor, was a deacon in the Chester Road Baptist Church, in Wrexham, and it was he who first advised Himbury of the vacancy at the college in 1950.

Principal John Griffiths died suddenly in 1947, before his first term as principal was completed. Edward Roberts, professor of both Christian doctrine and philosophy of religion, was then elected unanimously as principal and served in that role until January 1959. Himbury's history of the college recounts Roberts's early life and career but says little of his then-current roles. In his personal recollections Himbury chose to "say very little," while Hugh Matthews's history details the changes Roberts made to the preaching class, which, among other things, excluded the rest of the faculty from the process. Matthews observed that prayers and hymns were no longer part of the class, such that "the whole affair was cold and clinical and lacked anything like an atmosphere of worship."[34] There were clearly tensions between Principal Roberts and his staff. One issue seems to have been that the staff did not live on or near the college, leaving the principal to manage any situation that arose after hours.

Principal Griffiths's position as tutor in church history was taken up in 1944 by Dr. Emlyn Davies, who was to have some influence upon Mervyn Himbury, though not as much perhaps as it might have been. Davies had a position in London at the time and had previously been SCM secretary for the South West of the United Kingdom. Himbury had known him for some time. He was a striking figure physically and when he came to the college "he transformed the place," Himbury recalled. He was not, however, strongly committed to academic work and was frequently away on preaching commitments. In Himbury's view, however, Davies's greater fault was his capacity to criticize the principal openly:

---

33. Personal recollections of Mervyn Himbury.
34. Matthews, *From Abergavenny to Cardiff*, 30–31.

"he had no loyalty to his principal."[35] Himbury said that Ernest Payne had drummed into him the fundamental importance of loyalty to one's principal, even though there may be differences of opinion. Davies resigned from the college to take up a position in Canada in 1950, thus creating the vacancy that in due course Himbury would fill.

When Griffiths died and Edward Roberts was elected principal, a new tutor was needed. Rev. D. R. Griffiths, a nephew of the late principal, was appointed in 1945 and took up the role in 1946. This appointment arose from a new and somewhat convoluted method of consultation and selection, clearly a response to earlier controversies. Himbury said that Griffiths was "a tremendous help" to him in his later years as a student. Griffiths was also appointed financial secretary of the college, however, a role for which he was singularly unsuited. Himbury recalled many evenings spent with his tutor, and later colleague, struggling to bring the accounts into order for presentation to the college council. Himbury's own appreciation of the importance of sound financial management and responsible accounting is evident here.

Himbury commented on his tutors' teaching style, most of whom dictated from their notes. He recalled that after the war there was one student who had been a prisoner in Changi Camp, Singapore, and who struggled greatly under this method of teaching, presumably because it did not engage the students as adult learners.[36] Despite also being one to dictate from his notes, D. R. Griffiths was in Himbury's estimation a good scholar. He was "quiet and very concerned for accuracy" and had a commitment to a truly academic approach to biblical exegesis. He had also "a delightful human element in his character for those who would listen to him." For his part, Emlyn Davies did not dictate notes, but in Himbury's view "was no historian." He was "at least a good preacher" and "loved to shock."[37]

The honor board in the present students' union building at Cardiff University lists past presidents of the union society, including Mr. D. Mervyn Himbury BA for 1945–46.

From the beginning, he was keen to be part of the student union and had determined to become president. He succeeded in this goal, despite a resolution presented to the university senate that he should resign

35. Personal recollections of Mervyn Himbury.

36. In Himbury's own time as a teacher at the college, he was known to involve students in class discussion and other "innovative" approaches to teaching.

37. Personal recollections of Mervyn Himbury.

as president in view of his earlier academic failures. Professor Aubrey Johnson came to his rescue and the motion was defeated. Himbury only learned of this some time later.

It is not clear exactly what duties and responsibilities were involved in this role. While the president did not have a position on such bodies as the university council, there was an expectation of communication with the university administration regarding student concerns.

Clearly the role of president of the students' union was one of honor, but it also seems to have involved considerable work in sustaining and coordinating services for and on behalf of students. The most helpful source I have found in identifying the life of the students' union is the *Broadsheet*, a student paper first published in November 1946—that is just after Himbury concluded his term as president.[38] I obtained a facsimile of this first edition from the university library archives. It is a typewritten document of fifteen pages, edited by D. Mervyn Himbury. It was priced at two pence. The editorial begins with the rationale for the paper's creation:

> We have already seen, during this session, that members of the General Body of Students are taking a greater interest in the affairs of the Union than has been the case during the war years. The main object of this broadsheet is to give to the students as a whole a forum in which they may express their opinions and if criticism is made of any officer of the Union that officer will have the opportunity of replying through these pages.[39]

The creation of this paper was an initiative Himbury took as a positive step toward developing student life, albeit with a somewhat defensive tone as well. He wished to facilitate students' awareness of and participation in their collective life. He knew there were differences of opinion and perspective and expected them to be aired, with respect. He also saw the responsibility of the executive of the union to hear students' "grouses" and, so far as possible, to represent them to what was commonly called "the Administration," seeking remedy or rectification.

---

38. The paper reads as if Himbury remains in office as president, which clearly was not the case in November. Given that most of its contents refers to the previous academic year, and in light of the reference to Himbury having been ill for an extended period, it seems likely that it was intended to publish the paper earlier but was instead presented early in the new session.

39. University College of South Wales and Monmouthshire Students' Union Society, *Broadsheet*, 1, 1946, 1.

The editorial went on to note that it is possible for officers to "lose contact with the opinions of the student body," which can give rise to the perception that the union "is controlled by a few bureaucrats." Furthermore, the recent growth in student numbers as "ex-servicemen" returned to the university had made such communication more urgent still. Himbury's editorial went on to critique the habit of appealing to "the good old days," which he said had created a particular difficulty for the Debating Society. He then returned to the purpose of the new paper: "to present as far as possible a picture of college life today."

In the following pages, the secretary of the union at that time, Hywel Thomas, offered a satirical report titled "What's Happening," which begins with several intriguing comments about Himbury: "... our president has been seen gracing the Union Buildings several times of late, each time resplendent in a new tie." Furthermore, secretaries of various student societies were grateful for his willingness to sign checks for their activities: "Somehow he always realizes when one of these most important pieces of paper will be needed." The secretary's report goes on to note two interesting matters. First, "an increasing demand within the student body that facilities for research should be made available for all"—responding to the emphasis on research placed by the new Education Act. The secretary also noted an increasing concern about student finances, which led him to a detailed explanation of the constitutional responsibilities of the executive committee, the union council, and the union athletic board.[40]

These opening pages provide some impression of the breadth of student bodies and their activities, as well as the sense of contention and difficulty that was a part of student life at that time. The austerity experienced by students in this era no doubt led to much concern over finances. At the same time, the influx of returned servicemen (and presumably some women as well, though they are not mentioned) and the sense of vision and renewal of university life brought about by the recent government initiatives, brought new challenges for the student leaders.

The remaining pages of the *Broadsheet* include reports from several student societies, including the SCM. Although the *Broadsheet* reports that most departmental or faculty societies are no longer functioning, the editor (himself a history student) comments that the Historical Society appears to be functioning well and has plans for the new session. The Debating Society provided a long report of its own, occupying two full

---

40. University College of South Wales and Monmouthshire Students' Union Society, *Broadsheet*, 1, 1946, 2–4.

pages. Three pages detail the activities and achievements of numerous sporting clubs and teams, as well as listing the names of students who had received full sporting colors.

An interesting page in this publication reports on the formation of a new group, the Cardiff branch of Students Federation for International Cooperation, which "aims at improving relationships between peoples of every nation through propagating information concerning world affairs." This group was particularly hopeful that those who had served abroad would enrich and support its activities.

The paper also presents the formal minutes of the Cardiff University Students' Union council meeting. The final page contains four short paragraphs of diverse information: one reports that the Technical College is seeking full membership of the University of Wales and wishes also full membership of the student union. Another paragraph refers to the university publication *Cap and Gown*, in which Mr. Henry Loyn discusses constitutional issues. While another paragraph makes a joke about the secretary, the most intriguing paragraph states: "Many students will be pleased to hear that the President of the Union is back again after his long illness."[41] We do not know what this illness might have been, in the summer and autumn of 1946. Whatever it was, this newsletter and the indication of busy student life it reflects gives us some idea of Himbury's participation in and commitment to communication with the student body, and his desire to serve the well-being of students—a passion which was to shape the latter half of his career.

The "wholesome habit" of the University College Cardiff of sending the president of the student union to various conferences was mentioned earlier. It is recorded in his application to Regent's Park College, Oxford, that Himbury had been a delegate to the "Oslo Youth Conference." This was the second World Conference of Christian Youth, organized by the World Council of Churches, the World Student Christian Federation, the World Alliance of Young Men's Christian Associations, and the World Young Women's Christian Association. It was held in Oslo from July 22 to 31, 1947, with one thousand delegates from all continents. The theme of the conference was "Jesus Christ is Lord." Mervyn Himbury was one of the British delegates, representing the Baptist union.[42]

---

41. University College of South Wales and Monmouthshire Students' Union Society, *Broadsheet*, 1, 1946, 15.

42. Macy, *Report of the Second World Conference of Christian Youth*. I am indebted to Rev. Dr. Keith Clements for this information, as he has a copy of the conference

Undoubtedly this conference would have been immensely stimulating and broadening for Himbury, along with all the other students from around the world. Speakers at the conference included W. A. Visser 't Hooft (who became the first secretary general of the WCC in 1948), Pastor Martin Niemöller, Reinhold Niebuhr, Madeline Barot, and D. T. Niles. Among the many subthemes were such pertinent topics as "Freedom and Order," "Education in the Modern World," "The Christian Faces the Situation of the Jew," and "The Church Faces the World."

Approximately twenty years later Himbury offered a brief reflection upon that conference experience, in a short talk he presented on radio in Melbourne:

> The war had just ended, and I went to a Christian youth conference at which there were representatives from almost every nation in the world. It was a remarkable experience to meet with young people who belonged to nations that we had regarded as our enemies only eighteen months earlier.
>
> Conversation was not easy. We had all been well-trained in hostile attitudes which could not easily be overcome. Moreover, those of us who belonged to the European scene could not share the more optimistic views of those who came from America. So the great word of the conference was *tension*. We saw tensions everywhere.
>
> For me, therefore, one of the great moments came when one of the leaders of the conference came out with the remark, "You know," he said, "I give thanks to Almighty God every night that He is not as tense about us as we are about Him."[43]

In the academic year 1947–48 Himbury completed his bachelor of divinity degree, along with the various "pastoral" subjects provided at the Baptist college. The annual report of the South Wales Baptist College in May 1948 records that "Mr. D. M. Himbury, BA, has sat the Final BD Examination" and later notes that he "hopes to proceed to Regent's Park College, Oxford, for a further course of study." In his own recollections, Himbury stated that the external examiner for his BD was Ernest Payne, then a tutor at Regent's Park College, Oxford, who said to him, "You will go up to Oxford." It seems likely that Payne was instrumental in facilitating the scholarship that made this possible. Himbury recalled that if "a

---

report.

43. The radio segment was called "Pause a Moment." Himbury gave a number of these talks, for which the transcripts remain.

reasonable call had come along" he would have accepted it and gone into pastoral ministry; but it did not. Later in 1948 he went up to Oxford.

To Oxford

Regent's Park College is today a permanent private hall of the University of Oxford, providing accommodation for a diverse body of students studying at the university, including some who are reading theology with a view to ordained Baptist ministry. It is also a significant center for Baptist research. The name of the college provides a clear indication of its history: it was not always in Oxford, having been for a time located in Regent's Park, London.

Mervyn Himbury went to Regent's Park to undertake research in Baptist history, as a further element in his own ministerial education. The education of ministers was the college's primary purpose but also something under constant challenge. How should men (and later women) be equipped for ministry in Baptist churches, and was an academy, especially one closely linked to a university, the best context and means of this equipping?

The first Baptist educational institution in Britain began in Bristol in 1679, as a "society" or cooperative program for the training of pastors, and leading to the foundation of the Bristol Baptist College in 1720. By 1752 a similar initiative developed in London among the Particular Baptist churches, taking various forms and names, such as the London Baptist Society for Assisting Students, which functioned between 1792–1796. The society had no buildings or specific curriculum but did provide tutors to mentor the developing pastors. Soon after, new Baptist colleges were formed, at Horton in the north (1804) and in South Wales (1807). While there is some argument about how much the early Baptists concerned themselves with education, the formation of these societies and the development of these colleges supports the view that by the early nineteenth century there was considerable interest in the education of Baptist pastors. How and where this education was to take place was perhaps more at issue and this, among other things, reflected a concern about cost. As with the Welsh, the local British churches maintained an active interest in how their money was being used to educate their pastors.

What is now Regent's Park Baptist College began as the Baptist Academical Institution, located at Stepney in London from 1810 to 1827.[44] In the early years of this college, the annual reports included the publication of an apologia for an educated ministry, written by Robert Hall Jr., seeking constantly to persuade the churches of the need for and benefits of well-educated pastors. It was soon after that a major development in the wider educational context was to provide a stimulus and challenge to the fledgling college, with the formation of University College, London, in 1826.[45] Along with King's College (formed in 1829), University College was characterized as a Dissenting institution, for it was not part of, nor supported by, the Church of England, and imposed no faith test upon entry. For Nonconformists there was now an alternative to Oxford and Cambridge. Even though it did not have a theology faculty as such, Baptists in London were interested in joining the new university in some way. They saw it as more utilitarian than the preceding forms of university education, and therefore more amenable to ministry training.

In the succeeding decades many (though not all) Baptist students undertook a program of ministerial education which included a university degree. By 1865 the principal of Regent's Park College, Joseph Angus, was able to report that forty-three graduates had received a BA, MA, or LLB, while a further forty-six had undertaken at least some studies toward a BA.[46]

It was during this period that the Baptist "academical institution" moved to a building in Regent's Park. Holford House was a stately home built in 1832, in what was deemed "a more healthy and convenient neighborhood."[47] It provided thirty to forty student rooms, with capacity for further expansion of this number, and was close to the university. With considerable effort to obtain the necessary funds to rent the facilities, the college moved to Regent's Park in 1856, where it remained until 1927. The student body during this time included three groups: those

---

44. Clarke and Fiddes, *Dissenting Spirit*. Much of the historical detail in the following paragraphs is derived from this most recent history of Regent's Park College.

45. Interestingly, University College today uses the tagline "Disruptive Thinking since 1826."

46. This contrasts strongly with the situation in 1831, when it appears that of 841 Particular Baptist ministers, none had bachelor degrees, and while fourteen had master degrees and five had doctorates, all of these are likely to have been honorary awards.

47. Clarke and Fiddes, *Dissenting Spirit*, 61.

preparing for the entry examination for ministerial education, those engaged in ministerial education, and lay students studying at the university.

The decades that followed were a period of significant growth in the wider scene for theological education. In 1878 a consortium, which eventually included seventeen theological colleges, was formed, the Senatus Academicus of Associated Theological Colleges.[48] Regent's Park Baptist College joined this consortium in 1888. This institution provided a means to address a concern expressed within the wider Baptist union—that the link with the university meant that ministry students were actually studying less theology. In fact, this concern had already been addressed earlier by the college but the senatus offered the means to strengthen those responses. Ministerial education now involved five years of study, the last two being specifically theological, after the BA. Even then, the first year of the BA required study of Genesis in Hebrew and Luke's Gospel in Greek, as well as apologetic works such as Butler's *Analogy* and Paley's *Natural Theology*. The theological curriculum included examinations in theology, Old Testament, New Testament, homiletics, ecclesiastical history, and philosophy. Examination was undertaken cooperatively between the colleges of the senatus, and students could earn either the Associate of the Theological Senate (ATS) or the more advanced Fellowship of the Theological Senate (FTS).

Two other developments during this period are worthy of note. The first was that Spring Hill College, a Congregationalist institution in Birmingham and a leading member of the senatus, withdrew and moved to Oxford in 1886, becoming Mansfield College. The relationship between Regent's Park and Mansfield Colleges would remain significant as a means by which Baptist scholars could study at Oxford University. The other development was the creation by London University of a degree in theology, the London bachelor of divinity, through a newly-created Faculty of Theology. Seven of the existing theological colleges were identified as divinity schools, Regent's Park College being one of the first. Thus, students at Regent's became "internal" to the university itself. The first such cohort graduated BD in 1905.

The college Mervyn Himbury entered in 1948 continued with the name Regent's Park College but was now located in Oxford. The decision to move to Oxford in 1927 clearly determined the question of a relationship with a university, but it was no longer with the University of

---

48. Clarke and Fiddes, *Dissenting Spirit*, 66.

London. Consideration had been given to moving to Cambridge, but it so happened that in 1926 Ernest Payne, then a Baptist research student at Mansfield College, learned of the availability of a property in St. Giles, Oxford, and relayed this information to the principal at Regent's Park, Dr. Wheeler Robinson. In due course the decision was made to take up that opportunity, along with adjoining property on Pusey Street. The house in St. Giles became the principal's residence, and student facilities and classrooms were created on the Pusey Street site—the beginnings of what eventually became a full college facility formed around the quadrangle, as it is today. For the first ten years, however, the college had no buildings of its own in Oxford. Some students remained in London, while some lived in Oxford, initially at Mansfield College. The first college buildings were opened in 1938. The college photograph of 1937 includes twenty-one students from both London and Oxford.

Prior to Regent's Park College becoming a permanent private hall of Oxford University, Regent's students were matriculated through St. Catherine's Society, and many were associate members of Mansfield College's Junior Common Room. Nonetheless, the principal of Regent's Park College, Wheeler Robinson, was held in very high regard as a colleague and became president of the Society for Old Testament Study in 1929. He was appointed to the Faculty Board in 1933 and soon after made a reader in biblical criticism. The other tutors of the college at the time, Robert Child and Ernest Payne, were granted Oxford MAs in 1944, a further recognition of the college's contribution to the life of the university.

Mervyn Himbury enrolled through St. Catherine's Society. What is today St. Catherine's College was founded in 1868 as a "Delegation for Unattached Students," following recommendations of a Royal Commission in 1852 which sought to provide a pathway for male students who could not afford the costs of college membership at Oxford. The name of the society refers to St. Catherine of Alexandria. In 1962, St. Catherine's became a constituent college of Oxford University, and became coeducational in 1974. In 2020, St. Catherine's was the largest undergraduate college by membership, having 502 undergraduate students and 442 graduate students.

Though enrolled through St. Catherine's, Himbury was for all intents and purposes a student of Regent's Park College. His application for entry to Regent's was considered by the college council on June 19, 1948. The minutes of this meeting record that Principal Child presented four candidates for admission.[49] Some detail is recorded about each of the applicants. The following information is transcribed from the minutes:

> Himbury, David Mervyn, BA. Aged 25
> Church Membership: Hengoed Welsh
> Lewis' School, Pengam, 1934–1941; Cardiff Baptist College 1941–48.
> BA Hons. History. Completing this year his BD (Wales).
> Recommended by Professors Aubrey Johnson and Emlyn Davies, the Rev. G.R.M. Lloyd and the E. Glamorgan Baptist Association.
> Mr. Himbury stated that he was sitting for the Baptist Union Fellowship and desired, if admitted to Regent's Park, to take a research degree in History in Oxford.
> On the motion of Professor Rowley, seconded by Mr. Chowm, it was agreed that Mr. Himbury be accepted, subject to his securing a Baptist Union Fellowship, and on his assurance that he would undertake such course as might have the approval of the tutors of the College.[50]

The minute implies that the applicant was present for interview at this point, as Himbury is here quoted directly. Interestingly, the minute book contains a loose-leaf sheet, most likely the principal's notes for presenting the candidates to the meeting. Regarding Himbury, there is further information not recorded in the minutes: it is noted that he had already completed the "subsidiary" stage of his BD, including Hebrew and Greek; that he preached regularly, participated in the SCM, and was a delegate to the Oslo Youth Conference.

Himbury was awarded the Baptist Union Fellowship to provide for his studies. He entered Regent's Park College and is recorded in the student register as number 724. He was enrolled in the degree BLitt. The bachelor of letters was at that time the highest earned degree offered at Oxford, a research degree upon which graduates might build in their later careers, perhaps through publications. There was no MLitt or PhD. The university might award an MA to those who had undertaken further work, not by examination but as recognition of that contribution. The doctor of divinity was awarded to those who had produced an appropriate body of work.

---

49. Regent's Park College Council, *Council Minute Book*, 314.
50. Mr. Herbert Chowm was the treasurer of the college from 1934 to 1949.

Himbury recorded later that Principal Child was keen for him to study schools theology. Himbury saw this as an insult to the Cardiff Baptist College and the University of Wales. Ernest Payne urged him to do work in early Nonconformity. He undertook a dissertation on the role of the Christian magistrate, which he found fascinating. He "enjoyed reading and trying to understand it all," he said, "though not so much having to write it all up."

Although there was no formal supervision of research as it is understood today, Himbury worked with Dr. Claude Jenkins, regius professor of ecclesiastical history, whom he later described as "one of the most interesting men in Oxford." Typically, Himbury recorded some of Jenkins's eccentricities: "He was a man who at breakfast would fill his pockets with toast and he would nibble toast all day. I used to go to his rooms and sit down, there was a table between us and the pile of books on the table would go up and up and up until the end of term—I wouldn't see him! But at the end of term they would send in a few scouts and they'd clean the place out." An Anglican clergyman and theologian, Jenkins was the official Lambeth librarian from 1910 until 1952 and was indeed notorious for his collection of books. A photograph survives of the hallway of his house in 1934. It was estimated that he had some thirty thousand books in his home.

Sometime early in his career in Melbourne, Himbury offered the following reflection upon Claude Jenkins, in a short radio segment called "Pause a Moment":

> I had a remarkable old tutor when I was at the university. He was probably the best-read man I have ever known. Every week, like so many other students, I used to go to see Canon Claude Jenkins in his rooms at Christ Church.
>
> Once the door was opened, one was confronted by an amazing sight.
>
> Everywhere there were books with a narrow passageway between them leading to his study. By his chair was a little table. He would sit there while I sat on the other side, getting up now and again to peer over the pile of books on that table which grew to a remarkable height as the term went on.
>
> He read widely and voraciously on every subject you could imagine. Yet I always remember his last words to me as I was about to come down from the university.
>
> "Master Mervyn," he said, with his usual quaint old-world expression, "you will find great joy in your books but always

remember that if there is ever a choice between reading a book and speaking to a person who may need your help, put the book away."

Help us, O Lord, always to remember the importance of other people.[51]

Himbury's research project was titled "The Christian Magistrate, as Viewed by the Separatist and Dissenting Groups Before 1660." The thesis considered the origins of the Baptist movement along with several other groups. A typewritten copy is held in the archives of Whitley College.[52] It extends to some 180 pages, approximately sixty thousand words. Centrally, the thesis addresses questions of the nature of authority for those Christians who separated themselves from the state church in the seventeenth century. What did it mean to be the church? Within this exploration, there are various perspectives on the role of the civil authorities and the liberty of conscience in relation to the laws of the land. The project focuses on the era of Cromwell and his various efforts to reform both the Parliament and the church. The subject area thus included consideration of what might be expected from and within the civil society: Is a truly Christian society possible or is the "city of God" something distinct from the life we live in the world? For one whose passion was to be a preacher, these questions were of deep significance—what hope and what responsibility is offered to people in this life and, consequently, what is the role and mission of the church?

The method of study at Oxford involved regular meetings with a tutor, in which the student was to present an essay on a theme or source set at the previous meeting. Himbury's files include several long, handwritten sections which are almost certainly such essays, one on "The Christian Magistrate as Viewed by John Milton" and another "The Christian Magistrate in the Works of John Owen." These sections can be found in the thesis. In addition, the files contain a very large book with an alphabetical index naming the sources consulted in his research and handwritten notes from these sources. These are exceptionally detailed and (sadly) largely illegible as the paper is extremely thin.

---

51. This quotation is from the transcript of a radio talk given by Mervyn Himbury. The transcript, which has neither title nor date, is in his uncatalogued files, held in the archives of Whitley College.

52. Surprisingly, no copy or record of the thesis could be found at all, neither in the Angus Archives at Regent's Park, nor within the wider Oxford University catalogues.

It seems likely that Himbury was also supported and guided by Ernest Payne (1902–1980), who had encouraged him to apply to Regent's. Payne was one of the tutors there when Himbury first went up to Oxford. The principal was Rev. Robert Child, who had taken over from Wheeler Robinson in 1942 and was nearing his retirement (in 1954). Rev. Leonard Brockington had succeeded Robinson in teaching biblical subjects, especially languages, while Rev. Ernest Payne taught historical theology. Ernest Payne no doubt provided additional tuition and guidance to Himbury during his time at Regent's Park. Child, Brocklington, and Payne led the college through the years of the Second World War and the developments soon after—the time when Mervyn Himbury would come to Oxford.

Ernest Payne had served as secretary of the youth department of the Baptist Missionary Society from 1932 and later was its editorial secretary. He was part-time secretary of Regent's Park College from 1933 and has been described as Principal Wheeler Robinson's "right-hand man" in the entire enterprise of moving from London to Oxford, and construction of the college's first buildings.[53] Payne joined the tutorial staff of the college in 1940 and in 1946 was appointed a university lecturer in comparative religion and history of modern missions.

Ernest Payne was certainly one of the most influential British Baptist leaders of the twentieth century. He was a dedicated Baptist, an internationalist, and an ecumenist. He was a delegate to the first assembly of the World Council of Churches in 1948 and in 1954 was elected vice-chair of the council's central committee. He participated actively in the work of its Faith and Order Commission, and the British Council of Churches. Himbury wrote of him in his *British Baptists: A Short History*: "Baptists in the Southern States of America and in Australia have refused to join the World Council, whereas in Britain not only have they been represented at the great conferences but in such men as the present secretary of the Baptist Union, Dr. Payne, have contributed to the personnel and thought of the movement."[54] Author of many books on Baptist ecclesiology and missions, Ernest Payne also mentored many younger leaders for the future of the movement. While he left Regent's Park in 1951 to become general secretary of the Baptist union, a position he held until retirement in 1967, he retained an active involvement with the college and many

---

53. Child, "Ernest Alexander Payne," 2.
54. Himbury, *British Baptists*, 119.

of its graduates. Some years later he was again to be instrumental in the advancement of Mervyn Himbury's career, in his move to Australia.

Student life at Regent's Park College suited Himbury well. He was a resident and was soon active in the life of the college community. The annual report of the college for 1948–49 lists the current students: in total twenty-two men across five years of study. A further five men are listed as students at the Bristol college. These were counted as Regent's students, while preparing for ministry at Bristol before they were considered sufficiently qualified to come to Regent's. Mervyn Himbury is listed as: "D. M. Himbury, BA, BD. (*Baptist Union Scholar*) Cardiff College."

There were two strong student groups within Regent's Park College at that time: the Junior Common Room (JCR) and the Regent's Park College Preaching Society. Himbury was active in both from the outset.

The minutes of the JCR meeting held on October 12, 1948, begin as follows:

> The President was in the Chair and opened with prayer.
> He then extended on behalf of the House a cordial welcome to Mervyn Himbury and Bill Clarke, the new members. The president went on to explain that as there were now three St. Cath's men lodging in the College, it had been decided to segregate the business of the House into two meetings:— a. A House meeting dealing with specifically college and denominational affairs. b. A JCR meeting for the general affairs of the Common Room, which also affected the new lodgers.

"Lodgers" at the college were students of the university but not ordination students. Himbury was one such lodger. Nonetheless, at that time all "Regent's Men" were deemed "ministerial," and in fact Himbury's name is listed in the annual reports from 1949–50 onwards among the ministers educated at Regent's Park College.

These minutes indicate that Mr. Payne was invited to speak to the JCR about the recent Amsterdam congress of the World Council of Churches.

A month later D. M. Himbury was elected as auditor for the JCR, indicating his keenness to continue his participation in student leadership. Interestingly, every meeting of the JCR dealt with an item relating to sending parcels to Poland—usually paper, books, or other needed items, for the Polish Baptist Theological College. Early in 1949 the students agreed to resume an earlier practice of volunteering to assist with washing up after breakfast and supper.

Himbury is mentioned a number of times during 1949, on matters relating to contested procedures for student elections, the expenditure of funds for sporting equipment, and, at one point, a prank where he and another student presented the gift of a cake to celebrate their "engagement."

In March of 1949 at a special meeting the JCR agreed to send greetings "to the Free Church Colleges of Germany, or rather those to be visited by Mr. Payne in his forthcoming tour." This signaled a very significant event in Mervyn Himbury's own experience. Payne had proposed to lead a delegation of ten students from the British Baptist colleges. Six of these students were from Regent's, and one was Mervyn Himbury. The April 1949 minutes of the JCR include the following item:

> Mr. Himbury then gave a most interesting account of the visit of six members of the House to the Predigar Seminarium Baptista, Hamburg, during the Easter vacation. He brought the House the greetings of the Students of that Seminary.
>
> Mr. Whiting then asked Mr. Himbury whether there was any significance to be gleaned from the visit to his room in the early hours of Sunday morning of a young lady, Fräulein Schmidt by name, whom he had met during the mission of good will to Germany. Mr. Himbury succeeded in clearing his character to his own entire satisfaction.

I have a personal memory of Himbury speaking of this visit to Germany. Though it was by then almost four years since the end of the war, he was struck by how many of the students were hungry. This perception perhaps called to mind the conditions of his own student life in Cardiff during the war. His recollection to me referred to the importance of sufficient food if students were to be able to study.

Another significant part of the life of Regent's Park College was the preaching society. Its full title was Regent's Park College Rural Churches Preaching Station Society. This was the means by which the college arranged placements for its students as student pastors and visiting preachers in local Baptist churches. The society maintained very detailed records of these placements, as well as the minutes of its formal meetings. It is thus possible to track Mervyn Himbury's activity as a preacher and pastor during his time at Oxford.

The society's minutes for a meeting on November 30, 1948, record that "Approval of the House was received regarding the nomination of Mr. Himbury as Student Pastor at Woodstock." The secretary would then have submitted his name to the church immediately, in order to complete arrangements for the pastorate before the end of term.

It is not known how Himbury traveled to this village, but he did so throughout the next year as the student pastor. Perhaps he continued his bicycle riding practice from Cardiff days. There was also a bus service that ran between Oxford and the surrounding villages. He had already preached at several other churches by this time. The following is a gathering of the records of his preaching activity over the time he was at Regent's. Occasionally some commentary is made concerning the purpose of the visit. The location or names are of Baptist churches.

Table 4   Records of Himbury's Preaching While Resident at Regent's Park College

Date	Church	Commentary
October 17, 1948	Wolvercote	
October 31, 1948	Botley	D. M. Himbury
November 21, 1948	Eynsham	
November 28, 1948	Woodstock	
January 16, 1949	Woodstock	SP (Student Pastor)
February 6, 1949	Woodstock	SP
February 27, 1949	Littlemore	a.m. BMS deputation
March 6, 1949	Woodstock	SP
April 24, 1949	Woodstock	SP
May 8, 1949	Wheeler St., Birmingham	(Congregation Welsh)
May 22, 1949	Woodstock	
June 5, 1949	Woodstock	SP
October 9, 1949	Chester Street, Wrexham	a.m. and p.m.
October 23, 1949	Woodstock	SP
November 6, 1949	Woodstock	SP

Throughout 1949 he was preaching regularly, along with his academic work. The visit to Wrexham in November was no doubt related to the expectation of a "settlement" there when he concluded his studies.

The minutes of the preaching society indicate a general concern for the local churches and the appreciation of those churches for the ministry provided by the college students. The annual meeting of the society held on January 25, 1949, was chaired by the principal, with other staff present also. The following comment from the minutes of that meeting indicates something of the importance placed on relationships between the college and the churches and the value placed on this preaching supply:

> Rev. E. A. Payne thought that the society should know that at the Annual Rally of the Oxford Fellowship held last summer, the churches made it known that the ready services of the Society were greatly appreciated and the work of the Student Pastors was especially commended.

At its meeting on March 8, 1949, the society moved to advise the plan secretary of the Oxford Fellowship that it would be pleased to offer ten services per Sunday during the Trinity term. Collectively the students were committed to this form of ministry and Mervyn Himbury was an enthusiastic participant in it.

The minutes and reports of the society over several years reflect a concern for the Woodstock Baptist Church in particular. The college annual report for 1949–50 includes this paragraph, in the report of the preaching society president, J. L. Nainby:

> Woodstock is not without its difficulties, as numbers attending the services have decreased. This in itself should be a challenge to the faithful ones who give their loyal support to the Sunday Evening services and the Mid-Week meeting. The Anniversary Services conducted by the Rev. F. H. Rollinson of Chipping Norton were attended by members of other churches in the Fellowship. This occasion was one of encouragement to the church members. The work in the Sunday School has been maintained satisfactorily.[55]

These brief comments give some insight into the work of the student pastor and the challenges faced in that context. For his part, by the end of 1949 Himbury was busily preparing his thesis and looking to completion of his years of study in the first half of 1950.

The 1949–50 annual report of Regent's Park College included the following brief but significant statement: "Mr. Mervyn Himbury, BA, a

---

55. Regent's Park Baptist College, *Annual Report 1949-50*, 43.

Baptist Union Scholar, is settling at Wrexham."[56] Having completed his course, Himbury would have moved to a pastoral settlement, there to fulfill his long-held dream of being a Baptist preacher. This was, in one sense, the conclusion of his ministerial education—but in another sense, just its beginning.

Wrexham

Chester Street Baptist Church in Wrexham is one of the oldest Baptist churches in Wales. Various groups of Dissenters are known to have formed in Chester during the years of Cromwell's Commonwealth. W. T. Whitley records that during this period parliamentary commissions were sent into various parts of the country "to overhaul the ecclesiastical establishment, eject incompetent men, and install others. In each case their work led to the plantation of Baptist churches."[57] The commission appointed to examine Wales was based in Wrexham and found that the region had been "shamefully neglected," with more than four hundred parishes without a resident minister. The commission appointed additional ministers and schoolmasters, including a number who were already, or would soon become, Baptist. In addition, the commission itself appointed new persons to "approve" further ministry appointments and, again, several of these were Baptists.

In his work *The Welsh Baptists*, T. Myrfyn Bassett notes that "there were indeed some Baptists around Wrexham in the mixed church founded by Morgan Llwyd at the time of the Commonwealth."[58] Himbury observed, in his recorded recollections, that this church had included a number of Dissenting groups, including Congregationalists and Quakers as well as Baptists. He suggested that this was the place out of which the Quakers grew. There remains a graveyard from this time, which confirms that these groups were present. For various reasons, however, the other groups moved away, while the Baptists remained, and the church came to be identified as a Baptist church.

In the custom and practice of British Baptists, Himbury was both inducted and ordained at Chester Street, on June 21, 1950. We know that he lived at this time with his uncle, Idris Thomas, who was pastor of

---

56. Regent's Park Baptist College, *Annual Report 1949–50*, 14.
57. Whitley, *History of British Baptists*, 81–82.
58. Bassett, *Welsh Baptists*, 100.

another church in the area. Mervyn Himbury was making the sometimes-difficult transition from an academic life, with its focus on intellectual concerns and the largely unstructured days that allowed, to a much more "everyday" context, among people whose concerns were more practical and immediate. Himbury simply wanted to preach. For this he needed a congregation; but he had to learn also that those people had needs and gifts to contribute, and it was through learning to be their pastor that he also became a great preacher. It was not only about the content of his sermon but the context and the way his sermon connected with the people.

On this basis, it is vital to recognize this year at Wrexham as part of his ministerial education. While he had long engaged in regular preaching, including that time as student pastor at Woodstock, now he had the challenge and the time to draw together all that he had gained through his academic life and all that he was learning from and with his people, to affirm and practice his vocation as a Baptist pastor.

It was not to last. Within just a few months of Himbury's settling in Wrexham, the South Wales Baptist College received the resignation of Professor Emlyn Davies, tutor in church history. Davies had accepted a call to teach in Canada. Several friends and colleagues wrote to Himbury, declaring that he was the only person to replace Davies. Himbury was in a dilemma: indeed, this was a role he might have hoped to fill some day, but he had only just begun at Chester Street. Furthermore, in their approach to him, the church had said that they hoped he was not seeing this appointment as merely a stepping-stone to some other appointment, more or less an interim appointment. Himbury had assured them this was not the case: as he put it, "all I want to do is preach."[59] When he finished his dissertation at Oxford, he recalled, he had his doubts whether he was called to be an academic. He had academic interests, but "refused to do the hard chores which belong to such a life." This, he said in his recollections much later, had always been one of his problems; he did not like hard chores. Nonetheless, it is evident that when he chose to engage with a project or challenge, he brought all his talent and effort to its fulfillment.

Late in September of 1950 he faced a difficult choice, between ministry at Wrexham and teaching in Cardiff. The way this dilemma was resolved is a superb example of Baptist church discernment. Himbury refused to make the decision alone. He went to the church leadership,

---

59. Personal recollections of Mervyn Himbury.

the deacons. Very late in his life, he said that he could still see himself doing this. He said to them, "Brethren, I have this real problem and I have settled it—you are going to decide whether I stay here or go to Cardiff."[60]

Their response was graciously to accept his genuine openness to guidance, but together they decided that it was a matter of God's providence. They would wait to see if a call came from the college. If it did, they would accept it as a call to them as well as to Himbury: "And if they call you, you will go with our blessing; but you will not go without our blessing." Together, they agreed to wait upon the call from the college. When it came, Himbury accepted it with the blessing of the Chester Street people. The only condition the deacons placed upon his acceptance of the call to the Baptist college was that he should wait until January 1951, so that it might be said he had served the church in two calendar years.

So, early in 1951, he moved to Cardiff. Meanwhile, he had been planning to marry. He and Marion Phillips had intended to marry soon after he was ordained, and they were married soon after he moved to Cardiff.

---

60. Personal recollections of Mervyn Himbury.

Chapter 4

History Professor

The annual report of the South Wales Baptist College for 1958–59 begins as follows:

> I find that last year's report began with a mention of changes in personnel. Unhappily, that seems to have set a pattern, for since our last annual meeting we have had to bid a sad and fond farewell to Professor D. M. Himbury who, as everyone will know, has become Principal of the Victoria Baptist College, Melbourne, Australia. Many tributes were paid to him at the time of his departure. It only remains for us here to place on permanent record our appreciation of the fine service he rendered and the quite considerable academic prestige which his presence lent to the College.[1]

These words were written by the principal, Rev. Dr. J. Ithel Jones. Several pages later in the same report Himbury's successor, Professor Mansel John, offered his own tribute, with the parenthetical remark "and what a debt of gratitude the department of church history owes to him!" John goes on to describe the teaching load he had inherited. Eight students were pursuing the first-year diploma course, covering the first six centuries of the Christian era, with attention to forms of worship, the missionary expansion of the church, and the relationship of church and state. For a special study the Epistles of Ignatius were read aloud. Interestingly, a hint of "creative" teaching methods is given also: "in addition to essay writing, class discussion was encouraged."

---

1. South Wales Baptist College, *Annual Report 1958–59*, 7.

The final class, which was taken by students in their second or third year, engaged with the Reformation in detail and then the modern era, with a special focus on Britain. Final-year BD students engaged with document studies from the Reformation era, with special attention given to "Puritanism in England and Wales from 1560 to 1662"—Himbury's own area of research. For their part, the final diploma students read as special texts the *Epistle to Diogenes* and Luther's *Liberty of the Christian Man*.

These paragraphs give a clear indication of the work undertaken by Mervyn Himbury as professor of church history at the South Wales Baptist College from 1951 to the end of 1958. These classes were taught under the auspices of the Cardiff University College and were examined through the university. There, and in the decades of his teaching in Melbourne, he was commonly referred to as Professor Himbury—a recognition and appreciation of his ability to bring history to life for his audiences, not only in the academic classroom but from the local church pulpit or small groups in many places. Thirty years later, in 1989, "Professor Himbury" gave a series of nine talks at the Collins Street Baptist Church on "Reformers, Baptists, and Other Peculiar People."[2] Then in retirement, Himbury continued to bring the benefits of his scholarship to the ministry of his local church.

One other report is worth special mention. The 147th annual report, relating to the 1956–57 academic year, celebrated the publication of the college history, marking its terJubilee. The chair's report praises the tutorial staff, beginning with "Professor Himbury whose memorable history of the college will find a place in many homes and studies."[3]

A special segment of that annual report is devoted to the history of the college. The principal, Rev. Edward Roberts MA BD, urged the annual meeting to record its "profound sense of gratitude to Professor D. M. Himbury for his notable service in writing and publishing the history of the college, in connection with the Ter-Jubilee Celebrations." It is then noted that in the annual general meeting many tributes were paid "for the excellence of this work, and the proposition of thanks was carried with acclamation." Himbury then responded, testifying to "the great interest and pleasure" he found in the research involved.

---

2. Cassette recordings of these lessons survive in the church archives. It seems likely that this series was similar to the course he offered about this same time for the Council for Adult Education, a community education service in central Melbourne.

3. South Wales Baptist College, *Annual Report 1956–57*, 6.

It is also interesting to note how Mervyn Himbury began his own tutor's report: "Though the course followed by all students was that laid down by the Faculty of Theology of the University, every possible opportunity was taken of introducing topics of particular relevance to Baptist churches and their ministry." We may infer from this opening remark a concern on the part of the college (and Himbury himself) to maintain both its relationship with the university and to continue to provide for the needs and interests of its Baptist constituency: ministerial education. These concerns were to shape his life and work as a professor of history within Baptist communities, in Wales and in Australia.

It was expected of staff at the South Wales Baptist College to be actively involved in local Baptist churches. This was something Mervyn Himbury gladly undertook. For all the years he was a tutor in Cardiff, he served the Croes-y-Park Baptist Church, which is located in Chapel Lane, Peterston-super-Ely. It is set in a semirural location, on the outskirts of Cardiff.

John Briggs has written helpfully about the value and significance of Baptist history, considering "what our yesterdays have to say to our todays and tomorrow." He notes the dangers of separating "Baptist" history too much from that of the whole church of God, and of too great a "remembering," a focus on the past that does not attend to where the Spirit of God is leading into the future.[4] Nonetheless, Briggs argues that "within the pages of history can be found encouragement in stories of successful community-building, service and outreach, but also cautionary indications of times in which the church's integrity had been severely challenged by its failure in faithfulness and vision."[5] It is helpful to bear these comments in mind as we consider the many contributions of Mervyn Himbury as a Baptist historian.

It is clear that Himbury's teaching involved the integration of a number of topics and themes: Baptist origins and Baptist identity, worship and the sacraments, the relationships between the various Christian churches, and between church and state. Both as a teacher and a denominational leader he was continuously reflecting upon the nature and purposes of ministerial education, and these were the themes of his publications over several decades.

---

4. Briggs, "Memory, Vision and Mission," 38.
5. Briggs, "Memory, Vision and Mission," 52.

Baptist Origins and the Christian Magistrate

While it is not possible here to summarize in detail the entire thesis Himbury wrote for his BLitt degree at Oxford, the central themes he identified in that study proved foundational to much of his later work and interests.

The thesis itself is titled "The Christian Magistrate as Viewed by the Separatist and Dissenting Groups Before 1660." It comprises some 180 typed foolscap pages. It is a work of immense detail, drawing upon original sources and collating a range of perspectives from the various radical Puritan and Dissenting groups that developed during the tumultuous decades of the 1640s and 1650s. Himbury's approach is largely descriptive, with only occasional commentary and direct critical analysis. A scholarly analysis is evident in the classifications and depiction of the various approaches, along with some discussion of sources and attributions; but the various positions outlined are not evaluated, nor is there any attempt to comment upon the significance of these movements for Baptist life in the present. That task is left to teachers and other writing. It is a great pity that this thesis has never been published. Here is a rich resource in Baptist history which might enrich contemporary reflection upon Baptist identity and theology.

The thesis outlines the perspectives of numerous Separatist and Dissenting groups toward the office of the magistrate, with a particular interest in how that role related to the life of the churches.[6] In his conclusion, Himbury identified two key themes in the various perspectives and positions of these groups. The first of these was their "doctrine of law," which determined their views of magistracy as such. Second was their eschatological beliefs, in the sense of what they might expect in this life and this world, if human societies were aligned with these ideas of law and its purposes. Obviously, another key element was their understanding of the nature of the church and the ways in which it should be governed—and those areas or activities in which the church should not be subjected to the civil power.

In addition to these aspects, another element mentioned in Himbury's expositions of the various positions, though not named in his

---

6. The role and responsibilities of a civil magistrate was a subject of specific concern for the early Baptist groups, who debated whether a person could both be a Christian and a magistrate. This can be seen, for example, in the "English Declaration at Amsterdam" of 1611: A Declaration of Faith of the English People Remaining at Amsterdam in Holland, 1611, paragraphs 83–85.

conclusion, was the view of human nature implied in these views. The nature and function of law, as apprehended through conscience and reason, and what might be expected in human society, are at least in part understood in light of what might be called a theological anthropology, and this was another element in the thinking of these radical believers. In considering these ideas and movements, it is to be remembered that they are cast against the background of immense political and religious turmoil. In just a few short decades, the King of England was overthrown and replaced by a Parliament, itself opposed during a civil war; the era of Cromwell's "Commonwealth"; and then the time of Restoration.

A range of views is evident right from the beginnings of the Baptist movements. The earliest Baptist leaders, John Smyth and Thomas Helwys, differed in their theological understanding of the way Christian believers should relate to the civil authorities. A brief outline of their positions allows us to identify the key elements in much that developed in the succeeding decades. Influenced both by a strict Calvinist view of human nature and by his association with Mennonites, Smyth considered that it was only through the operation of the Holy Spirit that any human can do the will of God. A strict opposition of law and grace, seen also as a separation of Old Testament and New Testament perspectives, led to the opposition of the carnal and the spiritual. Helwys considered that Smyth's position denied the very nature of God and led to antinomianism. While agreeing that Christ has set us free from "ecclesiastical laws and the laws of the Old Testament," he argued that this does not mean we are free from all law.[7] There is one law given to all humanity, Jews and Gentiles, revealed in Scripture but needing to be interpreted by the Holy Spirit. Humans must be free "to yield themselves" to this guidance.

Here is an important implication of the early Baptist commitment to freedom of conscience. It was not always a matter of freedom *from* constraints but also included the freedom *to* obey the law or other authorities. From this position a view of the Christian magistrate is derived. Himbury concludes, "it is the task of the Magistrate to execute justice according to the moral law of nature, but he has no right to meddle in ecclesiastical matters." Helwys's associate John Murton is then cited, explaining that the magistrate has both a sword to punish the wicked and rewards for "weldoers": "And therefore this Ministry and sword is

---

7. Himbury, *Christian Magistrate*, 61.

appointed onely [sic] to punish the breach of worldly ordinances which is al [sic] that God hath given any mortal man to punish."[8]

For these early Baptists and Independents, then, it is not that the magistrate has no place in the church: rather, there was clear effort to identify the respective areas of responsibility, and thus ensure religious freedom. The magistrate has a right to obedience in secular matters, but neither the king nor the magistrate has any right to try to reform or rule the church: this is the realm of God's rule, through the Word and the Spirit. Furthermore, this separation of the secular and the realm of religious belief led the Baptists to a position of complete religious toleration. They rejected any position that imposed "truth upon the unbelieving."

These ideas were further explored in a detailed study of the works of John Milton and John Owen, both leading Independents. Owen particularly emphasized that the magistrate was to exercise his powers "for the welfare and prosperity of the Church, not so much to govern the Church but rather to sustain the context in which the Church may function."[9] Milton, a great champion of liberty of conscience, further elaborated the purpose of magistracy. In Himbury's estimation, Milton "regarded magistracy as being of the very essence of human society." To do away with it would not only end the Commonwealth "but also human society itself making life impossible."[10] In explaining the powers of the magistrate, however, Milton demonstrated an understanding of human nature, wherein outward social disorder (which is to be the magistrate's concern) is indicative of an inward failure, which is the church's concern. Himbury notes Milton's enthusiasm for the "divinely and harmoniously tun'd" Commonwealth of England, in which the king is to be subject to Parliament.

During the time of the Commonwealth, Himbury found, Baptist groups "exerted an increasing influence in England."[11] Fundamental to their position was a doctrine of divine law, which was understood in terms of human freedom. There was some debate over the extent of this freedom, for there remains a moral law to which all people owe

---

8. Himbury, *Christian Magistrate*, 61. The reference here is to John Morton, *Objections Answered by way of Dialogue* (1615) and *A Discription of what God hath Predestined* (1620). Authorship is attributed to him by Himbury, whereas Whitley asserted that it was Helwys.

9. Himbury, *Christian Magistrate*, 79.

10. Himbury, *Christian Magistrate*, 85.

11. Himbury, *Christian Magistrate*, 92.

obedience. Furthermore, Christian freedom does not imply an individualistic independence. Christians are bound to one another, and so too, each local community of believers does not stand apart from others but is bound to them in fellowship. These Baptists, then, saw the role of the Christian magistrate as the keeper of the moral law, thus creating or enabling "the conditions in which the church might make its witness more effectively."[12] To this end, Northumberland Baptists had petitioned Cromwell to establish a government "in righteousness," suppressing such things as profanity and idolatry, so that they might enjoy a peaceful life according to God's word.[13]

Inherent in these ideas, however, there is a tension between what was seen as the temporal power and the spiritual kingdom. For the Baptists, the magistrate should support and enable the mission of the church in the world. The Baptists had no desire to undermine the civil powers, but only insofar as that power was exercised justly and lawfully. As the unrest and turmoil of this period developed, the hopefulness on which these ideals rested was sorely tested. As a result, many Baptists joined the "Fifth Monarchy Men," a group formed in the apocalyptic expectation of the inbreaking of a new dispensation of Christ's kingdom. Meanwhile, they saw themselves as called to suffer in and for the world, not seeking to gain power or government over the present order.

From these ideas the thesis then turns to those groups whose theology is described as "the religion of the Spirit," as they emphasized "that the Christian must subject the whole of his life to the guidance of the Holy Spirit."[14] While this idea might not sound uncommon today, what is intended here is an emphasis upon inward experience, such as in the rise of Quakerism or a group known as the Family of Love. Each person was to appropriate the kingdom of God inwardly. Another group, known as the Diggers, affirmed a millennial expectation, coupled with a strongly negative view of contemporary English law. For them, while law was necessary to preserve peace and freedom, contemporary English law, deriving from the Norman conquest, was inherently evil. The union of church and state had made magisterial power tyrannical. Nonetheless, those seeking to live by the guidance of the Spirit were not to revolt

---

12. Himbury, *Christian Magistrate*, 97.
13. Himbury, *Christian Magistrate*, 98, Note 20.
14. Himbury, *Christian Magistrate*, 119–27.

against this order. Rather, their own lives should be so aligned with God's way that the exercise of magisterial powers would not be necessary.

Two further groups developed in this time as well and attracted the support of many Baptists. The Levelers emerged in 1647 and, in Himbury's estimation, was the group which gave a clear political expression to the theological ideas shared by many of the Dissenting groups.[15] The central concern of this group was "to secure for all people those rights for which the ordinary parliamentary soldier had fought"—namely that all people should be free.[16] This freedom could be achieved in one of two ways: by conquest or by agreement. The latter is the way of God, the Levelers believed. There should be a contract or understanding, an agreement between the governed and the governor. Their critical idea was the concept of an "Agreement of the People," which would provide the basis for human flourishing. Like the Diggers, the Levelers believed that such a development would restore the freedoms that obtained before the Norman conquest of Anglo-Saxon England. A parliamentary republic would require the abolition of "distinction of orders and dignities." Without such distinctions and the tyranny they enabled, the magistrate should function with the necessary authority to create and preserve "the due respect and obedience in the People which is necessary for the better execution of the Laws."[17] These were the ideas of John Lilburne, who was imprisoned by the House of Lords for expressing them.

Interestingly, the Levelers did consider that the magistrate had some rights in religious matters—theirs was not so strict a separation of the spiritual and the secular. While God alone can persuade or convict people in matters of faith, Levelers such as Lilburne advocated that the Commonwealth should promote the Christian religion by providing for religious education. Himbury noted that there was a problem with the Levelers' views, however, a tension within their view of the magistracy. On the one hand they saw it as "a secular ordinance" and on the other hand their eschatology looked for a contemporary society in which government had "certain responsibilities for ordering the spiritual life of the

---

15. Himbury, "Religious Beliefs of the Levellers," 269–76. Published in *The Baptist Quarterly*, this article was written by Himbury drawing upon this section of his research.

16. Himbury, *Christian Magistrate*, 144.

17. Himbury, *Christian Magistrate*, 148.

people."[18] For his part, Cromwell rejected the idea of the Agreement of the People.

The final group considered was the Fifth Monarchy Men, a millennialist group. In Himbury's words, they "never dissociated themselves from the Dissenting churches, but, retaining their loyalties to the sects, joined in preparing for the beginning of the rule of Jesus as King."[19] Seeing themselves as the only true church, they wished no effective relationship with the state. In expectation of the coming visible rule of Christ on earth, they separated themselves as much as they could from the existing church and every function of the state. More moderate forms of these ideas emerged, toward the magistracy of the fourth monarchy. Himbury details the views of Peake, who accepted "the powers that be" in terms of the good that they may do. Nonetheless, the real or proper task of the magistrate, "for whom political power should have little significance," is to join with the church in "witness to Christ's true Magistracy and Ministry."[20]

At the conclusion of his study, Himbury noted that most Dissenting groups of this era had a strong sense of the imminent return of Christ. The Levelers, however, sought to order Christian society through the agreement of the people and a Christian magistracy that did not require such divine intervention. In spite of their differences, however, all these groups "agreed with most Christians of the time in viewing human government as an essentially religious activity" and believed that a "true Christian magistracy" would one day be realized.

From this conclusion we gain little indication of whether Mervyn Himbury, as a twentieth century Baptist, considered these hopes and ideals valid or misguided. What significance he drew from them for the challenges of his own time we do not know. What we do know, however, is that at some point he began working on what might have been a book drawn from this research. There are files containing approximately fifty typed pages of a manuscript entitled "Christ's Holy Community," an incomplete work drawing upon various sections of the thesis.[21] In addition, early in his time at the Cardiff college he published two succinct papers similarly drawing upon this research. The first of these has the title,

18. Himbury, *Christian Magistrate*, 153–54.
19. Himbury, *Christian Magistrate*, 157.
20. Himbury, *Christian Magistrate*, 165–66.
21. There are handwritten pages as well, some clearly deriving from his study at Oxford. The sections for this work were typed up at Whitley College.

Christ's Holy Community and can be taken as an outline of the key themes for that larger work. The subtitle of the article is "Aspects of the Doctrine of the Church held by the Particular Baptists in the 17th Century." Key points from this article include:

- The Baptists with the other Separatists searched the Scriptures for God's law concerning his church. Yet, the Baptists were by no means as legalistic as the Independents were in their attitude to the problems of both church and state.

- The belief that the visible church is "Christ's holy community" is constantly reiterated by both the Particular and the General Baptists.

- The act of baptism represents both the subjection of the church to the law of its foundation and its essential sanctity.

- A detailed exposition of Hanserd Knollys's vision of the mystical unity of the whole church: Knollys is forced to consider how this spiritual unity must be translated into ecclesiastical practice. (From subsequent writings, it is clear that Knollys was one of Himbury's heroes from this era.)

- While the Baptists insisted upon the autonomy of the local church, especially as against the views of classical Presbyterianism, they did not preclude the establishment of an ecclesiastical relationship between their churches, though this was not fully defined.

- As the church, Christ's spiritual kingdom, is separate from the world, the members of the church claim no rights within the secular state other than those which belong to all citizens, whether elect or pagan.

- All Baptists asserted their belief that the invasion of the affairs of the church by the civil state was a denial of the very nature of the Gospel.

- All Baptist confessions of faith insist that it is the prime duty of the magistrate to "tender the liberty of men's conscience." This belief sprang not from an assertion concerning the rights of man, but rather from their view of the nature of the church.

- It is only in secular matters that the state has the right to interfere in the lives of its subjects.

- Believing as they did that there could be no true religion apart from the personal relationship between man and God, expressed in the act of baptism, the Baptists were always concerned to emphasize that their churches were gathered on a voluntary principle, knowing no compulsion save that of the Spirit of God.[22]

Himbury continued to be interested in the ideas of the Levelers and in 1954 published an article about them. In that article, he drew upon the study of John Lilburne and William Walwyn by M. A. Gibb, who described them as "looking for perfectionism in history [but] watering down the eschatological teaching of Christianity."[23] Walwyn shared the anti-clericalism of the Baptists and Independents, admiring their willingness to provide material support for those in need and their advocacy not only for their own liberty but for "the just liberties of this nation." Himbury asserts that "many Baptists and Independents joined them and others supported the movement with moral and financial aid," though by 1649 the sects became alienated from the Levelers.

The article also describes John Lilburne's theological ideas, noting his language "that typifies the Puritan movement," naming Christ as "the only Priest, Prophet, King and Lawgiver of His Church." Clearly reflecting the focus of his own research, in the latter part of the article Himbury describes Leveler thought as centrally characterized by "their view of Law, and in this they show themselves the heirs of the traditions of the Separatists and Dissenters."[24] They wished to see the law of the land reflecting what they believed was the law of nature, though unlike other groups they did not identify this with the Mosaic codes. They looked back to what they believed was an era of natural freedom in Anglo-Saxon times. They hoped for the restoration of that situation through the institution of a Christian Commonwealth, within which a Christian magistracy was God's ordinance, thus mediating the relationship between church and state. It was this vision of both magistracy and church which justified (in

---

22. Himbury, "Christ's Holy Community." Dennis C. Bustin has noted with appreciation Himbury's account of Knollys in this article, drawing particular attention to the importance in ministerial formation of study of the original biblical languages. See Bustin, *Paradox and Perseverance*, 269.

23. Himbury, "Religious Beliefs of the Levellers," 269.

24. Himbury, "Religious Beliefs of the Levellers," 273–274.

their view) "their attack upon the government of England and, particularly, on Oliver Cromwell."[25]

Himbury's conclusion to this article provides a much clearer sense of his evaluation of this and other such movements. Here there were tensions which could not in fact be resolved.

> The great problem of the Levellers was to resolve the tension between their belief that magistracy is a secular ordinance and that therefore there can be no intimate relationship between Church and state, and their, commonly held, assumption that human society being a creation of God, its government must assume certain responsibilities that are, by their very nature, religious.[26]

This conclusion seems to suggest that the only possible resolution for those holding these political views was a more thorough-going secularity, which was indeed the way in which political thought developed in succeeding centuries and, in different ways, in Britain and Australia.

Churches in Fellowship: A Short History of the English Baptist Associations of South Wales

This small book, which sold for a mere one shilling and sixpence in 1960, was written in 1959 just after Himbury had left his beloved homeland. It is indeed a work of love. In his preface he declares, "The discussion and devotions which I have shared with you are among the treasures I have carried in my heart to the other side of the globe."[27]

The work provides clear insight into Himbury's understanding of Baptist church life and signals matters that were to shape the remainder of his career. The themes of this short history are church extension, the relationships and responsibilities of local churches to one another through "associations," their engagement in social and political matters, and the decline in church attendances, giving rise to the need for a different approach to ministry.

At the beginning of the nineteenth century, the dominant language in South Wales was Welsh. There were no English-language Baptist churches in South Wales where new industrial developments saw English

---

25. Himbury, "Religious Beliefs of the Levellers," 275.
26. Himbury, "Religious Beliefs of the Levellers," 276.
27. Himbury, *Churches in Fellowship*, 3.

workers and their families now settling. In 1806 two Baptist churches were formed, in Merthyr and Cardiff, and by 1860 there were almost twenty in the region. Twelve of these churches formed an association, expressing a key element in Baptist ecclesiology—that the churches, also self-governing, are not isolated or entirely autonomous. They exist in fellowship and mutual responsibility. Himbury notes that the decision to form the Glamorgan and Carmarthenshire Association was quite specific in not mentioning the Lord's Supper. The churches refused to divide over the existing differences regarding open or closed Communion.

Although this was a time of much religious enthusiasm and revival, Baptist church growth was slow but steady. From just over two thousand members in 1859, the association grew to twenty thousand members in 128 churches by 1913.

Himbury detailed a number of activities of the association. "Circular letters" were a means of communication and shared formation, addressing matters of common concern such as the moral purpose of the new government schools and their impact on the Sunday schools. In the 1870s and 1880s the association established a Home Mission Society to support the weaker churches, including funding pastors for those unable to do so for themselves. The churches of the association also addressed many social and political issues of the day. Generally, these statements were closely aligned with the policies of the Liberal Party. In the 1870s they strongly supported the removal of religious tests for university entrance and in the early twentieth century they supported the movement for disestablishment of the Church of England.

Following the great revival and growth in 1905, the association divided in 1911 into the East and West Glamorgan English Baptist Associations. A vital part of the developments in this period was the establishment of minimal standards for appointment of pastors: the association would only support appointment of ministers on the accredited list.

Further developments were the discipleship campaigns initiated in the 1930s, which failed to gain broad support, while the emphases on evangelism and church extension continued in the face of massive unemployment and poverty.

The latter part of this book, under the heading of "Retrospect," details the steady decline of Baptist church membership. For the West Glamorgan Association, Himbury calculated an average loss of one hundred members per year, though 1936–37 saw a loss of four hundred members. By 1958 there were only 6200 members in the association. In that same period, the number of Sunday school attendees halved.

Himbury's conclusion to this short history is particularly significant, not only for that local group of Baptists but for what would be the focus of his life and career as a theological educator. Indeed, the reader senses his own anguish when he observes that those few who now attend services are already church members: "Souls do not come to be saved, they must now be looked for."[28] Preachers must now become missionaries in their own lands. What would this mean, then, for the training of Baptist pastors? Clearly this question was front of mind for Himbury in his new setting and role.

Baptismal Controversies

Himbury's depth of scholarship in Baptist history and his skill in communicating that knowledge is richly evident in a long essay published in the volume *Christian Baptism: A Fresh Attempt to Understand the Rite in Terms of Scripture, History, and Theology*. Once again, his conclusion provides a helpful indication of the key themes and elements covered:

> The history of baptismal controversy in Britain has not always been a happy one; it has been the cause of much bitterness and has led to extravagant denunciation of both sides. Numerous non-theological factors have influenced the course of discussion in every period. Yet it has also produced works of great learning and has provoked all sections of the Christian community to define, with theological exactness, their own view of the church and sacraments. Many of the arguments used remained virtually unchanged from the seventeenth to the nineteenth centuries, though the late eighteenth- and nineteenth-century writers tended to lay much greater stress on the right manner of baptism than did those of the earlier period.[29]

The themes indicated in this conclusion are addressed in detail through three distinct periods between 1640 and 1900.

During the time of the Commonwealth and Restoration much of the focus was upon baptism in relation to the being and nature of the church, "a company of visible saints," so called by the Particular Baptist

---

28. Himbury, *Churches in Fellowship*, 23.
29. Himbury, "Baptismal Controversies, 1640–1900," 305.

Confession of Faith of 1644. Though there were some crucial differences between the Particular and General Baptists in this era, both groups agreed that baptism is an "ordinance" of the New Testament. Upon the direction of Christ himself, this practice is to be continued "until the end of the world," as a sign of believers being incorporated into Christ, in the fellowship of his death and resurrection. They also agreed that it should be done in the Triune name, as against some earlier affirmation of baptism in the name of Christ alone. They agreed also on the mode of baptism, "immersion or dipping of the person." Though they did not at this time specify who was to administer this rite, generally they nominated the minister for this responsibility.[30] Between the two groups there was considerable discussion of the eternal destiny of children who died, in regard to how they were or might be included in the covenant of salvation. This question arose acutely for all who considered baptism as a sign of inclusion in the covenant community, now understood as the church in succession to God's covenant with the Hebrew people.

Himbury observes that these ideas were acutely controversial in this period. The denial of infant baptism "was a cause of political upheaval" and many of the debates he characterizes as "acrimony rooted in fear." Following on from discussion of the proper subjects of baptism was debate about the mode. Here there were several different issues. While there were "many Anglicans and Puritans who accepted that *dipping* was the New Testament mode of baptism long before it became customary among Baptists," this was not in itself a basis for returning to that practice.[31] From another group, however, there came a rejection of all forms of "water baptism." Those who affirmed what was called "the religion of the Spirit" argued that baptism was not about water at all, no matter how it was administered. For them, water divides the church, whereas the Spirit would renew and empower the church.

The next period considered was the seventeenth and eighteenth centuries, during which Himbury notes considerable public disputation as well as much scholarship concerning the issues already nominated. These debates were pre-figured in that between the Particular Baptist William Kiffin (1616–1701) and Daniel Featley, "a man despised by Baptists and later imprisoned by the Presbyterian faction," in 1642.[32] Featley

---

30. Himbury, "Baptismal Controversies," 277–78.
31. Himbury, "Baptismal Controversies," 283.
32. Himbury, "Baptismal Controversies," 286.

published his analysis of Baptist views in 1644 as *The Dipper Dipt*.[33] It is suggested that controversies such as this led to the publication of the 1644 *Baptist Confession of Faith*, commonly known as the "London Confession" and which included in its heading "of those churches which are commonly (though falsely) called Anabaptists."[34] Himbury's delight in unusual humans and their ways is evident in his discussion of another character of this time, John Tombes, vicar of Leominster from 1630–1649 and again 1649–1662. Tombes held strong views against pedobaptism and absented himself from the church building when the rite was to be performed. In considering the arguments of both sides of these issues, Tombes argued for a much wider and inclusive dispensation than the Abrahamic covenant, and so rejected the suggestion that Christian baptism is the successor to circumcision. For their own part, while holding a common understanding of the nature of baptism, divisions arose among Baptists over the accompanying rite of the laying on of hands: whether this should be practiced, and by whom. Another lively debate arose in this time and continued well into the next centuries over open or closed Communion. Was the Lord's Table open to those who had not been baptized by immersion? Kiffin argued for closed Communion, though insisted that the table was indeed open to all disciples, since any who were truly disciples of Christ would in obedience be baptized. On the opposite position was John Bunyan, who saw baptism more as a subjective "strengthening" of the faith of a person but was not a prerequisite for Communion. These views were more extensively explored by Robert Hall in *The Terms of Communion*, in 1815, presenting a comprehensive argument for open Communion.

In reviewing this second period and the continuing divisions over baptism, Himbury noted a more "calmly academic" mood, with several changes in emphasis.[35] Later discussions were more concerned with the mode of baptism before proceeding to discussion about who were the

---

33. The full title of this work was *The Dipper Dipt: or the Anabaptist duck't and plunged over head and ears, at a Disputation in Southwark*. A frontispiece to the work depicted a naked woman being baptized by immersion. Critics of Baptist practice suggested that such nudity was immoral and contrary to the sixth and seventh commandments. For their part Baptists considered that they were following the ancient practice of the church.

34. The Baptist confession of faith named here is commonly referred to as the "London Confession 1644" and is published in many places, such as Lumpkin, *Baptist Confessions of Faith*, 153–73.

35. Himbury, "Baptismal Controversies," 294.

proper candidates for the rite. Another feature Himbury noted in later works of this time was the tendency to focus more on refuting the arguments of pedobaptists than on the arguments for a Baptist view. So a famous work by Abraham Booth, *Paedobaptism Explained*, "consists largely of quotations from anti-Paedo-Baptists, which are used to justify Baptist opinions; a method often used since that time."[36]

The final section of the paper, relating to the nineteenth century, reflects on what Himbury called "the great revival of baptismal controversy" and provided him with some amusement. An immense amount of material on the subject was published, ranging from "great academic tomes to single sheet tracts sold usually at a shilling or so a hundred." A series of sermons by John Keble provided a fine Anglican exposition of the nature and efficacy of baptism, including the affirmation that a child so baptized is a Christian "forever," unless that person should choose to deny the grace granted to them. Baptism thus signifies the covenant between God and the person baptized. It is a work of faith, in which the church "speaks for the child, through the godparents it appoints," while God's own affirmation is mediated through the priest, who is "but shadow and token of our Lord Jesus Christ." Keble stressed the importance of the consecration of the water for the efficacy of this sacrament.[37]

Another great preacher presented a very different position. C. H. Spurgeon preached a sermon critiquing "baptismal regeneration," which doctrine he claimed was taught only by "the corporation which with none too much humility calls itself *the* Church of England."[38] This doctrine Spurgeon contrasted with the teaching of Jesus, in which salvation is not effected through a ceremony. This sermon created "a remarkable stir in theological and ecclesiastical circles," Himbury records. W. T. Whitley had already identified as many as 150 replies to Spurgeon, which Himbury considers an underestimate. The acrimony that ensued was even greater than that seen in the seventeenth century.[39]

Of a much more academic nature was the immense work by R. Ingham, *A Handbook of Christian Baptism*, more than six hundred pages in length, published in 1865, and followed in 1871 by *Baptism, Its Subjects*, a further seven hundred pages. Ingham offers a New Testament view of

---

36. Himbury, "Baptismal Controversies," 297.
37. Himbury, "Baptismal Controversies," 300.
38. Himbury, "Baptismal Controversies," 301.
39. Himbury, "Baptismal Controversies," 301–2.

baptism as a profession of discipleship of Jesus Christ and provided by God as the means of entrance to the body of Christ, covered an immense range of topics and opposing views. The mode of baptism is to be based upon the meaning of the Greek term βαπτίζω, to immerse. Evidence is drawn from Greek lexicons and other writers, reflecting a debate earlier in the century between Baptists and the British and Foreign Bible Society. Considering the large part of this work addressed to opposing views, Himbury remarks that "it is difficult to think of any objection, textual, historical or practical, that he has ignored."[40] A final element Himbury noted in this period was a renewed interest in archaeological studies as a source for baptismal theology, illustrating the mode of baptism as immersion.

The conclusions already noted led to two final comments. First, Himbury says that Baptist apologetics in these times often tended toward a certain legalistic attitude. He then offers the more positive hope that reflection on the immense material developed in these earlier times can provide a helpful resource for more modern discussions, while our own concerns can provide a useful basis for re-examination of these historical formulations.

British Baptist History

All the preceding works, together no doubt with his teaching materials from the courses in Cardiff, contributed to Himbury's book *British Baptists: A Short History*, published in 1962.

Like other works already considered, this book demonstrates Himbury's extraordinary grasp of an immense amount of detail, presented in a very readable manner and yet very succinctly, all within just 143 pages.

It is worth noting some points of comparison between this work and, for example, a similar book by W. T. Whitley, the founder of the college to which Himbury went in Melbourne. Published in 1923 and more than twice the length of Himbury's "short history," Whitley's work devotes six of his ten chapters to the early centuries. Chapter 7 considers "The Larger Horizon," with the founding of the Baptist Missionary Society and the beginnings of the seminaries, while chapter 8 moves into the Victorian era, and chapter 9 considers "The Overseas Dominions." It is only in the final few pages that Whitley turned to "Baptists in the world"

---

40. Himbury, "Baptismal Controversies," 304.

and "the Baptist contribution to life," considering Baptist influence in areas such as legal or medical practice. Here, though, we come across a succinct summary of his vision for Baptist life, in a quotation from a fellow immigrant to Australia, F. W. Boreham:

> Witness to the reality and glory of the unseen; educate the conscience of the community; apply the principles of Christianity to present conditions, and consecrate our citizenship to the service of every movement that makes for reform.[41]

Himbury's history, while still focused on the Baptist churches, offers a somewhat broader perspective and introduces themes which were to be of continuing significance in his career. We see Himbury's expertise as a teacher of history, clearly presenting the core issues, with just enough detail to explain the significance of each phase and development. He begins with a chapter he called "The Context of the Baptists." Here he notes Troeltsch's categories of "church" and "sect," but then suggests that many Baptist historians would reject the implication that their movement was some kind of innovation or novelty. Rather, they draw a continuous line to the days of the first disciples, while regarding "the growth of institutional Catholicism as a spiritual aberration."[42] In every age there have been those who sought renewal of the church's witness, though Himbury rejects the claim of those who call every such group Baptists. Nonetheless, the Baptist insistence upon belonging to the whole church, throughout its history, is critical.

After describing some of the radical movements of the early sixteenth century, Himbury observes that "the determination of the relationship between the Baptists and the Anabaptists is one of the greatest problems that confront modern church historians."[43] It is a debate that is not concluded, he adds. He then considers the activities of the early Baptists such as Helwys and Murton, including their publications, the various baptismal controversies, the foundation of Baptist churches in Wales and Ireland, Baptist life during the Civil War, and the beginnings of Baptist life in the American colonies. The following chapters engage

---

41. Whitley, *A History of British Baptists*, 358. Unfortunately, Whitley did not identify the source of this quotation, apart from naming Boreham, plus the words, "Hobart, 1908." The quotation is not found in any of Boreham's early books, so it seems likely that the origin was some other publication, perhaps an occasional address or an article in a church paper.

42. Himbury, *British Baptists*, 8.

43. Himbury, *British Baptists*, 16.

with Himbury's areas of special interest, the growth of "non-conformity," and the period when Baptists underwent persecution following the Corporation Act of 1661, which prescribed forms of public worship. While Charles II allowed some brief "indulgence," it was not until James II's Declaration of Toleration in 1687 that their freedom to gather was guaranteed. The period of the later seventeenth and early eighteenth centuries was a time of much less vigor among Baptists, with considerable internal disputation. Then followed, however, "the great awakening," led significantly by the preaching of George Whitefield and John Wesley. With this time there came a resurgence of Baptist life, including efforts to unite the Particular and General Baptists—something not actually achieved until late in the nineteenth century. In this era of new life, attention turned to the training of ministers and various forms of missionary outreach, most notably the formation of the Baptist Missionary Society. In 1804 the York and Lancashire Baptist Association appointed a tutor for training pastors and various colleges were soon formed, including the Academical Institution at Stepney in 1810. With these movements, Baptists began to move into the wider world, beginning with the work of William Carey in India and from there further outreach into China. Baptist witness developed also in the West Indies, parts of Africa, USA, Canada, Australasia, and South Africa.

This careful historical outline might be seen as the background for three particularly interesting chapters, which I think represent Himbury's deep interest and conviction as a Baptist historian and pastor. The first of these concerned the question of the relationship between each local Baptist church and the wider Christian church. The second was the theme of Baptists in the secular world, and finally the defining focus of Baptist life as it is expressed in worship, particularly in preaching and the sacrament of baptism.

The chapter headed "The Baptist Church and the Churches," begins with the question of whether each local Baptist church is a church unto itself—the much vaunted "autonomy" of the local church. On the contrary, Himbury argued, from the outset Baptists understood the church as a community of people called together by God (as they expressed it, "separated from the world") to be a visible body of Christ, existing in a mystical unity with the whole church. The earliest confessions affirm there is indeed but one church, made visible within all the individual or local churches. The practical issues for the Baptists, however, in this period of intensely difficult separation from the existing forms of church, was how their local groups of believers would relate to one another. How should that mystical unity be expressed? Their answer was to develop associations, through which the congregations would express both support for and accountability to one another.

The first such association was formed in Berkshire in 1652, though several churches had formed a link of this kind in South Wales in 1650. Similar groupings developed elsewhere throughout England and in Ireland. The General Baptists developed such associations a little earlier than the Particular Baptists. The General Baptists' *Orthodox Creed* of 1678 affirms the assembly of all the bishops, elders and brethren, representing all the churches, "make but one church."[44] A similar affirmation was made by the assembly of the Particular Baptists in 1689. The association was both theological and pragmatic. One of the key objectives of the various associations was to develop forms of training for pastors, to share in the ordination of new ministers and to maintain some form of mutual accountability on matters of doctrine and polity. In these early decades and centuries there was a strong sense of discipline, both moral and doctrinal. Such matters were regularly examined within the local churches and, unfortunately, led at times to significant tensions and divisions. "Independency" became a serious problem during the eighteenth century. With the period of the awakening, however, and a renewal of congregational life, a fresh emphasis on the purposes of the associations emerged. In 1812, for example, a meeting within the London Association proposed ten practical purposes, ranging from prayer for the outpouring of the Holy Spirit on the churches and the world to support for the academies (newly formed) and means of supporting older ministers "almost beyond their labors," Sunday schools, and offering advice on where new churches might be developed.

So much for the practical purposes of the union or association of churches. On the theological side, Himbury noted that the definition of its doctrinal basis was one of the greatest problems. There was no desire "to formulate a creed binding upon all its members, but rather to express the mind of the member churches."[45] In this way, Himbury touches upon one of the fundamental tensions in Baptist identity and ecclesiology: a commitment both to association and freedom, both for every Christian disciple and for each local church, within the discipline of Christ himself

---

44. Himbury, *British Baptists*, 109.
45. Himbury, *British Baptists*, 114.

as understood through the Scriptures. These tensions remain throughout all parts of the Baptist world. He noted that in the United States of America there was somewhat more emphasis on the autonomy of the local congregations, while in Germany he considered the association or union had greater powers than in the United Kingdom. He also mentioned differences in practice with regard to ordination, particularly in Australia and a few other places where the rite is conducted by the union rather than within a local church.

Two other topics are considered within this theme. The first was the development of the worldwide association of Baptists, a kind of union of the unions. Especially under the inspiration and drive of J. H. Shakespeare, the Baptist World Alliance came into being in 1905 at a congress held in London. In Britain, however, there had already been movements toward association and united action among the free churches, in such matters as action against unjust laws, as well as the formation in 1846 of the Evangelical Alliance, which included Baptists in its formative leadership.

It is significant that in this discussion of the relationship between churches Himbury devoted only one paragraph to the question of ecumenical relationships. Writing in the midtwentieth century, this is both surprising and quite telling. Again, it indicates a point of tension in Baptist ecclesiology. Himbury stated that while the existence of the Ecumenical Movement and the formation of the World Council of Churches could not be ignored, "for Baptists all over the world this movement toward Christian Unity has created problems."[46] After noting different responses in various parts of the world, ranging from active participation to strict non-participation, he explains, "Baptists recognize unity as a characteristic of the true church, but are equally concerned that it shall be apostolic, taking its meaning and practice from the New Testament."[47] It is precisely here that the challenges arose for those who would train ministers to lead Baptist churches: how would they assist congregations to discern what it means to be apostolic communities in fellowship with other Christians, beginning with other Baptists and extending to the whole church? This was the first of the key issues which would shape Himbury's career as a theological educator.

---

46. Himbury, *British Baptists*, 119.
47. Himbury, *British Baptists*, 119.

The second powerful challenge addressed in this book was perhaps *the* pressing issue at the time of his writing this work—Baptists and the secular world. This question was, of course, the subject of Himbury's own research in relation to the seventeenth century, focused on the role of the Christian magistrate as one expression of these issues. In the twentieth century, however, these issues took on a very different shape, with the emergence of the secular age. Himbury's approach is primarily historical, naturally, but seeks to sketch a framework within which contemporary issues might be considered. The primary issue in the earliest period was the understanding of civil law and recognizing the role of government, but under the law of God. Divine and moral law precedes the civil law. Therefore, Baptist history can be seen as a continuous desire for the reform of civil society and its laws in the light of the divine purposes for human life and society. Implicit in this tradition is a view that affirms human life in society rather than withdrawing into a separatist holy huddle. Thus, Himbury noted the Baptist support for the emancipation of enslaved persons and the end of the slave trade, in the 1830s, as well as support for universal suffrage. In Britain, Baptist engagement with many social issues was very closely mediated through the policies of the Liberal Party, including the repeal of the Tests and Corporations Act, in 1828—an act which precluded nonAnglicans from holding any public office—and later challenges to laws relating to registration of births, marriage, and entrance to universities. Baptists were also strongly supportive of educational reform, seeking to remove the requirement than only Anglican doctrine might be taught in schools. As Himbury summarized all this concern, the "underlying problem" was church establishment. Baptists supported the efforts of the Liberal Party from 1839 onwards for disestablishment—achieved in Wales only in the 1920s. In the American colonies, Baptists and Quakers exercised a profound influence in support of religious liberty and "played no insignificant part in seeing that the Constitution contained no religious test."[48]

Himbury observed that the secular world presents new challenges for Baptist witness. In Britain, for example, Nonconformist groups have had less active influence upon political life as church attendances have declined and as pressing social concerns, especially poverty, have been "largely solved"—a view that might today be challenged. With a vision

---

48. Himbury, *British Baptists*, 133.

for the whole world, however, there remain burdens and issues with which Baptists must engage.

The final chapter in this work turns to the inner and spiritual life of Baptist churches in worship. Characteristically, the chapter begins with preaching and various attitudes to what constituted a good sermon. After naming some earlier developments, Himbury wrote movingly of the great Welsh preacher Christmas Evans (1766–1838) who "brought to preaching a sanctified imagination and could move a congregation to tears of joy or sorrow."[49] Many other noted Baptist preachers are mentioned, culminating with "the towering figure of Charles Haddon Spurgeon" (1834–1892) who "could make the word of God live in the minds of his hearers."[50] Himbury states that in the twentieth century this tradition of preaching had unfortunately declined, though he notes a parallel between the evangelistic ministry of Billy Graham and the ministries of Christmas Evans and C. H. Spurgeon.

In the final move of his history, Himbury returns to the subjects of baptism and the Lord's Supper as central aspects of Baptist worship and spirituality. There is a sense, he declares, "in which the whole development of Baptist life is reflected by the attitude of each generation toward the act and doctrine of baptism itself."[51] For example, as we have seen, earlier generations were acutely concerned to define who may receive the sacrament of the Lord's Supper in terms of whether and how they had been baptized. Himbury also noted a renewed interest in Britain in the twentieth century in the character of both baptism and Communion as sacraments in which God is actively involved—a movement toward a Baptist sacramentalism which has developed much more strongly since then.

Attitudes to, and the practice of, hymn singing was another source of historical controversy, a subject which has its own contemporary expressions as well. While the Particular Baptists accepted this practice earlier, especially in Wales, the General Baptists added their voices somewhat later.

A final topic in this context concerns the architecture of Baptist places of worship, something of interest to Himbury at precisely the time he wrote his book, as the design of a new college chapel was being

---

49. Himbury, *British Baptists*, 136. It seems obvious that Himbury himself drew inspiration from the example of Christmas Evans, albeit a full century and more later.

50. Himbury, *British Baptists*, 137.

51. Himbury, *British Baptists*, 137.

considered. He noted the simplicity of places of worship, with a central pulpit and the Communion table in front, accessible to the people. Only in later centuries did a baptistery become a feature of such buildings, in lieu of baptism in a stream or pond.

Drawing together the many strands of this detailed and yet concise book, Himbury names the act of baptism as symbolic of the ethos of Baptist church life: here a believer "who knows that Jesus Christ is his savior enters the waters of baptism, to receive the gift of God and membership of the Church of Jesus."[52] This essential spiritual relationship, between the believer, the church, and baptism expresses the character and appeal of Baptist life: "their attempt to recover the primitive purity of the church and to express this in the modern world."[53]

Mervyn Himbury, history professor, continued to uphold and propound this vision of Baptist life and spirituality throughout his teaching career and ministry in local churches. Several further and smaller works express these themes and need to be mentioned here briefly. In 1972, as a member of a study commission of the BWA, he was invited to present a paper at the annual gathering in Jamaica, on "Baptists and Their Relations with Other Christians in Australia." As it happened, he was unable to attend the meetings, but sent his paper, nonetheless. The paper includes considerable detail, including especially a contrast between the attitudes toward ecumenical relationships in New Zealand, where he found strongly affirmative engagement, and Australia where he noted that there had been "very little excitement" over the formation of the World Council of Churches in Amsterdam in 1948. A detailed summary of arguments for and against affiliation with the world council, as presented to the Triennial Assembly of the Baptist Union of Australia held in Victoria in 1962, is presented, together with an account of the ongoing difficulty Baptists had experienced in these relationships. A version of the paper was later published.[54]

In 1976 he contributed an essay on "Baptist Spirituality" to a volume titled *Christian Spirituality: An Ecumenical Reflection*.[55] The essay deals almost entirely with early Baptist life. Once again we see Himbury's skill in presenting detailed material is clear summary, naming the critical

---

52. Himbury, *British Baptists*, 143.
53. Himbury, *British Baptists*, 142–43.
54. Himbury, "Baptists and Other Christians."
55. Himbury, "Baptist Spirituality."

issues, common beliefs, and the diverging approaches of various groups. The following sentences provide an excellent example both of those skills and the themes of his work:

> The first Baptists were concerned to stress that salvation was by personal faith alone and that this was the sole ground of baptism and church fellowship. Within that fellowship the believer demonstrated his faith by his disciplined life and by his enjoyment of the means of grace, established under the covenant of the New Testament. He is free to be under the law of Christ known through the canonical Scriptures.[56]

In one short paragraph he presents the ideas of Christian identity, salvation, the nature of the church, baptism, the means of grace, Christian freedom and responsibility, and the authority of the Scriptures. Following a brief discussion of the principles of association, expressed in Baptist unions or conventions, he returned to these key themes, again indicating the tensions already noted from his history of British Baptists:

> Baptists have always lived in the tension between their stress on the personal experience of salvation and their high doctrine of the institutional church and the sacraments. On the one hand they seek liberty for all men, that the believer's confession of Christ may be voluntary and free from any constraints; on the other they stress the intimate fellowship of believers within the church which involves conformity with the beliefs and practices of the fellowship.[57]

In a particularly telling comment he goes on to refer to group pressures which may, despite protestations of freedom, demand conformity with doctrinal orthodoxies or participation in specific forms of evangelism or social action: "Those who seek spiritual freedom can often create their own spiritual tyrannies."[58] These tensions and dangers are all part of Baptist spirituality, both in the past and in the present day.

Early in his retirement, Himbury contributed to a symposium commemorating three hundred years since the death of John Bunyan, with an essay titled "John Bunyan and the Tradition of Baptist Preaching."[59] He began with the affirmation of the utmost significance attributed to

56. Himbury, "Baptist Spirituality," 291.
57. Himbury, "Baptist Spirituality," 293.
58. Himbury, "Baptist Spirituality," 293.
59. Himbury, "John Bunyan."

preaching by the early Baptists, in common with their Puritan forbears but with a stronger emphasis upon charismatic leading. Then follows an account of a number of these early preachers, from Thomas Helwys to Hanserd Knollys (1598–1691). Cambridge educated, Knollys was dissatisfied with the lack of results arising from his preaching in the Anglican church. Himbury described how Knollys "preached himself into the fellowship of the Baptists."[60] Henry Denne (d.1660) was another former Anglican who joined the Baptist movement in 1643 and became a traveling evangelist who was reported to have gone "up and down the countries spreading his corrupt opinions and dipping."[61] Denne engaged in public debates over baptism with Featley.

Drawing upon his study of the tumultuous years of the Commonwealth period, Himbury notes the persecutions suffered by the Baptists after 1660. When many preachers such as Bunyan were imprisoned, lay preachers were appointed. Some churches adopted ingenious schemes to defend their preachers, including the installation of a trapdoor in the Bedford church (Bunyan's church) by which the preacher might escape. Such was the context of Bunyan's preaching.

Himbury briefly described Bunyan's conversion and experience of calling, which were not atypical of the era: "The dual emphasis on the objective word of Scripture and the inward testimony of experience is typical of Baptist attitudes."[62] Bunyan was also typical of his Baptist contemporaries "in his rejection of the narrow legalism of many Puritans for the more dangerous path the Baptists trod."[63] Bunyan did not follow the narrow Calvinism which, in the preaching of many Baptists of the time, put more emphasis on the argument than on the proclamation, the message for its hearers. This was something Himbury himself would also affirm. Bunyan's great contribution was in two areas, Himbury concluded: his "broad sympathy toward all Christians" and "the imagination with which he expressed the deep truth of the Gospel." Even so, Himbury's assessment of Bunyan was that his concern to confront the unbeliever with the challenge of faith in Christ was "ultimately achieved more by the written than the spoken word."[64]

---

60. Himbury, "John Bunyan," 40.
61. Himbury, "John Bunyan," 40.
62. Himbury, "John Bunyan," 42.
63. Himbury, "John Bunyan," 42.
64. Himbury, "John Bunyan," 43.

As a professor of history, Mervyn Himbury engaged in rigorous analysis of the origins of the Baptist movement, always seeking to place these developments within the life of the whole Christian church, but also drawing insights into the ways both church and society are interrelated. His writings, as summarized in this chapter, reflect both his scholarship and his commitment to serve the Baptist churches with a sense of the gift of their history and unique identity. In all this work, Himbury directed specific attention to the nature of the church as a community of baptized believers and the essential role of preaching within the church. In these aspects we see the integration of his own calling: to serve the contemporary churches, as preacher, as historian, and as a teacher who nurtured those who would also serve the churches as preachers.

Marion and Mervyn Himbury, wedding day, 1951.

The Himbury family soon before leaving for Australia.

Regent's Park College, faculty and students, 1949.
Mervyn Himbury is on the far right, middle row.

THE ORDINATION OF

D. MERVYN HIMBURY, B.A., B.D.

of CARDIFF BAPTIST COLLEGE
AND REGENT'S PARK COLLEGE, OXFORD

AND INDUCTION

TO THE PASTORATE OF CHESTER STREET
BAPTIST CHURCH, WREXHAM

—o—

Wednesday, June 21st, 1950

Cover page of the Order of Service for Mervyn Himbury's ordination, June 1950.

The opening of Whitley College, February 1965. Left to right: Miss Rachel Thomas, Dame Pattie Menzies, Mrs Marion Himbury, Mrs Amelia Lewis, Maelor Himbury, Prime Minister Sir Robert Menzies, Principal Mervyn Himbury. (Miss Thomas and Mrs Lewis are aunts of Mervyn Himbury.)

The Mervyn Himbury Theological Studies Centre, Whitley College.

Ystrad Mynach Stars Rugby Club, 1913–1914.
Reginald Himbury is on the far right, back row.

CHAPTER 5

Theological Educator
A Tale of Two Colleges

WHEN MERVYN HIMBURY ARRIVED in Melbourne in 1959, Australian society was experiencing profound and widespread change and the Christian churches participated enthusiastically in many of those changes. This was the backdrop to Himbury's new ministry with the Baptist College of Victoria.

Australia in 1959

Following the Second World War, the Australian Government undertook a vigorous program of "nation building." Population growth was the first objective: "populate or perish" was a political slogan of the time. The baby boom which followed the end of the war continued well into the 1960s. Immigration was the other major part of the population plan and immigrants were sought from the United Kingdom and from Europe, particularly. There was a cultural and racial focus, seeking white-skinned people from democratic countries. Asian immigration was explicitly resisted under the "White Australia Policy" established in the earliest years of the Australian Federation and only gradually abandoned in the 1960s and 1970s. The Australian population grew from 7.4 million at the end of the war to 8.3 million in 1950, 10.1 million when the Himbury family came in 1959, and had reached 12.6 million by 1970. The growth rate of around two hundred thousand per year generally included at least one hundred thousand immigrants.

The state of Victoria participated fully in this growth. From a population of two million in 1945, Victoria grew to 2.2 million in 1950, 2.7 million in 1959, and 3.4 million in 1970—an average increase of fifty thousand every year during that time.

The pervasive political ethos of the period aimed at peace and stability. The Australian Government was formed by a coalition of the Liberal and Country parties, led by Robert Menzies, who would be Australia's longest serving prime minister. Against the background of the Cold War, and with a population relieved to have resisted the Japanese forces in the lands and oceans to the north, there was a strong emphasis upon resisting communism and building the strength of the nation. One vital element here was the establishment of the ANZUS Treaty, signed in 1951. Although Menzies himself was profoundly committed to the British ethos and heritage, the nation had come to see the United States as its first ally and readily embraced a treaty which committed Australia to support the USA in conflict, as it also implied that the US would come to Australia's aid in time of need. This treaty symbolized a very significant shift in identity for the nation. Throughout the following decades Australia would welcome more and more the influence of American culture and political interests. That shift would be evident in Baptist church life as well.

Peace and stability were also symbolized in the housing developments of the era. The rapidly growing population needed homes and these decades saw the development of suburban housing estates ringing all the Australian cities. The advent of motor cars built in Australia by General Motors and Ford, and marketed as "the family car," supported this expansion. As a result, many communities developed with large proportions of young families, burgeoning kindergartens, and schools. Sporting clubs and youth organizations flourished.

Another part of the post-war development was the vision for growth and stability in the Asia-Pacific region. The governments of Australia, Canada, Ceylon, New Zealand, Pakistan, the United Kingdom, Malaya, and North Borneo (as they were then) formed "The Colombo Plan," which aimed at partnerships of mutual support, to strengthen the institutions of government, food supply, and health care. The plan offered scholarships to developing leaders from member countries to gain practical training in Australia—with the expectation that these leaders would return to their home countries as ambassadors for good relations and trade with Australia.

Education was an immensely important element in Australian life during these decades. When Robert Menzies died in 1978, William McMahon (one of Menzies's successors as prime minister) remarked that he believed Menzies's greatest contribution to Australia was the Commonwealth Scholarship Scheme. This scheme provided financial assistance to students of academic merit, to enable them to complete the final years of secondary education. It then provided similar support for outstanding students to attend university, paying both fees and, on a means-tested basis, a living allowance. These scholarships made it possible for the daughters and sons of working-class families to attend university, for the first time in the nation's history.[1]

Schools and universities were thus crowded. The children of the baby boom and those of immigrant families formed classes of as many as fifty or more, in schoolrooms intended for perhaps thirty children. There were not enough qualified teachers, and each state created a scheme to fund teacher training very generously. Meanwhile, people with just a few university subjects were recruited as teachers. Many trained as primary school teachers were enlisted into the secondary schools, and special schools were created for "technical" education for boys.

In Victoria there was only one university until 1958, when Monash University was created on the southeast suburban fringe of Melbourne. Demand for tertiary education continued to grow, and LaTrobe University was created in 1964 on the northern edge of the metropolis. With the creation and growth of universities nationally, the Commonwealth funded many students with scholarships. There was also a very substantial program of grants for buildings, including investment in student housing. Capital grants to create residential halls and colleges led to rapid expansion in these facilities—and provided a significant opportunity for the development of a new Baptist college in Melbourne.

At the time of the Australian Federation in 1901, the Australian Constitution provided no recognition of the indigenous peoples of the land, referred to as Aboriginal peoples. Their custodianship of the land over more than sixty thousand years remains unrecognized in the Constitution. Whereas the separate states or colonies had various programs to care for this part of the population, usually through what was termed "protection" or "advancement," in reality these activities were generally disastrous. People were herded into "reserves," frequently far from their

---

1. I was one such scholarship recipient.

own country. Until a referendum changed the Constitution of Australia in 1967, the Commonwealth Government had no powers in relation to Indigenous Australian peoples, and they were not even counted in the population census. From the later 1950s, however, and increasingly in the 1960s, awareness of the American Civil Rights Movement and the anti-apartheid struggles in South Africa gave impetus to a movement for change, leading to exceptionally strong bipartisan support for the referendum and subsequent constitutional change, and from the 1980s onwards, claims for landrights.

The awareness of political and social movements in other parts of the world was itself the result of another massive change in Australia, with the advent of television in 1956. Television brought the world into every person's loungeroom and, together with motor cars, created new opportunities for leisure and the celebration of the weekend, considered a quintessential part of Australian life. As Tom Frame has observed, "ownership of motor cars had a dual effect on church-going. On the one hand it meant that people could more easily travel to church; it also meant that they were able to escape their town or suburb in search of recreation."[2]

Religion was a strong feature of Australian life in this period. Studies of church attendances suggest that they reached a peak in the mid-1950s. In 1951 the leaders of four major Christian denominations issued what they called a "Call to the People of Australia," urging a stronger commitment to church attendance and the moral practices of a Christian life.[3] In part as a response to the perceived threat of communism, both internationally and within Australia, this call was supported by civic and political leaders. But it did not achieve its purpose. Church attendances began the long and continuous decline seen since then.

There was also a significant change in the religious make-up of the population. Despite being formally disestablished in the colony of NSW in 1836, the Anglican church had held a dominant position since colonization. In the post-war period, however, the number of Australian Christians that identified as Roman Catholics increased significantly. Here, too, there was a significant change. Migrant Catholics from Italy and many other parts of Europe brought a more relaxed and less puritanical approach than the prevailing Irish Catholic ethos. Changes following the Second Vatican Council transformed many aspects of Catholic

---

2. Frame, *Losing My Religion*, 66.
3. Frame, Losing My Religion, 64–65.

parish life and contributed significantly to the growth in ecumenical relations. Greek Orthodoxy also enriched the communities, especially in Melbourne. Numerous church-affiliated activities prospered with large numbers of young people, such as church sporting teams and associations, and activity programs such as Girls and Boys Brigades, Scouts and Guides, and many others.

Specific mention must be made of the evangelistic impetus of the churches at this time, particularly through the Billy Graham crusades in 1959 and 1961. Billy Graham came to Australia in the very same month as the Himbury family, in February 1959. Tom Frame has described the 1959 crusade as "an incredible phenomenon that went against the cultural mood."[4] More than three million people attended a total of 114 rallies, including one at the Melbourne Cricket Ground where 143,750 people formed the largest crowd ever gathered at that stadium. Many flocked to "come forward" to commit themselves to follow Jesus Christ. Altogether some 130,000 people made this decision, as it was called, during the 1959 crusade. Although over the longer term the decline in religious affiliations continued, in the immediate years following the Graham crusades there was a measurable influence in Australian society. Stuart Piggin has documented some of these elements. For instance, the increasing incidence of ex-nuptial births throughout the decade of the 1950s slowed only in the final year, 1959. The number of criminal convictions increased throughout the 1950s at twice the rate of population growth, but did not increase between 1960 and 1962. Consumption of alcohol actually declined by 10 percent during 1960 and 1961, a dramatic reversal of the established trend. Piggin does not attempt a strict causal explanation of these factors, but simply asserts "something happened in Australia at the same time as the Billy Graham Crusade."[5]

In addition, Meredith Lake has shown how the Bible continued to have a visible presence in Australian life. In government schools, there were programs of religious instruction, as well as student groups such as Crusaders and Inter-School Christian Fellowship, and on university campuses groups such as the Student Christian Movement and the Inter Varsity Fellowship. Feature films such as *The Robe* (1953) and *King of Kings* (1961) were highly successful. On radio and television, there were programs of daily devotions and many nationally syndicated religious

---

4. Frame, Losing My Religion, 66.
5. Piggin and Linder, *Attending to the National Soul*, 286–88.

drama and worship broadcasts. Mervyn Himbury frequently contributed to some of these religious programs, both on radio and television. In every hotel room in the country there was a copy of the Bible. Until late in the century, more than three-quarters of all weddings and almost all funerals were conducted by ministers of religion.[6]

Notwithstanding the official and general respect for the Christian religion, the majority of people did not attend church regularly. As Meredith Lake observes, "between 1972 and 2014, the proportion of Australians attending worship at least once a month fell by more than half from 36 to 15 percent."[7]

Within this overall picture of Australia in the mid- to later-twentieth century were the Baptists, who comprised around 1.5 percent of the population; but they were a church-attending people, committed to education both within their local churches and in the wider community. This was especially evident in Victoria when the Himbury family arrived in 1959.

The Baptists of Victoria

David Bebbington has observed that the Baptists of Australia display two features "typical of this kind of nation . . . early British affinities gave way to American cultural domination, and regions revealed markedly different tones."[8] In support of the second observation, he describes the conservative theological leanings of Baptists from Queensland, Tasmania, and New South Wales, while those in Western Australia and Victoria are considered "more centrist in their Evangelicalism." Only South Australia is described as "broad, liberal and modern."[9] These observations, published in 2010, are broadly accurate, though the regional diversity named earlier must also be recognized within the states as well, and nowhere is this more evident than in Victoria. The heritage of Victorian Baptists included a broader theological openness than is implied by Bebbington's brief comment.

As already noted, Baptists form a very small percentage of the Australian population, but there were churches formed from very early in

---

6. Lake, *Bible in Australia*, 284–88.
7. Lake, *Bible in Australia*, 288.
8. Bebbington, *Baptists Through the Centuries*, 249.
9. Bebbington, *Baptists Through the Centuries*, 248–49.

the life of the colony of Port Phillip, in the fledging village of Melbourne. The Collins Street Baptist Church was formed in 1843, just eight years after John Batman entered the region and took up lands belonging to the Wurundjeri people. The colony grew rapidly, especially through sheep farming and the gold rush between 1851 and the later 1860s, bringing a large influx of people, and immense prosperity, to the region. The Baptist Union of Victoria was formed in 1862.

Baptist life in Australia is organized on a state basis and it was not until 1926 that the various state unions of churches formed the Baptist Union of Australia, a body which coordinates some activities but has very little impact upon local Baptist church life.

Ken Manley's history of Australian Baptists provides helpful insights into the character of the Baptist denomination at the time of Himbury's arrival in 1959. Many of the features of Baptist life reflect the national ethos described earlier. Manley recounts the engagement with and support of the war effort (1939–1945) and then, in a section headed "Baptists on the March," the continuation of a militant and strategic approach during the post-war years.[10] The idea of crusades was a dominant element. At the same time, the influence of American, and particularly Southern Baptist, approaches to local church life and evangelism contributed much to the changes and developments, so much so that Manley's chapter heading quotes the observation, "Australia looks to America." The evangelistic crusades supported by Australian Baptists reflect this shift in cultural influence. The Welsh evangelist Ivor Powell spent three years in Australia, from 1951 to1954, conducting crusades in every state. By the end of the decade, however, the name on every Baptist's lips was Billy Graham, from the USA.

Manley summarizes the growth in church membership during this time, along with the rapid expansion of Sunday schools. In 1954, Baptist membership in Victoria was 8333; by 1961 it was 10,246 and by 1966 it was 11,360. Nationally, Baptist membership grew by 10.26 percent between 1956 and 1959, and 11.39 percent between 1959 and 1962—much greater than the rate of population increase, though clearly immigration was a contributing factor. Manley noted some of the specific elements that shaped local Baptist church life as a result of the Billy Graham crusades. As many as 11 percent of those making commitments to Christ in the Graham crusades were already, or identified as, Baptists. Local church

---

10. Manley, *From Woolloomooloo to "Eternity"*, 510–17.

pastors adopted a more directly evangelistic focus in their preaching. Southern Baptist groups were invited to Australia and Australian pastors made return visits to the USA, especially under the "Missouri–Australia Crusade" in 1964. Many Victorian churches participated in these events and in the "Pan–Australia Crusade" held in 1966.

Other aspects of Baptist church life in this time are well summarized by Manley's depiction of the 1950s as a "family-centered decade."[11] Children and youth were the focus of so much activity. Youth work in Victoria included Baptist Youth Fellowship meetings in Melbourne and arranged visits between city and country churches, explicitly intended to ensure that Baptist young people would meet and marry those from within the denomination. More generally, Manley notes that youth work fostered denominational identity.[12] Vacation Bible schools were another feature of local church life imported from the United States and effectively adapted to the local context.

Perhaps the most significant feature of the "rising tide" of Baptist life in these decades was the all-age Sunday school. This movement was promoted by the Federal Board of Christian Education and Publication, formed in 1956 and based in Melbourne. It produced Sunday school materials for the Baptist churches throughout Australia and New Zealand.

In Victoria, the Baptist commitment to education was also evidenced through the creation of grammar schools: Carey Baptist Boys Grammar School in 1923, Strathcona Baptist Girls Grammar School in 1924, and Kilvington Baptist Girls Grammar School in 1948.[13] These schools were seen as providing particularly for Baptist families.

Another very significant feature of Victorian Baptist life in these decades was the work of "Home Mission," involving what was later termed "planting" new churches. Along with the growth of new suburbs, the Home Mission purchased land and undertook various, and sometimes innovative, means to establish churches. Several existing churches commenced Sunday schools in new housing areas, as the basis for new churches. The Home Mission engaged a builder who, over a decade or more, had constructed more than fifty buildings for new churches. This work was led by Rev. Jack Manning, who would later become general

---

11. Manley, *From Woolloomooloo to "Eternity"*, 521.

12. Manley, *From Woolloomooloo to "Eternity"*, 523.

13. Carey and Kilvington later became coeducational and each of the schools has shortened its name.

superintendent of the Baptist union during some of the most significant years of Himbury's principalship.

The Baptist union leadership was under some revision. In 1960 the Baptist union created the office of general superintendent, and Rev. Tom Keyte was called to that role. This appointment was of strategic significance for the college as Keyte was also a leading member of the college council. The other key members of the leadership were Manning, as Home Mission superintendent, and the Union secretary, J. C. (Cliff) Thompson. In the ensuing period the Baptist union was served by four departments: Department of Church Extension (which incorporated the Home Mission), Department of Christian Education, Social Services Department, and the Missionary Department. From 1952 a "cooperative budget" had been established to sustain these ministries and a full-time stewardship director was employed to enlist support and funds from the churches.

In 1961, the closest date for which statistics are available, there were 147 Baptist churches in Victoria.[14] Many were older, inner-city or country churches, but others were emerging in the burgeoning new suburbs. Over the subsequent decades, the growth of many of the new churches mirrored the decline of the inner-city churches, perhaps reflecting transfer growth as well as real increase.

In summary, then, we may characterize Baptist identity in this period as involving a combination of various factors: the British Baptist heritage; the strong influence of the Evangelical Alliance, formed in 1856; a growing influence of Southern Baptist models for local church activities; and educational aspirations and a pragmatism which gave rise to creative outreach in many areas. In Victoria, an additional feature was emerging—what was called "New Settlers" work, which welcomed numerous Baptists from non-English-speaking countries and formed congregations where the people could worship in their own languages and styles. This work grew as a distinctive feature of Victorian Baptist life over several decades, as it was also in New South Wales; these being the two states which received the largest proportions of immigrants.

This activity and growth clearly evidenced the need for skilled and committed leadership: local pastors who would shepherd the churches. It is no accident, then, that significant attention was given also to the subject of ministerial training in the Baptist College of Victoria.

14. Annual handbooks were not produced by the Baptist Union of Victoria for the decade 1951 to1960.

The Baptist College of Victoria

With the rising tide of Australian nationalism in the 1880s, Baptists in Australia began to seek local training for their pastors. Many were familiar with Charles Spurgeon's "preacher's college" in London and envisaged something similar in Australia. The Baptists of Victoria decided to form a college, which they hoped would serve the entire nation. Thus, in 1891, the Baptist College of Victoria was founded, with Rev. William Whitley as its first principal. Whitley was a historian and came to Australia with a sense that this was indeed a history-making venture. While in Melbourne he completed a PhD from the University of Melbourne on the theory of Federation, an acutely relevant topic in the 1890s. The college began in rooms of the Collins Street Baptist Church, with just four students. There were so few students that for several years it seemed the college would fail; but Whitley was able to revive things during the first decade of the new century. William Holdsworth had joined the faculty and would succeed Whitley as principal in 1911, a position in which he served until 1938.

The move to establish a Baptist theological college was supported by the creation of the Victorian Baptist Fund, which was intended not only for the creation of a theological college but also to enable the development of new churches, to assist struggling churches, and to support retired ministers. This fund was to prove both a blessing and, as its capital diminished, an acute problem for the college. The perception that funds existed to sustain the college meant that many of the churches saw no need to contribute to its support. When the Baptist union established a cooperative budget, the college was not included. As a result, as the twentieth century progressed, the college continued with very little financial support.

A similarly generous provision allowed the college to develop its own facilities when, in 1911, a Baptist church member gave to the Baptist union two terrace houses and adjoining buildings in North Melbourne for the use of the college. One of the houses became the principal's residence, while the other provided classrooms, the library, and offices. An adjoining building housed student accommodation, where each student could have a study-bedroom. Behind was a building known as "the hut," which housed the kitchen and dining room. Two women came into the college to cook the meals, while students were responsible for cleaning their own rooms and, on Saturday mornings, cleaning the bathrooms and attending to the gardens.

These were the college facilities when Mervyn Himbury arrived in 1959. Here the family lived for their first six years in Melbourne. By now, the accommodation was inadequate for the number of students, and the buildings very run down.

Himbury was preceded as principal by Albert Grigg (1895–1961), appointed in 1939. Grigg had held the college together through the Second World War and then the challenging years of reconstruction, suffering a stroke in 1947, and again in 1954. While the principal was incapacitated and it was unclear whether he could return to his position, the college established interim arrangements which remained in place until Himbury was appointed. Grigg retired early in 1955. Himbury thus came to a situation where considerable uncertainty and instability had existed for some years. At the same time, very significant moves were underway to establish a new college.

The Old College

In 1955 the Baptist union established a college commission of five members who were to undertake three tasks: to assess the needs of the college, to submit a plan to the executive council for raising the necessary funds, and to advise on how the college could be made adequate to the future needs of the denomination—clearly implying that it was not so at the time.

The commission explored the idea of a university college. It was envisaged that, by some means, students of the Baptist college would be recognized as students of the University of Melbourne—at that point the only university in Victoria. Such a college would need new buildings. It was not appropriate to attempt to rebuild in North Melbourne as this was outside the university precinct. A project of this size would require a major development in fundraising for the entire denomination—which determined to establish a new college as a project to celebrate the centenary of the Baptist union in 1962.

For the years 1955–1958, a professorial board effectively replaced the role of a principal in overseeing all aspects of the college life, while the commission undertook planning for the future. In 1958 the college brought to the assembly the recommendation to invite David Mervyn

Himbury to be the next principal. His name had been warmly commended to them by Dr. Ernest Payne while on a visit to Australia and New Zealand.

The college in 1959 was staffed by two professors, Basil Brown (1914–2011) and John (Jock) Watson (1907–1981).[15] Brown had been appointed to the college in 1953 and continued until 1978. During the years without a principal, he was said to have "kept the College alive and directed the education of the present students."[16] Brown taught biblical and historical subjects, but later was able to specialize in New Testament. Watson was appointed in 1954 as professor of theology and taught subjects in philosophy as well. Both Brown and Watson were experienced pastors and preachers and exercised their gifts in preaching in the churches and guiding the ministers in training.

As was common in this era, there was a standard "college course" involving four years of study. Otzen's history of the college describes the course as it was in the decades prior to Himbury's arrival:

> The standard course leading to ordination was for four years: it followed the LTH course of the Melbourne College of Divinity in the first three years, with students sitting a Baptist College examination, then proceeding to the Melbourne College of Divinity for their examinations. Students also took at least two University subjects, such as History or Psychology, to broaden their education; tutorials in Arts and Science subjects were offered by the College.[17]

Principal Grigg had encouraged devotional and fellowship activities between the Baptist students and those attending other colleges, particularly the Methodist, Presbyterian, and Congregationalist students.

There was an entrance examination, which included a requirement of Greek at intermediate level (equivalent to Year 10). At that time, not all students were required to have matriculation.

To complete the licentiate in theology, students undertook subjects in Old and New Testament, church history, and theology, as well as subjects in "pastoralia," as it was termed. Biblical languages were also required, including four years of New Testament Greek, examined within

---

15. In common with other theological colleges in Melbourne and in Britain, the permanent teaching staff were designated as professors.

16. Otzen, *Whitley*, 110.

17. Otzen, *Whitley*, 87.

the college. Homiletics was taught within the college and students were expected to take that subject in each of their four years of training, such was the priority placed upon preaching. Elocution and church administration were also taught as internal college subjects. In addition, students were regularly assigned to or invited to preach in local Baptist churches, sometimes as relief for ministers on leave. This activity generally provided some pocket money for the students but also allowed them to become known in the churches.

From the very early years of the college, those students able to do so had been encouraged to undertake some university subjects; but in the years after the Second World War this became more common. Many determined to complete a university degree immediately after completing their college training. These experiences gave particular impetus to the vision of a university college. What was meant here was that theological study should have the same rigor as university studies and thus should be able to hold its place within all the disciplines of the university.

A final feature of the college at Errol Street concerns the food. As already noted, the college was limited in financial resources. One means of support was the provision of food from the annual Harvest Festivals in some of the suburban churches. For some time, this meant a ready supply of fresh food as well as preserves. Later in the year, however, little remained except for foods that would keep a long time—such as pumpkin. The pantry behind the kitchen became known as "pumpkin alley" and the menu had to include various ways of presenting this vegetable.

Otzen further described the state of the college at this time as "deeply impoverished in many ways." Typical of this impoverishment was the situation of the library, "still making do for the buying of new books with a mere £50 per year, supplemented by £30 per annum donated by the Lonsdale Street Particular Baptist Church."[18] A student served as a part-time librarian. Students borrowed from the principal's personal library as well.

Some years after the establishment of Whitley College, Mervyn Himbury wrote about his decision to come to Melbourne and what he first encountered. These words must be read with an awareness of some irony:

> I came to Melbourne from Cardiff in 1959 to escape from the terrifying fact that I was settling down into the world of an

---

18. Otzen, *Whitley*, 91–92.

academic historian, a fate worse than life in Australia. I must confess I was not sure what I ought to do but I knew I would never be content until I had done it.

It was in this atmosphere that I accepted the invitation to become the Principal of the Baptist College of Victoria. I knew nothing about the place save that one kind friend informed me that the major task of the principal of that institution was to act as matron. This I confess was not a lifelong ambition of mine. While on the journey I was also informed that the principal's residence was unfit for human habitation. This was possibly true, but I found it suited me well. . . .

I still remember the first theological student I met on my first visit to the college property. He was working in the library. This I found incredible if not heretical as it was the middle of the summer vacation. I shall always treasure his first word to me. I asked him what he was studying. He looked up with deep soulful eyes and said, "Geomorphology." My vocation was truly tested and, now, when I feel the burdens of office heavy, I whisper to myself the same word as an existential injection, "Geomorphology."

My first task in Victoria was to weigh up the situation which I understood at the time when the Victorian Baptists were weighing up me—a much more formidable task. The assets I inherited were easily assessed: a Victorian building in venerable and dilapidated condition, twenty odd theological students, (the ambiguity being integral to the statement), a vacant plot of land with a mortgage inexorably and, it seemed, eternally attached to it, and half a dozen men who were prepared to be fools because they were cranky about a college.[19]

The reference to a matron of the college would have resonated with Himbury's experience at the Cardiff college, where house management was an ongoing difficulty for numerous principals, until Principal Ithel Jones's wife, Nana, took over that role with great efficiency. From the outset, Himbury ensured that no such duties would be expected of his wife. The reference to a block of land was to the site in Royal Parade, Parkville, which had been purchased in 1957 for the purpose of the new college.

Such was the situation into which the Himbury family was welcomed in February 1959.

19. These words are drawn from notes found in Himbury's personal files and may have been part of an address or reflection offered at a college function. The notes are undated, but are headed "Whitley and I." A small amount of this material was published in the student magazine, *Monocle,* under the same heading.

Arrival in Melbourne

The Himbury family traveled to Australia, along with hundreds of other British migrants, on the *Orion*, which called at Port Said, then Fremantle, Adelaide, and Melbourne. At Fremantle they were surprised to be met by a welcoming delegation of Baptist people, who struck them as elegantly dressed, the ladies in coats and hats. They were somewhat disturbed, however, when one of their hosts advised them that he felt sorry for them, as the college in Melbourne was close to a state of collapse and the house provided for the principal was not fit for human habitation. Distressed by this news, they shared it with one of their hosts in Adelaide, where they had received a similarly warm welcome. The host suggested these comments were not accurate but observed that perhaps they had come from a disappointed candidate for the position Mervyn was now to take up. From the beginning, they found themselves amid surprising human warmth and some equally surprising pettiness.

They arrived in Melbourne on a Saturday night, presumably February 7. "The welcome we had in Melbourne was superb," both Marion and Mervyn said.[20] Since their arrival was to be quite late in the evening, it had been decided among the Baptist leaders that just one of them, Rev. Sam McKittrick, would meet and transport them to their accommodation for the night. No one had shared this thoughtful idea with the members of the Welsh Church in Melbourne, however, and a crowd of Welsh people were gathered on the dock to meet them. It was the early hours of the morning before they eventually left.

For the first two weeks in Melbourne, the family stayed in the suburban home of the Baptist union secretary, Cliff Thompson. A warm friendship was formed in those days. On their first day in Melbourne, McKittrick took them to worship at the Camberwell Baptist Church. Mervyn recalled how they were looking forward to experiencing an Australian service—only to find that the pastor spoke with a broad Irish accent and the service was very similar to a suburban Baptist service in England. That evening they attended Canterbury Baptist Church. In both places they were struck by what they described as "a really middle-class show . . . that was one of the differences—hats and gloves."[21]

They were staying with the Thompsons because the house at the college needed re-decoration, which was not yet finished. When they did

20. Recollections recorded by Rev. Marita Munro.
21. Recollections recorded by Rev. Marita Munro.

see the house, they were warmly impressed. It was a Victorian house with wrought iron work, very high ceilings, and was very cool. Just at that time there was a heat wave. Marion Himbury remembered a newspaper headline stating that children were being taken to the Royal Children's Hospital with dehydration.

They found one room was in poor condition but decided that they did not immediately need that room. They considered the house beautiful, with glass doors, large marble mantel shelves over the fireplaces, and crystal doorknobs. "We were very, very happy in the house."

Within the year, they also welcomed Dewi Michael Himbury, born on November 4, 1959.

So began Himbury's life as the college principal. Now it was for him to discover the landscape of that role. Here there were many conflicting forces and expectations to negotiate.

The Tasks at Hand

The academic year began in early March, with the twenty or so students coming into residence and the teaching beginning. Most students would undertake the licentiate in theology course with the Melbourne College of Divinity, but if they were already graduates, they could take the bachelor of divinity. Essentially the same classes were taught for these students, with additional topics or advanced reading set for the BD students.

At that time all tertiary teaching was arranged in year-long subjects and examined in November. Himbury would teach two subjects each year, one being early church history and the other Reformation church history, which extended into the modern era. Later he arranged to co-teach the Reformation history subject with his Presbyterian colleague Professor George Yule (1919–2000), at Ormond College.

A crucial part of his role was to run the weekly sermon class, which took place at the Collins Street Baptist Church. There can be no doubt that Himbury regarded this as a central, if not the definitive, part of his contribution as principal. He would preach a sermon for the weekly service held on Saturday mornings, and offered that sermon outline to his students, many of whom would be preaching at a local church the following day.

Regular meetings with his teaching colleagues, for planning and to discuss students and their progress, was another critical element in the principal's role. Doubtless in those early months and years Himbury was both finding his way, guided by the professors who had been there for many years before him, and also seeking to bring fresh vigor and support to a team which had held things together under considerable stress for five years or more. These meetings, however, were held more on an as-needs basis than the regular round of faculty meetings which are characteristic of college life today.

There were generally twenty students in college during these years, sometimes a few more. The student photograph for 1960 has twenty-seven students. Most were required to live in the college, which was often a source of disgruntlement for those who were seeking to marry. Ordination candidates could only marry with the principal's permission and this was generally given at the end of a student's course, though sometimes when a student had just one year to go. Many students were engaged for two, three, or even four years before being allowed to marry.

The question of married students' accommodation continued to be a matter of discussion and concern. The college had several applicants who were already married and some who were already pastors of churches.[22] Married students who lived in the metropolitan area traveled to the college for classes. Others lived in country towns far away from Melbourne. These were called extramural students and a special program of study was devised for them. Some undertook the LTh studies and exams, while others took college subjects only. Himbury was supportive of this program but considered it inferior to what was needed for those pastors' preparation for ministry. He recorded lectures on a huge reel-to-reel tape-recorder, and these were posted to the students, who passed them to one another.

A significant feature of Himbury's leadership of the college during these early years was his encouragement to gifted students to seek further qualifications overseas. In the wake of the visits from Southern Baptist leaders, there was growing interest in what seminaries and colleges in the USA had to offer. Through the course of the 1960s a number of graduates from the Baptist College of Victoria made their way to Southern Baptist seminaries to develop specialized areas of ministry. Not all returned, but of those who did Philip Chislett, Arthur Jones, Alex Kenworthy, Doug Rowston, and Ron Ham (who went to Union Seminary in New York) all went on to make distinctive contributions to Baptist life and ministry.

---

22. These pastors had usually completed a course of study at a Bible college and now came to the Baptist college for ordination studies.

The new principal of the Baptist college was invited to preach in many places, often for special occasions. There are no records of all these preaching assignments, but we can cite some examples. He preached at the opening of the new buildings of the Ashburton Baptist Church in July 1959 and for the annual assembly of the Baptist Union of Tasmania in Hobart later that same year. His stirring sermon, "Give Me This Mountain," preached to some two thousand people at the opening of the new buildings of the Baptist Theological College of New South Wales, was long remembered.[23] On most Sundays he would have been preaching for at least the morning service and often also the evening service. In those early years in Melbourne, he began to play golf with a group of other pastors on Monday mornings—generally their "day off"— and they would often discuss preaching and their ideas for sermons.

Just as the principle of association was an integral part of the Welsh Baptist ecclesiology, so, too, partnership was a critical element in the life of the Baptist college, and maintaining these partnerships fell very much to the principal. Foremost in these partnerships was the place of the college within the Baptist Union of Victoria. The college principal was ex officio a member of the executive council of the union and reported to that body on behalf of the college, as also to the annual assembly of the union. In that time, the assembly lasted through five days, including within it the annual ordination service, a highlight of the college year. There was a college session in the assembly, when the president of the college council, treasurer of the college, and the principal each presented reports. On occasions these were challenging and difficult times. The college sought always to serve the churches of the union but existed in tension with some of its influences as well.

Some of these tensions became very clear to Himbury within his first year. A conference on ordination was called for December of 1959 to discuss conflicting views of the need for and nature of ministerial training. This was to be the harbinger of a fundamental concern throughout Himbury's time as principal, as it had been for all the history of the college in Victoria, and is still today. The issues fundamentally concerned the place of academic study in relation to calling and what might be called "spiritual" qualifications. The report of the conference attempted to balance these concerns. Ordination should not only be based upon academic qualifications—as if it ever was. Rather, the "primary qualifications are in

---

23. Manley, *From Woolloomooloo to "Eternity"*, 571.

the personal life and capacity."[24] At the same time, the report encouraged *further* study for men in their years as probationer ministers, usually the year leading to their ordination, and Professor Brown was subsequently assigned the task of coordinating such studies.[25] Professor Watson already had a role in coordinating pre-college studies, as many of those seeking to enter college did not have the year-twelve matriculation certificate.

Himbury was acutely aware of the issues raised in this conference and had already begun to write about them. He was to publish several articles on the theme of training Baptist ministers in the years to come. At that time, he wrote a short piece for the student magazine *Upward Call* for 1959, offering both a historical perspective and his vision of what was needed in the present.

> Baptists have, throughout their history, believed in a *College-trained* ministry. Excluded from the ancient universities, by their confession, and the exclusive dogmatic tests which were an integral part of the British education system until the nineteenth century, they set up their own academies, which sent into the ministry a steady stream of gifted and equipped servants of Christ. Today wherever there are Baptists, there are also colleges so that the purity of the faith is upheld, and the increasing store of human knowledge brought to bear upon the witness of the Church. This is our task.[26]

Another immensely significant partnership for the college was the Melbourne College of Divinity. The Baptist College of Victoria was one of the theological colleges which had, in the earliest years of the twentieth century, explored the question of forming a Faculty of Theology within the University of Melbourne. In common with many universities founded in the mid-nineteenth century, the charter of this university specifically prohibited the promotion of divinity. As a result, the theological teaching programs conducted within the Anglican, Presbyterian, and Methodist colleges of the university were strictly not part of the University of Melbourne. The Baptist college was even more remote, both physically and institutionally. Negotiations toward entry to the University of Melbourne

---

24. Otzen, *Whitley*, 114.

25. At this stage only men were permitted into the ordination stream. Himbury himself did encourage women to study at the college much earlier than the Baptist union opened the pathway for women to be ordained, but he continued for a long while yet to refer to ministers as "men."

26. Otzen, *Whitley*, 114–15.

took place but eventually it was determined by the churches that this was not their preferred pathway. Rather, a parallel body would be established by the Victorian Parliament, with degree-granting powers and named the Melbourne College of Divinity (MCD). The MCD came into being in 1910, with Anglicans, Baptists, Congregationalists, Methodists, and Presbyterians as the founding communities. The MCD admitted students and set external examinations, initially for the bachelor of divinity, based on the expectation that candidates for ordination would first take a degree from the university and then proceed to theological study. Just as had happened in Cardiff, in later decades diploma level or licentiate studies were introduced as well.

The MCD was governed and legally constituted by a body called The College, which was made up of members appointed by the respective churches. Usually these were the heads of the various colleges and some other staff. On a rotating basis, one of the members would take office as president of the MCD and exercise the role that in a larger institution would be named chancellor. The president chaired the meetings of The College, maintained an oversight of its affairs (along with the registrar), and conferred degrees and awards at the annual graduation. The presidency was generally held for two years. Mervyn Himbury served as president of the MCD within a year of coming to Melbourne, in 1961 and '62, and again in 1970 and '71. It was during his second period of presidency that the MCD considered establishing an undergraduate degree in theology, which was to prove an immense opportunity for Whitley College.

By far the most important and productive of all these partnerships was Himbury's relationship and work with the members of the college committee, which later became the leadership of the college council. These men were all involved deeply in the life of the college long before Himbury came. It was they who set before the Baptist union the vision of a new college, and it was they who worked assiduously to make it a reality.

Himbury's files contain the notes from a recollection about the establishment of Whitley College, headed "Whitley and I." These notes have more the character of a speech, however, and include elements of his characteristic humor, which suggests that they are the transcript of a speech made on some occasion, most likely the first valedictory dinner at the end of 1965. A shorter version, with the same title, was published in the student magazine *Monocle* early in 1966.

The president of the college council (previously the college committee) was John Hopkins. He had trained for the ministry at the Baptist College of Victoria but had then developed a successful business in the manufacture and marketing of woolen hosiery. Himbury used to explain that Hopkins had a vision for relating Australian wool production with the need for employment in India to mutual benefit. Hopkins was a man of impressive presence and drive, with a no-nonsense approach to management and leadership. It was through the sheer force of his own vision that the Baptist Union of Victoria was persuaded to adopt the plan for a new college.

Rev. Milton Warn, first registrar of Whitley College, once remarked to me that Hopkins's vision derived personally from his appreciation of his pastors at Canterbury Baptist Church, who were intelligent preachers and addressed their congregations as intelligent people. He envisaged "MA Preachers," as Warn called them: pastors who were academically capable and could inform their congregations through preaching based on an educated study of both Scripture and the world around them. This was inherently the objective for a university college. Of John Hopkins, Himbury said:

> He was the man who first dreamed of Whitley. He is the only man I have ever met who could dream, bluster, scheme, shout, raise money and promise to give it away, simultaneously, while driving a car. I first met him at the docks wearing his Chev like a robe of office.
>
> I was to know him in many moods. It could be the affable beaming cherub but at times I saw his hair stand up bristling with understandable frustration, a remarkable sight and an even more remarkable achievement.[27]

John and Dorothy Hopkins were close friends of the Himbury family during their first two decades in Australia.

The other key person in the planning and fundraising activities of those early years was Geoffrey Stevens, also from the Canterbury Baptist Church and another businessman. He was an accountant and was well able to explain the funding models, budgets, and financial needs of the project. He was, also, a deeply spiritual person, committed to using his talents to support the Baptist churches of Victoria and especially the students and pastors. Of him Himbury observed: "There was Geoffrey

---

27. Drawn from Himbury's personal files.

Stevens, the man who welcomed me with the immortal, infernal phrase, 'We've got ourselves a rabble-rouser.' He was the eternal optimist who was constantly working out sums to prove how unjustified were his hopes."[28]

The "rabble-rouser" statement was made to other members of the leadership group after Himbury's induction service and was not meant for his hearing. He was not, in fact, happy about it—hence the word "infernal" there. But in other ways Himbury was quite happy to be seen to stir up his hearers, and the Baptists of Victoria and Australia, to a wider and more creative vision of the Gospel, and of themselves as a community of witness to that hope. After all, did they not derive from the radical Puritan "rabble" of the mid-seventeenth century?

Percy Iddles was secretary of what was called the Centenary Project Committee from 1958 and has left some detailed account of its formation and processes. The decision to establish "a major building program" as an appropriate means to commemorate the centenary of the Baptist Union of Victoria was made that year. The construction of a new college on the land already purchased in Royal Parade, Parkville, was approved by the general council of the union. Himbury appreciated Iddles for his enthusiasm and commitment to the project but recalled that, when returning from promotional meetings seeking support for the new college, Iddles's car was always very cold. He did not use the heater as he said he was afraid he might fall asleep at the wheel![29]

One of the most important men working with Himbury at this time was Bernard Tuck, both a distinguished lawyer and senior public servant, who was secretary of the college council. Himbury and Tuck would meet for long sessions planning the necessary shape of the governance of the college. A new constitution was needed, which had to be approved by the assembly of the Baptist union. This document was to prove a source of decades of trouble for Himbury and for the college, as it provided for the existing staff of the college (principal and professors) to remain in office without need for re-appointment by the Baptist union assembly. The constitution also provided basic position descriptions for various staff and essentially gave the principal all power and responsibility for the operations of the college.

Olwyn Abbott, a member of the Ashburton Baptist Church and a very senior manager in the National Australia Bank, was treasurer of the

---

28. Drawn from Himbury's personal files.
29. Drawn from Himbury's personal files.

college for twenty years, from 1950, and then president of the college council for the next twenty years. Abbott was perhaps a more conservative figure than the others mentioned in this group, but he was fiercely loyal to the college and its staff, and a fine strategic thinker. Himbury deeply appreciated Abbott and worked closely with him. Despite their differences in personality and style, they had an understanding with one another which was more than a working relationship.

Milton Warn, who served as registrar of Whitley College at its inception, once observed to me that it was part of Himbury's good fortune and wise leadership that in those two decades the college council was made up of many people in mid-life, who were just approaching the top of their careers. They already had significant standing in their professions and could bring that professionalism and gravitas to the leadership of the college. It is also important to add that Himbury was wise enough to learn from these colleagues and to follow their guidance, even when it was frustrating to his hopes and ambitions.

Clarifying the Objective: "The Aim of Ministerial Training"

Amid all the tasks and demands of the rapidly changing situation, Himbury continued to reflect upon the nature and purpose of theological education. Here it is interesting to note a shift in his language. In his history of the South Wales Baptist College, he used the expression "ministerial education." By this time the word "training" is used more and more, not as something new but rather as a significant shift in emphasis. I noted earlier his statement that coming to Melbourne meant for him a release from the prospect of remaining an academic historian. Early in his time in Melbourne he wrote, or perhaps finished writing, and published several significant contributions; his *British Baptists* and *Churches in Fellowship*.

Soon after the opening of Whitley College in 1965, he wrote two more important papers. In these the focus had moved to the very specific concern with the training of Baptist ministers. Comparison of these two papers is very illuminating. One is a largely historical work which, like many of the other works discussed, offers only a brief but important comment at the end regarding its significance for his contemporary context. The other is a profoundly situational piece, published in the denominational paper and engaging with the immediate challenges to the training offered at Whitley College. This shift in both focus and style indicates an immensely significant development in Himbury's life at this time.

In 1966 Himbury published an article in the *Baptist Quarterly* on "Training Baptist Ministers." There are two striking features in this piece: first, the quality of the historical survey, again providing the detail of scholarship characteristic of his other writings. The other element arises from that history, as the focus is almost entirely upon preaching. The training of Baptist ministers here is about their formation and education to be preachers. The focus is set in the opening sentence: "The Puritan tradition which did so much to mould many of the forms of English preaching was founded on the belief that the preaching ministry was so great and holy that those who were called to exercise it needed the best training that could be offered them."[30]

After surveying the educational background of early Baptist leaders, such as Smyth, Denne, and Knollys at Cambridge, and the Welsh preachers Powell and Myles who had been to Oxford, Himbury noted that many early Baptist preachers were (as the 1644 confession said) "esteemed... to be unlearned and ignorant men."[31] With no formal training programs, individual pastors took it upon themselves to mentor new ministers. During the eighteenth century, some Baptists remained "suspicious of any emphasis upon ministerial education, [while] the outstanding ministers commended all efforts to improve the educational standards of the ministry."[32] Then came the evangelical awakening with fresh impetus in ministerial education. Himbury's observation here is crucial: "The motive which inspired the early advocates of the academies was essentially evangelistic and missionary." The nexus between these two movements is evident "when one notes the dates of the various enterprises."[33]

When considering the curricula of these early academies, however, Himbury makes a critical observation:

> The techniques of preaching and pastoral work were not the prime concern of the academies and their contribution in these

---

30. Himbury, "Training Baptist Ministers," 338.

31. Himbury, "Training Baptist Ministers," 339, quoting the 1644 Baptist Confession of Faith.

32. Himbury, "Training Baptist Ministers," 341.

33. Himbury, "Training Baptist Ministers," 343.

fields were incidental rather than essential. The curriculum was essentially academic, aimed at giving the student an acquaintance with the body of knowledge which would be of service to him in understanding the Christian faith and preparing his mind so that he could benefit by theological books that were becoming increasingly available, but *presupposing that he had gifts already which would accommodate themselves to the practical needs of the ministry.*[34]

The words in italics indicate that there was a recognition of the personal and spiritual gifts essential for ministry, but it was taken that these were divinely given and nurtured within the churches from which the pastors came, before their formal ministerial education. These gifts would enable the minister to profit from that education, not only during the years at the academy but also in subsequent years of practice and reflection.

Moving then to more recent times, Himbury noted that this approach has been challenged, especially by American seminaries, "where courses on the practical discipline of church life have assumed major proportions and professional staff appointed to undertake them."[35] By contrast, in Britain ministers learned to preach primarily through the sermon class and perhaps some lectures in rhetoric, and these continued to be the responsibility of the college principal. After some detail of these elements of training, Himbury then asserts that despite criticisms—usually arising from lack of resources—"the Baptist colleges of the nineteenth century were remarkably effective. *The Times* in 1877 pointed to the superiority of the training received by Dissenting ministers, to that given to candidates for the ministry of the established church."[36]

In his conclusion, Himbury returned to several earlier themes. The colleges, now a widely accepted part of Baptist church life, continue with the primary task of ensuring that every minister has a strong grounding in biblical and theological understanding, in order that they might "build up the saints in the faith of Jesus" and present the Gospel to the world "in a way that is relevant to its own doubts and needs."[37]

Whereas in this paper Himbury continued to allow a minor place for what he called techniques of ministry, a year later he returned to these

---

34. Himbury, "Training Baptist Ministers," 344–45. Emphasis added.
35. Himbury, "Training Baptist Ministers," 345.
36. Himbury, "Training Baptist Ministers," 347.
37. Himbury, "Training Baptist Ministers," 363.

questions in a much more direct way, amid what was clearly a challenge to his own position and to what was seen as an over-emphasis upon academic subjects at the new Whitley College. This article, published in the *Victorian Baptist Witness*, was the first of many times over the next decades when Himbury tried to explain the necessary balance between academic and practical aspects of ministerial training. The use of the term "techniques," sometimes with a disparaging tone, and a concern with the idea that ministerial education was seen as a matter of learning the right "facts" or information, were to become recurring themes in his leadership and struggles, both within the college itself and in its relationship with the Baptist churches in Victoria.

The one-page article is called "The Aim of Ministerial Training."[38] He began with two key arguments, including a few phrases from one of his earlier papers. First, the Baptist minister is to be a leader, and training for leadership requires discipline. These disciplines involve (contrary to some current trends, he asserts) care for the institution of the church, building up its life and people. But there must also be a focus upon life "in the world, for it is here that [the minister's] Lord commissions him to go and make disciples." This assertion immediately leads to Himbury's continuing concern: what, then, is the role of a theological college? His answer is that the college "is not to give men techniques which they will apply to their ministries but to produce men who will find ways of being able to evaluate every situation they meet and deal with it." Again, he appeals to the nature of the Gospel: it is here that the "basic disciplines" of ministerial education are found. The minister must know the Bible and how to use it and be able "to think the thoughts of Jesus and the Apostles," as a living theological reflection, neither limited to the past nor to contemporary modes of thinking. The Holy Spirit enables this work, in an appreciation of the mystery of God's revelation. Thus, it is not so much knowledge of facts and opinions that makes a minister, but rather the training in how to handle and judge them—knowledge in the service of wisdom and love, one might say.

On this basis Himbury offers a careful balance between the practical and spiritual dimensions of ministry. Yes, there are practical tasks and skills: conducting the ordinances, educating the people, leading them in evangelism. Himbury the historian observes that over the centuries pastors have drawn upon "an almost infinite number of techniques" in

---

38. Himbury, "Aim of Ministerial Training," 8.

fulfilling their ministries. In the present age it is necessary to teach relevant techniques, but also to teach that these will become out of date. Preaching and pastoral care can be relevant only if ministers understand the world in which they live. So, the discipline of continuous learning is essential for this ministry.

Above all, Himbury asserts, is the discipline of love: love for the church and for the world God loves, which involves and is nurtured by discipline in worship. In passing, Himbury notes that developing this discipline is one of the most acute difficulties for contemporary theological colleges. The individualism that pervades modern culture and the fact that "so many men live out of college" mean that a life of common prayer and devotion are far more difficult to maintain. Here, in just the third year of Whitley College's existence, he named what was to become the trend for the future and, in one sense, the failure of the vision for the new college.

The conclusion is that the success or effectiveness of a carefully constructed curriculum rests not only with its educational life and facilities—rather, "the College stands or falls by the lives and work of the men who have lived there, whether they have had the opportunity of subjecting themselves to a true Gospel discipline for the sake of their Lord, the church and the world."[39]

A New College

Undoubtedly the establishment and opening of Whitley College was the defining event of Mervyn Himbury's career. Before he was appointed, the leadership of the college had indicated to Dr. Ernest Payne "that the College could become a University College, if a Principal with the energy and commitment to carry such a huge undertaking could be found."[40] Himbury fulfilled that undertaking.

Soon after the creation of the new college, Himbury instituted the periodic Holdsworth-Grigg Memorial Lecture, the first of which was delivered by Dr. Ernest Payne. With the publication of that lecture, Himbury included his own account of the birth of Whitley College.[41] It

39. Himbury, "Aim of Ministerial Training," 8.

40. Otzen, *Whitley*, 127.

41. The Holdsworth-Grigg Memorial Lecture, September 1967, by Dr. E. A. Payne, was entitled "Christian Tasks and Prospects in a World of Change," and was published

is not necessary here to record that story, except to note several crucial elements which profoundly shaped his function as the first principal of Whitley College.

The concept of a university college was never universally welcomed. Indeed, it was met with skepticism from within the leadership of the Baptist union, as well as many within the churches. Here several issues came to the fore: would the ministers trained within this college be academics or would they be people of spiritual depth and evangelistic zeal—the implication being that these were mutually exclusive. While Hopkins, Iddles, Stevens, and Himbury traveled around the churches promoting the vision for a new college and raising the necessary funds for its construction, fundamental doubts remained. One issue concerned the existing program of Commonwealth Government funding. The college sought and received significant support for the building of a university residential college, but among Baptists there were many who were wary of receiving gifts from the public purse. The question of government funding for church schools was one of the most hotly debated political issues of the time. Baptists were deeply committed to a separation of church and state and in Victoria the existence of Baptist schools brought this subject into sharp focus. An uneasy compromise had been agreed in 1954, accepting some government assistance for Baptist projects in community service and education.[42]

While the question of funding to build the college was addressed, much more critical was the issue of the support of the college's ongoing operations. For decades it had been acutely underfunded and now a much more elaborate operation was envisaged, with more staff and facilities to maintain. The operational budget predicted a shortfall of £7000. This seemed an "insoluble" problem, Himbury wrote, and some members of the union leadership suggested that the project be delayed.[43] Just as this critical possibility was to be considered, news came of the death of Mr. Charles Sanham, who left to the college a sum that would provide an annual income of £8000. Himbury described this legacy as providential and so "it was with a deep sense that the whole project was under divine blessing that the denomination assembled on September 1,

---

by Whitley College that year. In the same volume, Himbury included his essay, "Birth of Whitley College."

42. Otzen, *Whitley*, 109.

43. Himbury, "The Birth of Whitley College," 12.

1962, on the site of the new College, to unveil a foundation stone."[44] This event marked the centenary of the Baptist union. Himbury described the creation of Whitley College as a miracle.

Through 1963 and 1964, construction took place. Then on February 25, 1965, the prime minister of Australia, Sir Robert Menzies, opened the new college. Photographs of Himbury standing with the prime minister show a man justly proud of this astonishing achievement. The following day a service of worship took place when people from the churches could gather to celebrate and pray for the new college.

Along with all the challenges of building, furnishing, and engaging new staff to manage the college, one challenge remained: the need for students. Himbury and Warn were to recount the amusing realization of this need:

> The Registrar sat down in my room, "Well," says I, "that's done. But," I added, "haven't we forgotten something?"
> Then came one of those moments of inspiration for which Milton Warn is noted. "We haven't got any students," says he.
> "Good," says I, "that will make us unique."
> "Ah," says he, having the gift of second sight which compensates him, "that will mean there will be no one to pay fees."
> "Oh," says I, "let's get some, then."[45]

Thus began the first year of the college's operation in its new form, with seventy students and three tutors in residence.[46] Of the residents, a dozen or so were theological students, with others (married men) coming in for classes. A large section of the upper floor had not yet been completed, so the college was not yet at its full complement. In contrast to later years, when a college photograph was organized, the non-resident theological students were included with the residents. To Himbury they were all students of the one college.

---

44. Himbury, "The Birth of Whitley College," 13. Interestingly, Himbury's former Welsh colleague and predecessor at the South Wales Baptist College, Rev. Emlyn Davies, who had emigrated to Canada, was present at the laying of the foundation stone. Davies was in Melbourne as the guest preacher for the annual assembly of the Baptist union.

45. This quotation is from the notes found in Himbury's personal files headed "Whitley and I."

46. The term "tutor" here does not refer to a theological teacher, as it did in the British theological colleges, but to an academic guide for the resident university students, usually a person undertaking postgraduate studies and able to provide support and pastoral care for the resident students.

Though they had enjoyed the home provided in Errol Street, it was exciting for the Himbury family to move to the striking new house adjoining the college buildings in Leonard Street, Parkville. The home included four bedrooms and a modern kitchen, as well as a separate garden area providing some private space for the family. There were large parks and sports grounds at either end of the street. The oddly cuboid design of the house was striking and distinctive, alongside the round college building, and received some media attention.[47] For his part, Himbury chose to name the home after one of his early Baptist heroes, Thomas Helwys.

In addition to his role as theological teacher, working with the Baptist union and the MCD, the principal had responsibilities in relation to the University of Melbourne and its associated residential colleges. The "Heads of Colleges" group met regularly and were invited to numerous university events, including graduation ceremonies. Himbury attended many of these as well as official functions at other colleges, such as the opening of new facilities at Queens College and the dedication of the new chapel at Ridley College. If anything, these were very heady days, when his relationships around the city, in the media, and the university world expanded to include many people—artists and performers as well as political and other leaders. Dinner with the entertainer Barry Humphries was no doubt a very amusing occasion, while attending a reception for the prime minister of India, Indira Gandhi, was memorable in other ways.

The First Year

The many challenges of that first year are evident in the minutes of the executive committee and the college council. Himbury and his staff were aware of the need to establish the identity of the college among the other university colleges as well as among the churches of the Baptist union. Baptist students attending the university were encouraged to come to live at the college and others, non-resident, to take tutorials at the college, in addition to their university classes. Theological students were awarded bursaries to cover their residential fees but needed other means of support, and many worked in the kitchen to this end.

---

47. A popular design magazine, *Home Beautiful*, published a feature on the design and fittings of Helwys House.

From a contemporary perspective it is surprising to see (from his reports to the college executive committee) how much the principal was involved in the minutiae of administration, such as interviewing and managing the employment of cleaners and kitchen staff. In addition, there was clearly considerable tension with the "hostess" first appointed to manage these aspects of the college life. The first person to hold that position resigned after just six months in the role. After a short time, it was decided that the college would engage a commercial catering firm, an arrangement Himbury found considerably more acceptable—even if the students did not always agree. His view was that if the students complained about the food, most other things were going well! On the other hand, reflecting on his own student years and his observation of student life in post-war Germany, he did place a premium on ensuring that students ate well.

Himbury's daily life as principal, during term, established a clear routine. He would breakfast at home but would often walk through the college dining room at breakfast time, taking the opportunity to speak to individuals about various matters. In his booming voice, sometimes personal matters were no longer as personal as they had been. His intentions were to care for and support the students. One such occasion remains in my memory: a time in 1968 or 1969 when there were reports of very heavy bombing in Saigon, the home of a student from Vietnam. Himbury asked the student whether he had heard from his parents recently and offered him the use of the college telephone if he needed to be in touch with them.[48]

Then he would go about his duties in the office until 10.45 a.m. when morning tea was held in the senior common room; a weekday gathering of the professors and tutors. This became an institution, where guests might also be welcomed, and conversation ranged from student concerns to matters of social, political, or academic interest. Himbury insisted that morning tea included the provision of food, quite often cream cakes or other baked items. For those teaching classes, morning tea took place during a break in the sessions.

Himbury might take lunch in the dining room, though usually only if he had special guests, when they would sit at the high table. After the afternoon's work, he would meet the tutors and any invited guests in the senior common room, where they would gown and then process into the

---

48. By contrast, disciplinary matters were dealt with in private, always.

dining room for dinner, known as "Hall." Himbury always sat at a chair covered with a special college emblem designed and presented to him in the first year. Three courses for dinner were served, after which he would make any announcements he wished, and then lead the procession out. The students, who were also required to wear jacket and tie to Hall, plus academic gowns, stood during the processions (whether they had finished their meals or not). Hall was held five nights a week, which meant the expectation that Himbury would not dine with his family those nights. Usually, he would take coffee in the senior common room after Hall and then go home. On occasions, however, he would invite selected students and tutors to his home for a supper soiree, often with an academic guest. The conversation was often based on an area of the guest's interest or expertise.

Some matters seem to have generated a surprising amount of difficulty in that first year.

One of these, remembered as a source of frustration, was the design of a new college badge. At the executive meeting in February, the proposed design was rejected. At the next meeting, that decision was reversed and an amended design adopted. Then, after Himbury had presented the design to the students, the executive voted to rescind its approval and sought yet another design. This was just one of many frustrations that arose from a governance model in which executive committee members saw themselves actively involved in the management of the college. Himbury reported to them every month on matters such as the design of advertising brochures, guests to Hall, and so forth. In November of that year, the executive committee, "following considerable discussion," resolved that members of that committee "should refrain from opposing any recommendation proposed in its name before another body such as the College Council."[49] Leave to present a minority report might be granted, but the principle of "cabinet solidarity" was here established as a critical basis for the ongoing governance of the college.

Beyond these everyday aspects of college life, several major challenges emerged or developed during 1965. The first of these was the decision to add to the college staff the position of dean. As with other residential colleges, it was envisaged that this role would be held by an academic staff member of the university, who would live at the college and provide leadership of the tutorial program and general oversight of

---

49. Minutes from the college's executive meeting, November 1965.

the student welfare. The minutes indicate that approaches were made to several suitably qualified persons and the position was widely advertised, but eventually it was concluded that there was no suitable person in Australia. Himbury would need to seek such a person from overseas.

In addition, there was considerable concern that the college needed a librarian, who could lead the development of the library, which needed now to be expanded in many ways to support the resident students in a variety of disciplines.

Another critical challenge concerned the building developments imagined toward the completion of the original vision. To begin with, there were twenty-seven more student rooms to be completed on the top floor. What was called "Stage Two" of the project involved another building for student amenities, such as games and music rooms. It was reported later in 1965 that the window of opportunity for applying to the Commonwealth Government's three-year grants program was very soon to close. It was therefore urgent that attention be given to the plans for, and funding of, this project. Along with consideration of the amenities wing, there was also strong pressure to provide a pipe organ for the college chapel.

The college also began planning for the first of the Holdsworth-Grigg Memorial Lectures and determined to invite Dr. Ernest Payne to present that lecture in 1967. Himbury would thus be able to show his mentor the fulfillment of Payne's recommendation to the Baptists of Victoria that Himbury was the person to meet their need. Meanwhile, Himbury invited other noted leaders to visit the college, including Rev. Edwin Robertson, leader of the "Church and Life Movement," who presented a lecture to the college students on recent developments in European theology.

Matters of finance were a constant subject in the executive and council meetings. The terms and conditions for the principal and professorial staff were approved by the council, providing for sabbatical leave. The annual assembly of the Baptist union took place in October, where the principal and college officers presented the annual report and subjected themselves to questions from the floor (as was usual for Baptist union agencies). Himbury's next report to the executive committee expressed concern that in that extended session almost all the time was spent on questions relating to the staff salary and conditions. This was the first indication of what was to become an ongoing but largely unspoken sense of dismay or disapproval around the churches. The college staff were no longer as subject to the assembly as had been the case for seventy years previously.

The other defining event for the college in its first year was the death in 1964 of Alexander Crocket, and then of his sister Margaret Crocket in 1965. Their estate, primarily in real estate, was left to the college. Following legal advice, the college set up a process for liquidating the estate. In July 1966 Himbury wrote an article for the *Victorian Baptist Witness* announcing that these legacies, "of almost a million dollars, are the two largest gifts ever received by an Australian University College, and are amongst the largest gifts ever received by a Baptist institution."[50] The article went on to say that Baptist churches will realize "that the Crocket bequest relieves them of a financial burden in the maintenance of the College and will wish to support, as magnificently as they have done in the case of the College, the total work of the Union."

This passage seemed to suggest that churches no longer needed to give to the college and should instead support other aspects of the union's budget. That suggestion was to prove an acute difficulty for the college in the decades ahead. Though the churches had no strong history of supporting their college financially, now they were being told they were not needed at all. Together with the decision to remove assembly's capacity to review the appointments of the existing staff, the sense of pride in a new college quickly turned to a sense of distance, if not alienation.

In July of 1966 the implications of these developments were spelled out in no uncertain terms. Already, at the end of 1965, Himbury noted the declining support for the college from the union's budget. In the 1964–65 budget, the college had requested £7000, but only £6500 was approved and only £4904 was actually received. For 1965–66, £8500 had been requested; only £6500 was approved, and at the time of Himbury's report in October 1965, he was unsure that this amount would be met. At the college executive meeting in July 1966, it was decided to inform the Baptist union that the amount received in 1965–66 was "one hundred percent of the college's requests" and that "the college would make no claim on the denominational budget."[51] Rather, the administration of the Crocket estate provided the college with ample funds for its envisaged operations and developments. Negotiations took place toward purchasing adjoining properties on The Avenue, Parkville, and plans were

---

50. Himbury, "Bequests to Whitley College," 6.
51. Minutes from the college's executive meeting, July 1966.

formulated for a new wing. The college appeared rich and was now informing the Baptist union that its support was no longer required.

Early in 1966 the students of the college published a magazine, *Monocle*, which was to cause an immense amount of controversy within the Baptist churches. Unlike the old college magazine, *The Upward Call*, this magazine contained articles on subjects as diverse as the ethics of vivisection and the biology of human aggression, as well as satirical profiles of the ministerial students and their beliefs about heaven and hell. Photographs of students smoking a pipe or drinking beer were included. Himbury had to deal with such a torrent of protest that the magazine was eventually withdrawn from circulation. Several years later the theological students published their own magazine, *To Minister*, which sought to recapture the role of *The Upward Call*, but this was very soon abandoned also.

Himbury wrote a short article for the first edition of *Monocle* magazine, which was titled "Whitley and I," an adaptation of the material he used as notes for an address. After briefly recounting the miracle of the college's creation, he now asserted, "the story is only beginning. A college is not only money and buildings, it is men and tradition. The men, of great variety in outlook and ability, have come. The tradition is slowly growing."[52] He went on to say that more funds were needed to provide scholarships and facilities for the "secular university students" so that the academic community of the college might grow and flourish. Clearly the external view that the college was now rich with resources was not the experience of those running the college.

The impact of these developments in Himbury's own life was profound. He was the head of a new college which was noted all around the city for its innovative design. The college seemed poised for success, despite being smaller than the other more traditional colleges of the university. With this success also came a degree of hubris. In reporting to the annual assembly, Himbury would applaud the academic achievements of particular ministerial students (often to their embarrassment). The vision was being fulfilled, as many of those preparing for pastoral ministry were also undertaking university degrees. For the years 1967 and 1968, a ministerial student was elected president of the Students' Club. The Baptist college had become a university college.

52. Himbury, "Whitley and I," 5.

When Dr. Ernest Payne delivered the first Holdsworth-Grigg Memorial Lecture in 1967, he celebrated the fulfillment of the hope that had been mentioned to him a decade earlier when the college was seeking a new principal. Himbury had proven to be that person with the energy and commitment to fulfill their vision.

Payne's lecture set out something of an agenda for the college in what was indeed a tumultuous time socially and theologically. Payne's theme was "Christian Tasks and Prospects in a World of Change." After a historical sketch of the expansion and now decline in Christianity, Payne nominated four key tasks for Christian faith in the "climactic hour" of the twentieth century. First, he urged a more serious waiting upon God, for guidance and an outpouring of the Holy Spirit. Then he asserted that "the Christian Churches cannot meet today's challenges unless they improve their relationships with one another." Next, he named the need for "a more carefully planned strategy for both witness and service," reflecting both evangelism and care for the poor and hungry. Finally, Payne nominated the need for theological engagement with the changing patterns of society. New forms of ministry would need to be devised and ministers would need to be aware of the scientific and intellectual developments shaping the world in which they and their congregations lived.[53]

In reality, Payne was articulating the vision of those who established the new college, and these challenges were to engage Himbury and his faculty in the decades ahead. Many of his students shared this vision as well, often in the face of local congregations with other concerns or priorities. Something of this sense of concern and disconnection is evident in the article Himbury wrote for the student magazine *To Minister* in 1969, titled "The Imprisoned Ministry." Two paragraphs are particularly striking:

> The best of our young people ask for bread for the world and we give them the building stones of our Gothic churchmanship. They ask for life and we give them institutions. They ask for love-in-action and we give them theological formulae.
>
> A mood of despair is sweeping across our world. As man is imprisoned by his social order, whether capitalist or communist, so Jesus is trapped by His ecclesiastical order. While our youth grapples with problems of hopelessness, the Baptist Union will spend its time revising details of its constitution. Should a new

---

53. Payne, "Christian Tasks and Prospects," 8–10.

star shine to lead us to the re-birth of hope, many of us will miss its glory for we will be sitting in a committee meeting.[54]

The anguish of the college principal and his students is powerfully expressed here. The hope for new forms of ministry, engaging with youth who were caught up in the National Service Scheme for military service in Vietnam, the movements for change in numerous social institutions (including the universities), and the sense that the churches were simply not aware of or responsive to these concerns, all caused him deep distress. Nonetheless, he concluded with a prayer for "men who are fool enough to believe in such love [seen in the crucified Jesus] and brave enough to practice it and faithful enough to endure to the end."

In the face of these many concerns and challenges, Himbury realized that, in fact, he needed to take a sabbatical, which was proposed for the first part of 1967. Then arose the question of how the college would function without him and who would act as principal. It was decided not to appoint an acting principal—clearly a decision not to prefer one of the professors over the other. Instead, it was decided that the president of the college council, John Hopkins, would move into an apartment at the college for the period of the principal's leave and would function as "pro-principal." While away, Himbury would investigate possibilities for the dean position.

It was during this time, also, that he took up the invitation to preach in Brooklyn, New York, for the 120th anniversary of the Concord Baptist Church of Christ, from May 17 to 21, 1967. He had been invited by his friend, Rev. Gardner C. Taylor. This was an occasion and honor he would long remember and recount, particularly the lively response of the congregation once a senior deacon declared him to be "all right."

Indeed, the principal of Whitley College had reached a new phase of his life and career. Amid many demands and challenges, nonetheless, things were all right.

---

54. Himbury, "Imprisoned Ministry," 4.

CHAPTER 6

A Long and Winding Road

1970 to 1986

ESTABLISHING A NEW COLLEGE was in many ways to prove the easier task. The next two decades presented three interlocking challenges that would fundamentally define Himbury's career. It was now necessary to develop the college, which in turn required him to define its fundamental nature and purpose, and then defend its very existence. These tasks demanded all the determination and skill Himbury could bring to his changing role over the remainder of his career, in what can be described as a long and winding road.

Debating competitions were a feature of university student life in this era. Whitley College participated keenly in the intercollege debating competition. Internally each year a staff–student debate was also held. This event provided Himbury with the opportunity to exercise the debating style he had seen and participated in at Oxford, often involving great humor and some intellectual nonsense. On one such occasion, early in this period, the topic for debate was "That Whitley College is Square"—playing upon the colloquial use of the word "square" to mean old-fashioned and lacking in style. The student team took the negative case, and the leading argument was put that the college is in fact round. Furthermore, it was argued that, in all significant respects, Whitley College is identical with its principal and, to uproarious laughter from the student audience, the speaker asked Himbury please to stand so that all may see that, in fact, Whitley College is rotund. This argument carried a profound insight. In many respects, Himbury's own life had become identified with the college he had created—a kind of institutionalized personality—so much so that the story of his life in this period is inseparable from the developments and crises in the life of Whitley College.

What was it like to be the principal of Whitley College at that time? Himbury saw himself as a preacher, a teacher, and a pastor. He was also a husband and father. His fundamental life commitment was to serve the church, by preaching the Gospel and nurturing others who would do that too. These commitments, however, drew him inevitably into the complications and difficulties of other people's lives, their problems, misbehavior, and conflicting views and expectations. Thus, his days were often taken up with student concerns and meetings.

Students and Meetings

Late in October 1969, I and a friend from Whitley College walked from the college to the home of a former college student in North Carlton. That man had a troubled history, having been asked to leave several places where he had lived, including Whitley College. He had recently been released from hospital after psychiatric care. We were going to meet with our friend, but upon entering the house we found that he had taken his life.

The next morning, Mervyn Himbury met with us to express his concern for us. He also said that a question he had to wrestle with was the extent to which his action, in asking the man to leave college, had contributed to the man's anguish and death. Whether it was pastorally appropriate to say that to us—two students at that time—may be debated, but it indicates both his open vulnerability and his sense that we were at one in sharing this grief and regret. At times of deep, personal angst, Himbury simply said what was in his heart. That was mostly how he dealt with emotions.

This tragic event was just one of many times when Himbury had to deal with troubled young people, wrestling with many "demons" in their own lives and the immense tensions within the existing society. A fundamental feature of the background situation was Australia's involvement in the war in Vietnam and the related National Service Scheme, which drafted twenty-year-old men into the army. Himbury had written, just a year earlier, of the needs of this generation and the ministry of the college in serving undergraduates that "they are a serious lot . . . (who) work a lot harder than did most students in the pre-war era. . . . War, want, tyranny and hypocrisy in our society are bold and living issues in their lives."[1]

He acknowledged that his own role as principal of a university college involved far more than administration and teaching. He would also spend time listening to those who, once they trusted him, would "empty their hearts of the burdens they carry." Here we see Himbury the pastor, in bold and clear relief. He went on the say that by providing food on the table, books in the library, and tutors in the classrooms, Baptists were earning the right to serve this generation, even as Christ himself had "washed feet, ate with publicans and sinners and died on a cross for undergraduates who mock Him."[2]

For all that, his sense that the church, of which he was such a prominent representative, offered no effective answers for the troubled youth of the day was a source of his own anguish. Equally, he was distressed that the churches for which he was preparing ministers did not seem to share his concern. Over the coming years he was increasingly worried by the rate at which graduating and ordained pastors left the ministry. His sense was that many of the churches did not want the college's graduates—but neither was there any articulation of what was needed, what perhaps needed to change. For this reason, Himbury again turned to the question of how Baptist ministers should be trained. To this end, early in 1970 he undertook a study tour of numerous Baptist colleges and seminaries, in both Britain and the United States. He wrote a substantial report on the issues he discerned and his findings, in turn leading to commentary on the challenges facing the Baptist colleges in Australia.

At least some of Himbury's students had already captured the spirit of the era and, with Himbury's positive encouragement, were engaging in experimental and creative forms of local church ministry. Early in the 1960s, Alan Nunn had planted a new Baptist church in Doveton, where a "manse-chapel" building was developed rather than initially building a church hall, as was the established approach. Similarly, in West Melbourne, Ian Paxton had led the church to engage much more closely with the local community and its needs. They would abandon the old church facilities, lease some of the land to a petrol company and build a chapel annex to the manse. Another experimental approach involved several

---

1. Himbury, "Serving the Undergraduate," 1.
2. Himbury, "Serving the Undergraduate," 1.

students moving to a rural town to commence a ministry, again without church buildings, focusing upon community engagement.

As the decade of the 1970s proceeded, three critical features of student life challenged the essential vision of Whitley College as the Baptist College of Victoria. To begin with, the University of Melbourne was no longer the only university in Victoria. As student numbers grew rapidly, it became clear that Commonwealth Government funding for student residential facilities would not continue. Over time only a very small proportion of students would live in colleges and increasingly these became a privileged few. For those who did enjoy that opportunity, however, the years spent in college were often definitive for their lives and careers. As Himbury saw it, Whitley College could offer not just a place to live, but a Christian influence, example, and care. He sought to embody all three of these elements.

He was particularly interested in those he considered "characters," people of different views, sometimes countercultural in their politics and ambitions. Young men facing the National Service Scheme, some seeking exemption as conscientious objectors, received his personal support. Some who were unsure of their career choices, some who were struggling to adapt to the freedoms of living without parental supervision, and others who were living away from their home country would all know his support and understanding. Discipline was not something Himbury enjoyed at all. He left that to the dean of students and the tutors, and more than once would threaten to "throw out" a student and within hours retract that decision. No doubt the second chance that he had been given when he had failed his first years at Cardiff remained in his memory as the basis for grace toward other young people struggling to find their way forward.

Another critical change in the student cohort concerned the theological students, all of whom at that time were male candidates for ordination. Through the decade of the 1960s and 1970s, more than half of those applying to the college were men already married. This change, which had already been evident in Wales when Himbury was there, meant that the originating vision of the new college was already challenged. The idea of ministerial formation happening within a residential community, where pastors in training lived and learned with university students, was now possible only for some theological students. Quickly it became clear that most theological students were now older and had dependents and commitments quite different from undergraduates. They were at once more serious and studious, yet less engaged with the life of the college than resident "theologs," as they were termed. As it happened, some of the resident theologs were also men in their later twenties, fully a decade older than most of the wider undergraduate cohort. Several of these were elected to student leadership roles and contributed to the college as a supporting pastoral presence, able to mediate between the students and the administration at times of tension. Before long it would be noted that there were effectively two student bodies: those who attended the college by day, and those who lived there at night.

The third critical aspect of student life in the college concerned women. At a time when women were entering universities in ever-increasing numbers, most university residential colleges were for men only. In addition, the ordination pathways were open to male students only, although there was a form of ministry training open to women in the Baptist union, for what was called a "deaconess" ministry. Some of these women students began to attend theology classes at Whitley College, though generally only one or two at any given time. It must have been quite intimidating to be the only woman student among twenty or more male theology students and around one hundred or more other students taking lunch in the dining hall. The questions of accommodation for women students and married theological students, and in due course the question of the ordination of women, would contribute considerable tension and difficulty as the 1970s proceeded.

Along with student concerns, another regular feature of Himbury's life was a demanding round of meetings, many of which were related to other meetings and involved him presenting much the same report to two or even three different groups. The college was governed by a council, which was made up of the principal and professors, the elected officers of the college (president, secretary, and treasurer), members appointed by the Baptist union assembly, and numerous ex officio representatives of union agencies such as Carey Baptist Grammar School, the University of Melbourne, and other groups such as the Whitley College Women's Auxiliary. A subgroup of the council was appointed as the oddly-named "theological faculty," which governed the specific activities of ministerial education, approved the teaching program, and decided when a candidate was ready for ordination. The real power in the college, however, rested with the executive committee, which met monthly and managed the financial and property matters, as well as coordinating staffing and administration of the whole college. The principal presented written reports to all these groups and worked with the secretary of the council to prepare the agendas for each group's meeting.

The principal was also an ex officio member of the executive council of the Baptist Union of Victoria and reported to its monthly meetings, as well as to the annual and half-yearly assemblies. On occasion he might also present items to the general council of the Baptist union, which met several times between assemblies. Of particular importance was the general council meeting where ordinands were presented for approval by the council for ordination later that year. Over time, this became an occasion for opponents of the college to challenge the students with doctrinal questions.

Himbury was also ex officio a member of the advisory board of the Baptist union, a group whose primary function was to assist churches in search of new pastors and, in turn, to advise pastors seeking appointments. The advisory board met every month and Himbury served in this role for his entire time as principal. Himbury exercised the opportunity to recommend his students and graduates, commending them to churches, and wherever possible supporting them to obtain an appointment. He was known for doing so and his students continued to be grateful for it, as the system required someone to promote their cause, especially in the early years of their ministry.

The principal of Whitley College also participated in several other peak governance bodies. At the University of Melbourne, the heads of the residential colleges met regularly, though in a much more informal network than exists today. From this group one of the principals was invited to membership of the university council, a role Himbury enjoyed for some years, particularly during the time Robert Menzies, the former prime minister, was chancellor. On the theological side he represented the Baptist College on the Council of the Melbourne College of Divinity (MCD), again throughout his entire time as principal. This body met six times a year. Twice Himbury served as president of the MCD, for two-year terms (1961–62 and 1970–71), which would have involved him also in the executive committee for six years each time—as vice president, president, and past president.

From this sketch of the role of the principal we can see that Mervyn Himbury's life entailed engagement with several diverse groups, all claiming some governance or ownership over the life of the Whitley College.

At the same time, tertiary education itself was changing dramatically. For example, the move to continuous assessment challenged the older end-of-year examination model. Campus life was volatile during the Vietnam War years. In different ways, local church life was changing, especially as women joined the workforce and the unpaid army of volunteers were no longer available to support many traditional church activities. A more "professional" or managerial model of ministry was emerging, centered on a church office. The needs of children and youth in the rapidly-growing population presented new challenges. What kinds of people were needed to lead the churches into the future? How should ministers be trained for this time? These were just some of the questions with which Himbury had to wrestle. What became clear was the need to develop the college; but to do that it was also necessary to define its purpose, not just once but again and again, and in so doing also to defend its very existence.

Developing the College: The Women's Wing, New Forms of Ministerial Training, and Divisions Emerge

From the outset it was recognized that additional student amenities would be needed. A games room, music rooms, offices for the professors (who initially occupied rooms intended for resident tutors) and at least some further accommodation for visiting scholars were among the ideas considered. It was at first envisaged that these facilities would be developed on the land at the western edge of the college site, adjoining Mile Lane. Soon, however, other ideas emerged, most importantly the vision for a "women's wing." With a view to future developments, the college began to purchase adjoining properties, beginning with the stately home at number 50, The Avenue. The building was soon named Crocket House in recognition of Alexander and Margaret Crocket, who had left a very large bequest to the college. A substantial part of funding for the purchase came from a grant from the Australian Universities Commission, on the basis that a new building would provide a women's wing for the accommodation of female university students. Thus began a controversy that would cause much difficulty for Himbury through the next few years. Attempts to buy other adjoining properties were not successful, but another house further away, at 298 The Avenue, was purchased and for a time housed college students or staff.

Early in 1970, plans were made for the demolition of Crocket House and construction of the women's wing. With the expectation that the process would proceed, Himbury left Australia for a semester of study leave. His specific intention was to visit theological colleges and seminaries in Britain and the USA, to study their approaches to ministerial training with special emphasis on practical aspects of this training.

This was Himbury at his best as a theological leader. His own disposition was to be skeptical, if not dismissive, of some of the new emphases in what he called techniques in ministry. While he encouraged practical skills in preaching and pastoral care, he retained a fundamental conviction that ministerial education was more about the person in relationship with God and God's word than anything else. Nevertheless, such was his concern about the need for the church to respond to a rapidly changing society, and his sense that existing forms of ministerial training were not addressing those needs, that he undertook this study, on behalf not only of Whitley College and the Baptist Union of Victoria but (as his report indicates) offering what he found for the benefit of the other Australian Baptist colleges as well. We also see him concerned to learn from international experience, albeit limited to the two countries most influential in Australian Baptist life, Britain and the USA.

Study Leave

Himbury's study leave report details his findings at three Baptist colleges in Britain: Cardiff, Spurgeon's, and Bristol. It is notable that he did not consider Regent's Park College as offering anything significantly different to the already existing modes of training. He stated that the advent of a new principal at Manchester was his reason for not including that college in his study. This was perhaps unfortunate, as in fact the Northern Baptist College (Manchester) was very soon to commence a quite innovative alternative pattern of training under Dr. Michael Taylor's leadership, and Manchester University would establish a chair in social and pastoral theology. Within the decade, these elements would attract several of Whitley's graduates to Manchester for their doctoral studies.[3]

It was during this time in Britain that Himbury made his last visit to his family home, as his father Reginald Himbury died on May 2 of

---

3. Dr. Bruce Rumbold (later to be professor of pastoral studies at Whitley College) went to study at the University of Manchester in 1974 and I (later to be professor of systematic theology and then principal at Whitley College) went there in 1981.

that year. It was also to be his last visit with his brother, John, who died following a car accident later that year.

Himbury met with his former colleagues at the South Wales Baptist College, and discussed with Ithel and Nana Jones the prospect of them moving to Melbourne, where Ithel would take up the position as minister of the Collins Street Baptist Church later that same year.

To summarize his findings very briefly, Himbury noted in Britain the decline in church membership and the number of candidates for ministry, but also what he considered a "severe decline in academic standards."[4] Amid widespread student unrest in the universities, he found Baptist college students "thoroughly conservative in most of their attitudes." Among the colleges there was a growing concern for more practical training.

The Cardiff Baptist College had established a diploma program of pastoral studies which had been adopted by the university and was now taught by university faculty. Subjects included moral philosophy, problems and techniques of pastoral care, sociology, psychology, education, and communication. Himbury noted that students took this course seriously, though he judged it to have insufficient theological content. At Spurgeon's College a Southern Baptist teacher was offering courses in practical disciplines, especially evangelism. Himbury felt that the program was not well related to the local context and was disadvantaged by not being integrated into the degree or diploma programs. By contrast, at Bristol Baptist College a team of local ministers taught subjects in pastoral theology, in a program that Himbury considered to be both well-run and effective.

Himbury wrote at much greater length about his observations of seminaries in the United States, including some quite glowing remarks about aspects of the Southern Baptist Convention, in its organization and corporate identity. On the other hand, he commented extensively on the wider student unrest and disillusionment with the "American dream" and, interestingly, noted a concern for climate studies and the sense of impending climate crisis. These issues, however, were not so evident on

---

4. This statement and the following descriptions of ministerial education in the Baptist colleges in Britain are found in the unpublished version of Himbury's study leave report, which has the same title as the published version, "Forms of Baptist Ministerial Education." None of these comments were included in the published version, which is almost entirely devoted to his observations and reflections upon Baptist ministerial education in the United States of America.

the seminary campuses. He did note that in some places the students' concern to engage with wider social issues led to some loss of what he termed "the otherness of the Gospel," with a risk that their concern to communicate effectively to the world might so emasculate the Gospel that they have little to communicate. Some of these students also were questioning "the utility of the pastoral ministry," in a reaction against "the traditional American pulpiteer."[5]

The situation of the American seminaries was so different to that of the colleges in Britain or Australia. The seminaries were accredited to grant their own degrees and, in the case of the Southern Baptist institutions, were funded 80 percent of their operating costs by the convention.

Having noted these features, Himbury wrote affirmatively of the seminary programs in pastoral theology, counseling, and Christian education. These "practical disciplines"—a term he did not fully endorse—occupied a third of the seminary course. Furthermore, he thought it most important that they were "integrated into the total course." In addition, field work was a significant part of all students' schedules and was managed and supervised by the seminaries. Students were not merely sent into pastoral contexts as a means of gaining a living, as in Australia. Rather, the seminary staff provided direct personal supervision of this field experience. These observations were vital for what was later to develop at Whitley College.

Perhaps if he had been able to implement changes in line with these comments, appropriately adapted to the Australian context, many later difficulties might have been forestalled.

Himbury also commented on the use of electronic resources, such as closed-circuit television, in preaching classes. He did not consider these helpful, as they tended to focus attention upon how the preacher might appear. He concluded, "I have not seen a method of teaching preaching which is better than the old-fashioned preaching class in which a man is made conscious of the reactions of a congregation composed of his peers. Moreover, good preaching demands a grounding in the traditional disciplines of theology and above all an emphasis, not on the techniques, but on the aims, purposes and the theology of the sermon."[6]

Finally, he noted the paucity in the common worship life of the seminaries in both Northern and Southern contexts. Many students do

---

5. Himbury, Forms of Ministerial Education, 25.
6. Himbury, "Baptist Ministerial Education," 28.

not attend worship services. Furthermore, Himbury expressed a disappointment in the worship services in the churches. In many places he felt no experience of worship at all, but rather a focus on the church program. Only in very few places was there any meaningful prayer.[7]

In this report, presented to the college executive and council upon his return in August, Mervyn Himbury's role as a leader in theological education for Baptists in Australia is clear. He was no longer primarily engaged with his earlier work in Baptist history, though he continued to publish occasional articles or book chapters on some related themes. He began to refer to his ministry as administration, though I suggest he meant something more than that term often denotes. He was engaging in the difficult tasks he had named several times already, in seeking to discern the necessary forms of theological education for the future of Baptist church life in a rapidly changing world.

One further aspect of Himbury's observations, not recorded in this official report, was his informal consultation with married students resident on seminary campuses in the USA. Himbury spoke with the wives of students living in these facilities also. He formed the opinion that, overall, it was an unhealthy situation for the wives and children, albeit convenient for the student. The "fish-bowl" effect of being observed by faculty and other students induced pressures on marriages and family life. These observations led Himbury in the years ahead to oppose proposals for the college to provide married students' accommodation.[8]

While in the United States, Himbury met with three of his former students now undertaking postgraduate study there. Doug Rowston was doing doctoral work at Southern Seminary, Philip Chislett was studying for an MDiv at Northern Baptist Seminary, while Graeme Garrett was undertaking a ThD at Berkeley. Himbury's encouragement of these and other students, in a way that had never been done before, was further evidence of his vision for the future of the college and the church, and his appreciation of the international contexts of theological education. In this it is evident how much his vision and perspective had changed from that of his home context in Wales. He laid a foundation crucial to the ongoing life of Whitley College—a commitment to nurture the next

7. Himbury, "Baptist Ministerial Education," 28–29.

8. This paragraph is based upon my personal recollection of Himbury's commentary on these situations. He did comment on "the pressures which married seminarians experience" and stated that "these marriages can easily break down," in the published version of his report "Forms of Baptist Ministerial Education," 17.

generations of teachers, not only for Whitley but for other colleges as well.

In a further development of this report, published by the college along with *The Second Holdsworth-Grigg Memorial Lecture*, Himbury added a section posing questions confronting Australian Baptist colleges. He noted the temptation for Australian colleges to seek to emulate the Southern Baptist seminaries. He insisted, however, that "the ideal system of ministerial training for Australian Baptists can only be devised within their own country and by Australians."[9] The questions needing to be addressed included not only the kinds of courses to be offered but required a profound wrestling with the nature and mission of the church itself. He noted the division between those who see college training as a matter of inculcating denominational identity, with a view to preserving existing structures, and others who saw the need to educate ministers "to create a situation of which no one has yet dreamed."[10]

Once again Himbury used the terms "training" and "education" carefully to distinguish different approaches. He expressed concern that most Australian Baptist ministerial candidates "lack the cultural background to benefit from [their] ministerial course," which in turn affected teaching methods. Here he argued for the development of culturally appropriate teaching, developing skills and disciplines for the changing context. Significantly, he observed that if the ministry is "more than preaching," then these other forms of study will be vital.[11]

One crucial element in these developments was "the relationship of the pastoral work undertaken by students and their total training."[12] The dichotomy experienced by many must be overcome. In this section, Himbury was clearly acknowledging the need for what would be developed in the next few years as the Supervised Field Education program, which would integrate much more with the whole course of study, and in this he drew upon the insights derived from the colleges in Britain as well as those in the USA. For him, practical aspects of training needed to be more than the acquisition of techniques. It was vital that ministry practice and theological studies should go together—an integration of education and training.

9. Himbury, "Baptist Ministerial Education," 30.
10. Himbury, "Baptist Ministerial Education," 30.
11. Himbury, "Baptist Ministerial Education," 31.
12. Himbury, "Baptist Ministerial Education," 32.

Internal Struggles

While Himbury was overseas, the college was in some turmoil, even though to anyone living or studying there many things seemed to be progressing well. John Hopkins managed the college as pro-principal and Professor Brown coordinated the theological studies program, reporting regularly on the progress of the ordination candidates. The college had a particularly strong football team that year and defeated Trinity College in the second division final, a surprising achievement that was telegraphed to Himbury by the secretary of the Students' Club. For a brief period, the college was promoted to the first division. Himbury was delighted. His college had "made it" and done so in the way most popular among Australians—sport.

At the same time, the building proposals had run into serious difficulty. The entire project was subject to considerable time pressure. The Australian Universities Commission offered funding on three-year periods, the current period about to end. To have any chance of consideration for the next period, applications needed to be submitted well before the end of the year. The funding already received for the purchase of 50 The Avenue needed to be spent within the current period, and only for the purpose for which it had been given. These concerns were just some of the issues over which conflict emerged. The proposals for the women's wing on that site were much more expensive than anticipated. Detailed consideration of the ongoing costs of the new facility indicated significant increases in the college's operating budget, which was already underwritten by drawing upon bequest income. Baptist union officers argued that support of the women's wing did not fall within the terms of the bequests: the new wing would need to be self-funding.

Several other plans were mooted within the executive committee, including alternative uses for Crocket House. Himbury was not made aware of all these maneuvers but did gain some knowledge. He felt as if he had lost control of the college agenda. An anxious correspondence took place between Himbury and Hopkins: was the principal's position in jeopardy, given that (as it seemed) members of his own executive were now proposing projects contrary to his objectives? Himbury contemplated resigning. The executive minutes record that Himbury had written to Hopkins thanking him for a deeply reassuring letter. We can only surmise what might have been said each way, in a time of much less speedy communications.

Himbury returned to a critical situation. He made an immediate resolve never again to go away for a protracted time and thereafter took his study leave only in shorter segments. That decision indicates a fundamental lack of security in relationships within the college leadership. He could not trust that he would return to the college as he had left it.

To develop the college with further facilities required a clear sense of its mission and purpose. In particular, what was the relationship between the university college and its students—who were referred to by members of the executive as "secular students"—and ministerial education? Where should the priority lie? There were new pressures to provide additional teaching staff, in areas such as Old Testament and pastoral studies. There was the demand for student facilities, including those envisaged in the original plans and now also the women's wing. There was also the long-standing question of married students' accommodation. The executive minutes show that all these issues were discussed, and various priorities asserted, along with the need to make a timely application to the government if funding was to be obtained from that source. The president set these questions before a series of meetings focused on the future use of 50 The Avenue. It was clear that there were competing concerns between the development of theological education and the educational services offered to university student residents. The treasurer, O. C. Abbott, declared in this context that if there had to be a choice between these two, he believed the Baptist community would focus on the former. Several executive members presented papers outlining their own sense of priorities for the college. There were clear personal tensions as well.

When Himbury returned, he wrote his substantial report while trying to gain some perspective on all that had transpired. It was Himbury himself who in November of 1970 brought forward a new proposal: a building on the western edge of the Royal Parade site and integrated with the existing facilities. A three-storied wing would house a smaller number of women students—twenty-four, rather than the originally planned forty-two students. There would be offices and a seminar room for theological staff and students, thus providing the main building with released space for additional tutors and tutorial rooms. Student facilities for music, a gym, and television room were included, while the upper floors included two apartments for guests or other staff. In one move, many of the expressed concerns and needs were met, at considerably less expense. So it was thought. In the event, the rampant inflation of the ensuing years meant that the building cost far more than envisaged.

The paper in which Himbury set out these proposals, written for presentation to the college council, noticeably used the expressions "my officers" or "my executive committee," as he summed up the issues and problems that had been identified. In so doing, however, he was at once clearly holding them responsible for what had taken place and at the same time asserting his authority in the college. With this new scheme, he would be expecting their loyal support.

The compromise proposal was, in due course, agreed to—though not without difficult negotiations with the Australian Universities Commission—and over the next two years building went ahead. The struggles of the year, however, laid bare the inherent tensions within the vision and identity of the college. Developing the college presupposed its defining purposes, and these clearly were not universally agreed and understood. Himbury found that he needed to define and defend "his college," both from without and within.

From its inception, the college was subject to opposition from a small but active group named the Baptist Revival Fellowship. Their objective was to restore the Baptist Union of Victoria to its Calvinistic heritage, as they saw it, and the major means of doing so was to replace Whitley College with what they deemed to be suitable staff and a program not tainted by association with "secular" students, nor indeed the ecumenical association with the Melbourne College of Divinity. It was known that sympathetic students were recruited by this group to pass on their notes from college classes as evidence of the "liberal" theology being taught. Representatives of the group challenged ordinands when presented at the general council. The fact that the major source of ongoing funding for the college, and indeed all its assets, was held in the name of the Baptist union led them to believe that they could persuade the Baptist union to deprive Whitley College of its resources and move these to a new college of their own creation. In 1976 an Australian person trained at a conservative Baptist seminary in the United States was identified as a suitable principal for the new college—a direct and personal challenge to Himbury's position.[13] All of this provided a sense of opposition out of proportion to the strength of the group and the likelihood of their plan ever coming to fruition. Nonetheless, it remained a specter with which Himbury and the college had to deal constantly. He did so with dignity and commitment to the path he had undertaken. He sought to reach out

---

13. The Baptist union agreed to ordain that pastor in 1976, but he left the state soon after.

to the leading pastors in this group, making himself available to preach in their churches (which he did) and to maintain collegial fellowship with them.

In many ways it was the tensions inherent in the college itself that most required defense and further definition. Himbury's response to these issues was to press ahead with the development of the college. The building at 50 The Avenue was to be used for some students and tutorial staff. Ironically, the building would eventually be developed into The Mervyn Himbury Theological Studies Centre, opened in 1990. The questions of further staffing needed attention next, especially as Professor Watson was soon to retire.

Ros Otzen's history of Whitley College describes the period from 1975 till Himbury's retirement in 1986 as one of "unexpected changes."[14] That title might apply to the entire decade of the 1970s. Himbury suffered one setback after another, yet he persisted with his drive to develop the vision and mission of the college. He did so, however, without the support of two men who had been with him all the way: John Hopkins, president of the college, and Milton Warn, the registrar. Hopkins resigned in 1971 to take up the position of warden of International House, literally across the street from Whitley and in direct competition with it for resident university students. Hopkins could fulfill his own dreams for quality university student care, but Himbury felt bereft of his long-term ally. He did not ever publicly say so, but it is likely that he felt somewhat betrayed. In Hopkins's place, the council elected Olwyn Abbott, formerly the treasurer and another lifelong supporter. Abbott was much more deeply involved with Baptist union life and was able to manage relations with the union in a way Hopkins could not. This was a gift Himbury came to appreciate many times in the years ahead.

Milton Warn left to take up a suburban pastorate. He had served the college since its inception and was a loyal confidant to Himbury, a role he continued in succeeding years.

The new building, which came to be known as the west wing, was to be built in the years 1972 and 1973. It was not what Himbury had originally proposed, but it was to transform the life of the college. In 1972 the college officially became coed, though it was some time before this decision could be implemented, as the construction project stalled when the builder went bankrupt. What else could befall Himbury's vision?

14. Otzen, *Whitley*, 151–72.

Most of the university colleges were experiencing difficulty in recruiting and retaining students. Empty rooms threatened the budget. Within a short time of the west wing opening, it was clear that women students should also be housed in sections of the main building as well, and the college became genuinely coed.

The next traumatic development of the decade involved staffing the college. Here several of the issues outlined earlier came together. The Baptist union had appointed a new general superintendent, Rev. Norman Pell, who had served with the Billy Graham Evangelistic Association. Pell envisaged the future of the church in Australia as something like a continuous evangelistic crusade. Pell had many ideas for changing the ethos of Baptist life and for this he needed pastors of a similar mind. These ideas brought him into open disagreement with the college, which came to a head when Himbury proposed the appointment of a new professor of theology. Dr. Graeme Garrett, recently returned from the USA and serving as associate minister at Collins Street Baptist Church, was proposed for this role.

The college recommendation to the union assembly, however, was not unanimous. All agreed that they needed a professor of theology, but what was meant by "theology"? Pell argued that the college needed a teacher of *practical* theology and made this known, particularly to the ministers of larger churches in the eastern suburbs, some of whom had begun to develop an opposition to Whitley College which was to remain for decades to come. The appointment process went forward to the annual assembly. Not a word was spoken in opposition to the nomination in the assembly, but the resolution did not achieve the necessary two-thirds majority. It became known that an informal but nonetheless intentional process had led to this resistance. A long-standing difference between the college and the union over the balance of theology and practical training had produced this outcome.

Himbury was furious. He felt betrayed from within his own community, though his public complaint was that it was "un-Baptist" to oppose a matter without ever saying anything or owning up to the reasons for doing so. As Professor Watson had already retired, exceptional arrangements had to be made for teaching classes in theology. Dr. Ithel Jones assisted, as did some other suitably qualified suburban pastors. Dr. Garrett moved to a pastorate at Box Hill where he served with distinction and later began to teach at the college as an adjunct lecturer, until he was again proposed and appointed in 1977.

Meanwhile the college needed a new dean and senior tutor, to care for the residential community, as Bruce Rumbold prepared to go to Manchester, UK, to study for a PhD in pastoral theology. It was at this time that deeply disturbing events were happening in Queensland, where the young and charismatic New Testament lecturer, Dr. Athol Gill suffered a fate similar to Garrett's. He was already teaching at the Baptist Theological College of Queensland, but in this instance the union assembly had failed to reappoint him. Gill, with a very young family, was without a job. Though he did not particularly know Gill, Himbury was aghast at what had transpired. I recall the day when Himbury declared, at breakfast, "I've got to do something about Gill." That day he booked a plane ticket and flew to Brisbane to discuss with Athol and Judith Gill the possibility of coming to Whitley to serve as dean, with some expectation also of teaching New Testament studies.

Athol Gill became dean in 1974 and thus began a period of very strong growth in theological enrollments that was to last for decades to come. Gill was an attractive teacher, prophet-like in appearance and emphases, and quickly developed an intentional discipleship community in Clifton Hill, The House of the Gentle Bunyip, which both fed off and contributed much to the growth of Whitley College.

Along with the advent of women students in the college came the question of the ordination of women to the Baptist ministry. For Himbury this was not an issue at all. He had known this to be the practice in Britain and supported it, notwithstanding his habit of constantly referring to pastors as men. He was often shy in the presence of women and seemed to overcome this problem largely by ignoring them. But he quickly exercised his skills as a historian and established that in all the relevant documents, both of the college and the Baptist union, there was no formal or constitutional bar to admitting, training, and ordaining women. In 1975 the first woman candidate for ordination was accepted. Marita Munro was duly ordained in 1978, but not before a major struggle. Two Baptist union-appointed study commissions examined issues relating to ordination (what did Baptists mean by "the ministry" and how should such ministers be selected and trained?) and the ordination of women to this ministry. These reports provided some resolution to issues between the college and the union and paved the way for the ordination of those women already accepted as candidates. Himbury recognized that it would be unhelpful for him to be part of either of these groups, so other members of the college staff contributed to them. In these years, at least some of the tensions were able to be considered by theological and practical discussions and a common position agreed.

On another front, major changes were taking place within the Melbourne College of Divinity. Indeed, during Himbury's second period of presidency a working commission had investigated what was to be an epoch-making change for the MCD: the offering of an undergraduate, taught degree. Until this time, the primary offering was the BD, externally examined. What was envisaged was a degree taught and examined within theological colleges, under guidelines and accreditation by the MCD. This momentous proposal gave rise to the creation of the first ecumenical teaching consortium, the United Faculty of Theology, made up of the Presbyterian and Methodist theological halls (Ormond and Queens Colleges), Trinity College, and it was anticipated the Jesuit Theological College as well. Together, these institutions brought immense library and faculty resources, forming a quite impressive academic theological community.

Himbury was keen that Baptist students, too, should have access to this degree. His own experience in Cardiff had shown the broadening benefits of Baptist students studying with those from other Christian traditions. He was hopeful that Baptists might become part of the new "united faculty." Alas, it soon became very clear that many in the Baptist community would not accept their ministers being trained in a consortium with Roman Catholics.

Himbury knew not to pick a fight he could not win. On its own, Whitley College did not have the resources to qualify to teach the BTheol. Yet there was pressure for this opportunity to be made available to Baptist students for the ministry. The MCD assisted the situation by defining the minimum standards for college accreditation to teach the degree. Himbury again exercised decisive initiative. He approached the College of the Bible, owned by the Churches of Christ, and opened negotiations which, by 1975, led to the formation of the Evangelical Theological Association (ETA). The name distinguished this consortium from the United Faculty of Theology and emphasized its evangelical ethos. A joint teaching program began, involving some combined courses, with students and staff traveling between college campuses. Within a decade, the ETA developed a very lively program involving hundreds of students per year, almost all involved in the BTheol and, significantly, paying their own fees.

As this program grew, it also became clear that fewer than a third, and eventually fewer than a tenth, of these students were seeking ordination. Rather, here theological study was preparing people for ministry in many forms, from youth and community service to professional life in all sorts of careers. What was happening was in response to a felt need on the part of Christians expressing, as Himbury's successor Ken Manley was to observe, a failure of the Christian education programs of the local churches, or at least their acute limitations.

These developments offered a significant answer to the question Himbury had been asking for decades—the question of how leaders and pastors were to be trained for the church and its ministry in a rapidly changing world. These students were a response to that question. Whitley College was now offering university-level theological education for church leaders and workers, indeed the "ministry of the laity" as it was termed. This was a very significant development for the whole church in Australia. In contrast to Hopkins's vision that the people in the pews would be educated by an MA preacher, now in large numbers those people were accessing theological education for themselves.[15]

There were still several deeply disturbing issues within the college. Not all in the college executive welcomed the influx of so many students. The staff were clearly over-stretched and poorly paid, and did not, for example, have clear contracts providing study leave or other common award features. Furthermore, the college still did not have a member of staff teaching pastoral subjects. Dr. Bruce Rumbold had returned from Britain and was available to teach some subjects as an adjunct, but pressure mounted for an appointment in this area. Similar concerns existed in regard to Old Testament studies, where again several suburban church ministers provided the teaching. With a clear sense of the possibilities inherent in the strong student interest, but aware of how stretched their own workload had become, Graeme Garrett and Athol Gill wrote to the theological faculty urging the appointment of more staff.

Himbury responded to the pressures here by asking the college council to appoint two fellows, themselves long-standing members of council and academics in their own areas, to conduct a comprehensive review of the teaching activity and resources of the college. Professor Brian Spicer and Dr. Keith Farrer did so without fear or favor and the

---

15. This rapid growth in students attending theological and Bible colleges—but not for the purposes of ordination—happened throughout Australia in the later 1970s through to the early years of the next century and across almost all Christian denominations.

content of their report, presented in 1978, was quite confronting for Himbury.[16]

The fellows collated detailed information on the growth of enrollments, the courses being undertaken, the relationship with the College of the Bible, and the existing staffing. They also examined the teaching facilities. Their conclusions were that the facilities and teaching arrangements were quite inadequate. The college was highly dependent upon adjunct lecturers in many areas, especially Old Testament and pastoral studies. The report presented a plan for development of the faculty to meet the growth of enrollments, including appointment of a professor of Old Testament and a professor of pastoral studies. The report argued that Whitley College should develop its own faculty strength and not rely upon the College of the Bible to provide for areas in which Whitley might lack teachers.

The library also came in for strong criticism. A lack of space, both for books and study areas, as well as noise from outside, was noted, along with the lack of a coherent accession policy. A critical assessment of the library by an MCD commission in 1977 was cited.

The report also moved outside its immediate terms of reference, to critique the college's administration and its relations with the Baptist churches. On the former subject, it was argued that the informal mode of administration suitable in a small college would no longer satisfy needs and more formal modes of communication would be necessary. The lack of regular staff meetings was strongly criticized. The "complete dependence" of the college on one administrative staff member, Rosemary Dillon, was noted.

With regard to the churches, it was suggested that the college could identify pastors whose experience and skill might helpfully contribute to the training or supervision of pastors. Inviting the churches to assist the college by releasing their pastor for such activities would be one means of restoring trusting relationships with at least some churches. In addition, the report proposed that the Baptist union be invited to fund the new position of professor of Old Testament. Altogether, fourteen recommendations were made for enhancing the teaching life of the college.

The fellows' report clearly supported the proposals of Drs. Gill and Garrett and implied that Himbury had been slow to respond to the challenges of growth, and especially earlier proposals for an appointment in

16. Farrer and Spicer, *Academic Life of Whitley College*. The report was named an "interim report," though no further report of this nature was made.

pastoral studies, though in the latter instance it noted some good reasons for that delay. Following the presentation of the report, intense tension arose in the relationships between Himbury and his faculty, leading to a meeting called by faculty members with the chair of the council, Olwyn Abbott. While the faculty had intended to meet without Himbury present, Abbott insisted that he should be included and, in the event, there was a robust discussion.[17] The view was put by one member that Himbury was to be honored for creating the college as it now was, but that he was strangling its growth.

This was perhaps the only time when such a confronting and overtly critical meeting took place between Himbury and his faculty, all of whom were loyal friends and admirers, and at least half were former students. Himbury listened to the presentations, then offered some responses. Those at the meeting agreed that it was helpful that all were free to express their views. It was also agreed that it would be desirable that faculty meetings be held more intentionally, for the ongoing coordination of the theological program. The outcome from the report, however, was in the hands of the college council, not the staff.

Himbury lived with these tensions for the next several years. Meanwhile, Professor Basil Brown retired, and the college proceeded to nominate Athol Gill as his replacement. Gill was duly appointed professor of New Testament in 1979. The relationship between the two was one of curious mutual appreciation and tension. Himbury saw that Gill could attract many young people to the college and to his distinctive forms of community ministry among poor and marginalized people. In many ways he facilitated Gill's work, while in others he remained curiously unhelpful. Gill became involved with Baptist World Alliance work for human rights and was invited to various meetings overseas, increasingly in Latin America. For every such invitation, he had to make special requests to the college council. There was no provision in their terms of appointment for staff to have study leave or for travel allowances. The salaries were in fact lower than the recommended stipend for a suburban pastor within the Baptist union, and without the housing provided. In the view of the staff, Himbury was begrudging in his support. Himbury's own experience in Wales had taught him to be cautious with money. He was not afraid to spend money when it was needed. His position was that he stood between the staff, with their vision for even more growth,

17. I was present at this meeting, as I was an adjunct lecturer at the college at that time.

and an executive committee that was concerned to preserve the capital accumulated in the previous decade, especially in a time of high inflation.

The council moved to make appointments in line with the fellows' report. The college created the position of professor of Old Testament and, after a protracted selection process, Dr. Peter Broughton was appointed in 1980. The position was not funded by the Baptist union. Dr. Bruce Rumbold was appointed to teach pastoral studies part-time. The professorial appointment was not made until 1986.

A very positive initiative developed, however, regarding supervised field education.[18] Despite Himbury's own comment that it should be Australians who work out how to develop appropriate forms of ministerial training for their own context, Dr. William Hand, from Eastern Theological Seminary, Philadelphia, was invited as a visiting professor in 1981, to set up a program of supervised field education. He provided resources for such a program and soon after Rev. Grenville Hinton was appointed as the first director of the program. These actions implemented several of the proposals of the fellows' report.

One other aspect of the fellows' report is important to note. Whereas they were commissioned to study the academic life of the college, with particular reference to theological teaching, the report only mentioned the university college students once, in reference to the provision of pastoral care. What was now clear was that the college had two entirely distinct operations and bodies of students. The theological teaching operation utilized the same buildings as the residential home of students attending the University of Melbourne, but increasingly the college had two parts. It was Himbury, and in many ways only Himbury, who held the two parts together. While a small number of ordination students resided in the college, the original vision of a residential community housing both theological and university students was increasingly an anachronism.

The decade of the 1970s was one of many challenges and upheavals in the college and deeply challenging for Himbury. He had defended his college and seen it develop new facilities and experience staffing changes, quite surprising growth in theological student numbers, and the creation of an entire new degree program and teaching partnership. The question of ordination of women had been resolved and the first women ordained. The threat of the Baptist Revival Fellowship had receded. Much had been

---

18. Some years later the name of this program was changed to include the word "theological": supervised theological field education.

achieved in the development and defense of the college, and yet the fundamental question of its nature and reason for being continued to be a challenge.

On the home front, his sons had completed their education and were launching into their own careers. Himbury was approaching his sixtieth year and moving toward retirement. Before that time, however, more major crises would demand his attention and threaten to undermine his achievements.

In October 1980, the Baptist union assembly asked the college to examine its future. As Milton Warn, former registrar, put it, was Whitley now "a twin-stream College rather than an ever-widening river"? Indeed, should the two operations be separated?[19] For its part, the executive committee responded to the Fellows' Report and the subsequent discussions by affirming that the college "should remain one, under the one principal."[20] But this very wording shows that in fact it was Himbury, as principal, who was called upon to embody a unity which very few others saw or supported. This was to be his long and difficult task in the remaining years of his principalship.

From 1980 through to his retirement in 1986, it was no longer Himbury who was driving the changes and developments in the college. Rather, his leadership now took the form of coordinating and holding together the competing needs of the two arms of the college. The theological school was growing rapidly, despite the continuing lack of space and resources. Rooms needed to be rented in adjoining facilities to accommodate larger classes. Athol Gill, together with Rosemary Dillon, provided most of the administrative coordination. For his part, Himbury continued teaching church history, preaching in the churches, engaging with the exceptional rounds of meetings inherent in his role, and focusing upon the administration of the university residential college.

In 1983, he traveled to Britain for a shorter sabbatical. The college celebrated twenty-five years of Himbury's leadership as principal. Two observations are worthy of note. First, Himbury pointed out that despite the claims of some, the university college was not occupied by the children of wealthy parents, people from independent schools. A large number were dependent upon government living allowances. Himbury

---

19. Otzen, *Whitley*, 153.
20. Otzen, *Whitley*, 154.

asserted his own conviction that "it is important to be able to demonstrate that the Colleges serve the whole student population."[21]

A more personal reflection is deeply poignant. In response to celebratory gifts, he said:

> Kindness has been the essence of our experience over the past twenty-five years. My [Welsh] accent may betray my origins still, but my heart belongs here among the Baptists of Victoria. It is my pride to have had some part in the life and education of some magnificent people among the theological and non-theological students of the College and no one could ask for more than this.[22]

Himbury's critics would have noted the word "pride," for indeed he often seemed to boast of his students, even as the Apostle Paul would "boast" of the grace given to him in his calling. Together with use of the possessive "my college," his sense of ownership and pride invited resistance by some. To others, however, Himbury had every right to enjoy the outcome of what was a long and winding road, defining, developing, and defending the vision and life of the college he was called to lead. Most significantly, here he places the focus upon human kindness and the joy of seeing "magnificent people" find their way in the world.

Two further critical events were to mark his final years in office. In July 1984, the college took to the Baptist union assembly the unanimous recommendation that Professor Athol Gill be reappointed for a further term of five years. For the second time in Himbury's experience, the assembly did not vote with the required two-thirds majority in favor. Some criticisms of Gill's teaching and emphases in social justice were made, but many more concerns about the college more broadly influenced the outcome. There were those who maintained that Whitley College graduates did not remain in ministry and were not acceptable to the larger eastern suburban churches, who favored pastors trained in New South Wales.

The decision was devastating for Athol Gill and his family, as also for Graeme Garrett, who had known the same experience a decade earlier. Himbury had long known how resistant groups within a Baptist union could cause difficulty with a college appointment. His history of the South Wales Baptist College drew attention to these issues several times. There was widespread angst within the college and among many of the

21. Otzen, *Whitley*, 156.
22. Otzen, *Whitley*, 157.

churches. A speedy response was instigated by the East Doncaster Baptist Church, which gathered signatures from sufficient members of assembly to call a special meeting. In August, Athol Gill stood before the assembly to respond to his critics, most powerfully inviting the meeting to open the pew Bibles, as he demonstrated his passion simply to respond to what is actually in the text. He provided, also, statistical data demonstrating the longevity in ministry of Victorian ordained ministers, in contrast with New South Wales graduates, and was backed up by several pastors of larger eastern suburban churches who stated that they were in Victoria precisely because of the ethos and freedom that applied here, in contrast to their home state. The outcome of the meeting was overwhelming support for a motion to reappoint the professor of New Testament.

That decision, however, did not address many of the concerns underlying the situation. The leadership of the Baptist union recognized a wider concern, not merely with the college or members of the staff, but with the character of ministry and the training needed. In a sense, finally, the union was to pick up the issue Himbury had been writing about and wrestling with for the last two decades: but it did so with a sense that it was setting him aside and seeking a new era and a new vision for itself and the college.

The Baptist union appointed a "ministry consultative committee," which would include some college staff but also pastors and members from the churches, to comprehensively address issues relating to the needs of the churches, leadership and training into the future, and what kind of person might lead the college in its future role.[23] In effect, the union was seeking to determine what it would do with Himbury's legacy, even before he had retired. The terms of reference for the inquiry included, however, some of the long-standing and unresolved issues of Himbury's time, such as the possibility of providing residential facilities for married theological students. The report recommended consideration of this possibility, along with expressing concern for "the wives of men training for the ministry"![24] Presented to a special general council in November 1985, the report also outlined the essential qualifications for the principal of the college—clearly anticipating Himbury's retirement, though it was not due for another two years.

23. The report of this commission was presented to a special general council of the Baptist Union of Victoria in November 1985 and published as *The College and the Churches*.

24. Baptist Union of Victoria, *The College and the Churches*, 17–19.

Even before that special meeting, Himbury's old friend Milton Warn had encouraged him to accept that it was time to go. Taking the initiative in response to the reality of the situation presenting itself was strongly characteristic of Mervyn Himbury. He dealt with things as they were. In October 1985 Himbury gave notice of his intention to retire a year early, in 1986. He wrote to the president of the council:

> It is my belief that, while I would love to be involved in planning these changes [envisaged in the commission's report], this would not be right. Soon the College must have a new Principal who ought to have the freedom to participate in plans for the future. . . . I love Whitley so deeply that I am not only prepared to work and fight for it, but also to leave it, if it is for its good.[25]

Mervyn and Marion had already been considering where they might live. In 1986 they purchased a home in Kathleen Avenue, Pascoe Vale. The brick cottage had plenty of room for the couple and a lovely garden space where Mervyn could grow some vegetables and Marion could enjoy a flower garden.

In the intervening time, Himbury suffered a quite debilitating bout of influenza and was laid up for some weeks. Despite being overweight for many years, it was uncharacteristic of him to experience illness of this nature. It was only in later years of his life that he struggled with serious kidney problems. During that time of illness, I happened to call upon him while I was visiting Melbourne. He spoke with me about his concern for Dr. Graeme Garrett, whom he knew was deeply distressed by the situation of the college. Soon after, Dr. Garrett resigned from the college and left to become master of Burgmann College in Canberra. Himbury said to me that it troubled him to know that Garrett was so unhappy but that he felt he could not do anything about it. "I don't know what I can do to help," he said. Garrett was one of Himbury's "boys," a former student who had become a great preacher, scholar, and teacher. Now, he would move into another field of work and, later, another denomination. It was a separation that weighed heavily upon Himbury, as also Whitley College. It was a harbinger of change.

The Himbury era was coming to a close. The long and winding road would come to an end. Many issues remained unresolved, for another principal and faculty to deal with in their own ways. Principal Himbury

---

25. Otzen, *Whitley*, 159.

would need to leave behind some things he could not help or resolve, while affirming and valuing all that had been achieved in his college.

The celebration of Himbury's contribution took many forms, among both the students and staff. For its part, the college council presented a comprehensive resolution to the annual assembly, in recognition of Himbury's long service as principal (see Appendix A).

What this resolution did not recognize at the time was the foundation laid for the future faculty of the college, among his former students. In addition to Professors Garrett and Broughton, no less than ten of his former students would become faculty members in the following decades, while several others would be appointed to Baptist colleges in other states.[26]

---

26. The Whitley faculty members included Bruce Rumbold, Keith Dyer, Terry Falla, Simon Holt, Colin Hunter, Merrill Kitchen, Ross Langmead, Alan Marr, Marita Munro, Bruce Tudball, and me. In addition, former resident and tutor Ian Roos became the business manager and dean of the residential college.

CHAPTER 7

The Word in the World

MERVYN HIMBURY BELONGED TO the first generation to enjoy what have been called the "bonus years" of a long retirement, something very different from the normal experience of men who lived and worked in the coal mining valleys of South Wales. Like many pastors, Himbury did not so much retire as move to a different phase of ministry.

It is helpful to see his life in the decades following his time as principal of Whitley College through the lens of "action-reflection" theology, in which the experience of life and ministry contribute to further theological understanding and ministry practice. In these years of preaching, teaching, and some writing, we can see him re-affirming his life's mission, reflecting upon the priorities for the church in the modern world, and drawing attention again to the values and contribution of the early Baptists whose struggles and achievements he had studied and taught about.

His thoughts, as expressed in recorded sermons and history classes delivered particularly in his retirement at the Collins Street Baptist Church,[1] provide us with a clear sense of his spiritual and theological convictions and the meaning he saw in his own life and ministry.

After a short time of rest and some opportunities to travel, Himbury took up a position as associate minister of the Collins Street Baptist Church. Interestingly, there is no formal record of the church making this appointment. It was more of a personal invitation to shared ministry from the senior minister, Rev. Ron Ham. What is recorded is that from December 1987 onwards he regularly attended deacons' meetings and

---

1. These sermons and lectures were recorded on cassette tapes. I have transcribed the material presented here from those recordings.

continued to do so until November 1993. At that time, Rev. Jim Barr was formally appointed as associate minister. Though Himbury had officially concluded his term as associate minister, he continued to preach regularly and meet with the ministers on an occasional basis.

It was entirely to be expected that Himbury would serve in this way at Collins Street, the church where he and Marion had been in membership since arriving in Melbourne in 1959. As he noted in the "Personal Preface" to the history of that church, published in 1993, Collins Street Baptist Church was "the context of my life and that of my family." He had found most of his friends there and noted also the many significant occasions when he had preached, including "at the Induction Services of Merlyn Holly and Ithel Jones and also at their memorial services." He had served as moderator when Ron Ham was called and now, perhaps indicating the informal nature of his initial appointment as associate minister, he referred to Ron Ham's "graciousness in inviting me to be associated with him in the ministry of the church."[2]

Only when in very advanced years and suffering from considerable immobility did Mervyn and Marion move to another church closer to their home. While preaching at the Collins Street Church's 160th anniversary in July 2003, Himbury reflected that his and Marion's long association with the church had been "a very happy experience—and the only reason that we are not regularly here now is purely physical: It is a matter that is difficult to get here, it is difficult to get in here, it is difficult to get out of here, and it is so much easier to go to the little church around the corner, where at least we can make a more relevant contribution."[3]

During a period of almost ten years, Himbury preached often at Collins Street and exercised a significant role in pastoral care. He also undertook a variety of teaching activities, within the church and at the city campus of the Council for Adult Education.[4] His recorded sermons,

---

2. Himbury, *Theatre of the Word*, 3. Throughout that work, Himbury noted the appointment or retirement of several associate ministers of the church but does not refer to himself as having this role. It seems that he was recognized informally, by both pastor and members of the church, as one of their ministers and no formal appointment was needed.

3. Collins Street Baptist Church sermon cassette 667. The sermon title was "The Essentials of a Baptist Church." Himbury at that time was two days short of his eighty-first birthday.

4. This institution, now known as the Centre for Adult Education, was a forerunner to what is now commonly known as the University of the Third Age and local neighborhood study centers, offering short courses in an immense range of topics and

series of history classes, and published history of the Collins Street Baptist Church are a particularly valuable resource to draw upon as a means of gathering together the themes of his life and the significance of his ministry.

Whitley College: Retrospect and Challenge

One of the most significant events conducted at the conclusion of his principalship was a thanksgiving service held at the Collins Street Baptist Church in December 1985. Himbury preached a remarkable sermon on the theme "There is Death in the Pot."[5] This odd motif is taken from his characteristic choice of an Old Testament text with a quite peculiar image or expression. On this occasion, the text was from 2 Kings 4:38. Himbury's theme was drawn from verse 40, "It came to pass, as they were eating of the pottage, that they cried out, and said, 'O thou man of God,' there is death in the pot.' "

In this sermon, Himbury addressed many of the challenges he had faced, and the issues still confronting the college and its mission in both the church and the wider community. Himbury began by allegorizing the story of a "dearth in the land," to play upon the possibility of the college over-expending its resources and needing to send its students out to forage for ingredients and cook meals; but alas, the food "tasted so vile that everybody spat it out." He remarked that students complaining about the food was "a familiar thing," but then went on to say that it is literally true that "there is death in the pot." He said that all heads of university colleges wake every morning wondering about what might happen that day, as youth suicide "is always at the back of our minds." He commented that he had been blessed that there had been no suicides at Whitley in his time, though he referred to the death of one student who had died soon after he "threw him out of college" and who remained on his conscience.[6] Himbury then commented on the wider concern that many students "are put under such tremendous pressures that it is almost inevitable that some of

---

skills to interested members of the public, but not towards any formal qualification.

5. While researching other sermons preached at Collins Street Baptist Church, I discovered an unmarked cassette recording of this service and sermon. The hymn before the sermon was "Guide me O Thou Great Jehovah," sung to the tune Cwm Rhondda, and Himbury's voice can be heard singing enthusiastically a hymn and tune he loved so well.

6. This was the student whose death is referred to at the beginning of chapter 6.

them will break." Along with the risk of suicide there was the "silliness of students themselves," especially in drinking and driving, or driving too fast—and there was that double entendre as well, death in the pot. Apart from physical death, he noted "the death of ambition" or vocation, which he said could happen to theological students as well: "you see a man's vision fading and dying, where they become geriatric thinkers at twenty years of age."

What should be our response when there is death in the pot? "Throw it out" is an easy administrative answer, which may be done with food. But it should not be the Christian response to young people and their misguided behavior. "Throw them out . . . Let's have this place nice, clean, and hygienic for good Baptists to come and see. They don't act like us, therefore let's have nothing to do with them."[7] Here, Himbury was clearly confronting the attitude he had encountered in all those who did not support the college and imagined another kind of college, where only Baptists of a certain lifestyle might live and study.

Again, when depicting the response of Elijah, he offers a rejoinder to those whose focus was always upon administration and the preservation of the college's resources. Elijah proposed taking the last portion of meal they had left, in a time of famine, to put it into the pot of death. "He was a shocking administrator, was Elijah. He did not understand how to run a college. No wonder he had trouble. To throw good after bad . . ." But despite this humorous rejoinder, in Elijah's proposal Himbury saw a different response to the question of how to use college resources and considered it "an answer we have to take very seriously."[8]

Himbury said that so often the church wants to take things *from* young people: their impertinence, their aggression or stupidity, and their music; their games and their relationships; the way they play about with alcohol and experiment with sex. But what, he asked, are we going to give them? After twenty-eight years of running a college community, his conclusion is that it is no good being negative if we want to face our world of young people. "What are we going to give them? What are we going to put *into* the pot? How are we going to cure the death that is in there?"

Here we see the passion of Himbury's ministry, and his leadership offered to the Baptist and wider community, burning strong still: "I believe that we as a Christian church have a tremendous responsibility. Woe

---

7. Himbury, "There is Death in the Pot."
8. Himbury, "There is Death in the Pot."

to us, if we ignore the young people of our generation because they are not our type. We've got to do something about them."

He went on to say that we have our experience, including our Baptist heritage, with a commitment to freedom, and we have our compassion to throw into the pot—"to try to understand why some of these kids do these things." We also have our health and, above all, "a bit of love that we have, to give them." Again he appealed:

> You will not save the world by criticizing it. You will not save the world by condemning it. You will not help one young person by telling that person he's going to hell, or that she is missing out on the real thing. You will only do it when you throw the best you've got into the pot, however little it may be, and however precious it may be. It's the only way.[9]

He recounted the story of one young person who had completed her degree, with support from the college, and now was making her way in her career. As the Apostle Paul said that he did all he could that he might save some, so too "through Whitley, you may not save the world, but you can save some."

Again, Himbury returned to his critics. One senior minister had questioned why so much time was wasted even considering a university college, when "we should be talking about evangelism." Himbury said he could not understand the question.

Why? Here he confronted the question of what his career and ministry had been about. "There is only one reason," he responded. "Because Jesus said, 'Feed my lambs, and feed my sheep.' And if there's death in the pot, we must still find a way of feeding them." Himbury then turned to the concern to keep the churches going, which he parodied as "the problems of raising enough money to keep the doors open to raise enough money to keep the doors open." This, he said, will cause the death in the pot to seethe "and we ourselves will die by it."[10]

So he ended with an appeal to the contemporary church to offer all it has to give to and for the world. This service of thanksgiving acknowledged the privilege of knowing hundreds and hundreds of young people and "now and again I've been able to help them." He asked God's forgiveness for times when he, too, has been more concerned about his office or keeping the college going than about the students: and then, in

---

9. Himbury, "There is Death in the Pot."
10. Himbury, "There is Death in the Pot."

a most poignant moment, he declared that "Whitley can die—as long as the lambs and sheep of God are fed." His successor would not have an easy task, but it was a superb one.

Thus, he summed up his sense of mission and the continuing vision he offered to the college and to the church: "There is death in the pot, but out of that we can make a meal that will satisfy the needs of some people, and they will discover how God provides and how Jesus fulfills his word, and he will never leave them."[11]

In the years following his retirement from Whitley College, Himbury offered support to his successor, Rev. Dr. Ken Manley, but chose to remain at a distance from the college. For his part, Ken Manley wished to honor Himbury and hoped to involve him further. The most significant expression of honor came in 1989, when the building previously known as Crocket House was substantially refurbished and extended to create the Mervyn Himbury Theological Studies Center.

In this period of his life, Himbury experienced several physical ailments, including the need for knee replacements. His strength as a rugby player no doubt sustained him for many years, but his obesity in middle and later life caused considerable strain on his joints. Later still, he experienced quite serious kidney failure, needing regular dialysis, and in his final years the treatment for this difficulty needed to be carefully balanced with management for heart failure as well.

In the face of these challenges, however, he retained his cheerful and hopeful disposition, and a lively interest in his circle of family and friends, though it became increasingly difficult to keep in touch.

In what was the final year of his life, Himbury wrote a deeply personal note to his successor, Ken Manley, who had recently undergone major surgery, as well as completing the first volume of his magnum opus, a history of Australian Baptists.

> 3/3/08
> Dear Ken,
>   I have just heard from Geoff Blackburn of your health problems.
>   Marion and I will be praying for you that the healing power of Jesus will transform you.
>   Get well. We need your special gift. You have taken the first grand step in your history, but we need more if Australian Baptists are to realize their true identity.

---

11. Himbury, "There is Death in the Pot."

When by some miracle I got a first in BA History I thought, for a moment, that this could be my task but the Almighty had more menial tasks for me. You have so much more to contribute.

I take the opportunity of thanking you for your contribution to Whitley.

May God be with you and may he who has called you now give you health and strength for the tasks you have already begun.

Blessings,
Mervyn[12]

In the latter years of his life, Mervyn and Marion moved their church affiliation to the Moreland Baptist Church, near to their home. They appreciated a local pastor who visited them regularly. At the Sunday morning services, special chairs with arms, which allowed them to get up from the chair with greater ease, were placed at the back. There they sat looking over the congregation with benevolence, and from there, too, Mervyn would occasionally lead them in prayer. Both Mervyn and Marion were much-loved members of this community during this time, just as they too loved the people there.

In July of 2006, Mervyn became very unwell and spent some time in hospital. His pastor, Rev. Cheryl Williams, advised me of this situation and that it was about to be Mervyn's birthday. On that day, we visited him together and brought to him the elements of the Lord's Supper. After sharing this sacrament together, Mervyn commented on how unwell he felt and how unsure he was that he would recover. Then he declared, "What a hoot it would be, to die on your birthday!" He recovered, to enjoy several more birthdays.

From Principal to Pastor and Preacher

The recorded sermons and history classes delivered during these years at Collins Street provide a rich insight into Himbury's vision of Christian life and mission, but also allow us to see his pastoral care for the congregation and its members. One such sermon provides a superb indication of Himbury's pastoral insight as well as his characteristic skill as a preacher. On June 7, 1987, he preached a sermon on the theme "The Art

---

12. I am indebted to Ken Manley, who made this note in its handwritten form available to me.

of Forgetting."[13] As it happened, two elderly women from the church had died in the preceding week and another member, Dr. Keith Farrer, fellow of Whitley College, was in the coming days to leave Melbourne, to live in Britain. There was deep sadness in the congregation that day, to which Himbury addressed part of his sermon.

He began by saying that his sermon would break some of his own rules for preaching, taught to his students over many years. He would not have one text, but many.[14] His interest was in the subject of memory. In the next weeks he would visit the house where he was born and the church where he had had his first "great experience of God"; he would stand outside the Congregational Church where he had first preached a sermon, and later would visit the church where he had been ordained. "What a magnificent thing memory is, at times," he declared. If he did have an overall text for this sermon, it was an old prayer from an anonymous medieval saint:

> O Lord, help us to remember what we ought not to forget,
> and to forget what we ought not to remember.

Himbury commented on the "most awful stories" found in the book of Judges, stories of anarchy in Israel, "when the children of Israel did everything they could to offend against all decent social laws." Though there are occasional remarkable persons, prophets, and leaders, on the whole society is at its worst, for "the children of Israel did evil in the sight of the Lord . . . and they forsook the Lord, and served Baal" (Judg 2:11–13).

While he did not want to make God one who merely justifies our social morality, Himbury asserted that a society that forgets God is doomed to anarchy. There are some things, he affirmed, that we forget at our peril. To forget that behind the whole world there is a divine imperative is to forget order and to embrace chaos. Indeed, to forget God is to forget the very essence of our being.

Himbury spoke then of the value in remembering "the things that God has done for us through people." These are things we ought not to forget—citing the instance of the Joseph story, where Joseph assisted a fellow prisoner who, when released, forgot Joseph. Then Himbury turned to the immediate situation and spoke of the two members of the church who had so recently died:

---

13. This sermon is recorded on Collins Street Baptist Church sermon cassette 295.

14. Himbury considered it an offence against homiletical principles to waste a number of texts.

> I will for the rest of my life remember the quiet, so kindly things that Alice McAdam used to say to me, not in any fussy kind of way. But she was kind, and she knew the sort of right things to say without any of the ostentation that can characterize some people. She helped me.
>
> Let me confess there were times in my ministry in Whitley College when I could have thrown the whole thing in, and nobody helped me more at that time than Maida Thomas, I remember.
>
> I know that my own ministry is utterly different because of the memory of these people.

Such people may not be great in the sight of the world, but they bring to us a power, an insight and an understanding which is beyond the comprehension of most people. We ought not to forget. This thought led him to affirm the words of Psalm 103:2, "Bless the Lord, O my soul, and forget not all his benefits."

We can look back at all the great things that have happened to us and it makes all the difference. God has pardoned us, healed us, rescued us, loved us, cared for us: you go back again to the Psalm, where you have a whole list before you: "forget not all his benefits," the things that have been part of us, these great experiences.

"O God, help us to remember the things we ought not to forget."

Of course, there are things we ought to forget. To develop this idea Himbury turned to the reading from Philippians 3:1–14, where the Apostle Paul speaks of striving to achieve that which belongs to Jesus Christ: and urges his readers not to think he has already achieved this or already won the race. Himbury paraphrases Paul's words, "This one thing I do, however, is to forget what is behind me, and do my best to reach forward to that which is ahead." Himbury said that here Paul is speaking of all the things in his past which would come between him and his experience in Jesus Christ. These were not necessarily bad things: some were very good things. Himbury depicted a pride of race, "a Hebrew of the Hebrews." As a Pharisee, Paul was one who had been set apart to the worship of God, and "according to the Law, blameless." Yet he considered all this refuse, for the sake of Christ.[15]

Himbury noted that we may have many things that are good, in our past, but we have to decide between the good and the essential. To illustrate his point, he recalled his sea voyages to and from Australia. He had

---

15. Here Himbury was broadly paraphrasing Phil 3:13–14.

enjoyed watching the ship being loaded. Each person had limited space in their cabin—and here Himbury made a joke about his own size—so passengers could pack some of their luggage, valuable possessions still, but labeled "not wanted on the voyage." Those things would be stowed elsewhere in the ship. This image is invoked by Paul's idea of "forgetting what is behind me."

"We have to forget the childish things that prevent us from knowing the glory of Christ," Himbury said. Here he referred to a love of the miraculous, which can draw us into unscriptural ideas of God. Citing 1 Corinthians 13:9–12 and the need to give up childish things, Himbury spoke of childish days in the faith and an "inadequate sense of what is needed to be a Christian . . . to forget superficial things of Christianity, in order to enjoy the depths of the Gospel; to forget an inadequate vision of the church, that we had once, and to grow up into Christ, who is the head and upon whom the whole body depends."[16]

Moving to his conclusion, Himbury noted that it was one of the great tasks of the Spirit "to bring all these things to remembrance," to enable us to remember Jesus and his word, to remember who we are, and to have the strength to be and become who we ought to be. Thus, he celebrated what we ought to remember, and the wonderful gift of memory, but also affirmed the spiritual art of forgetting.

Return of the History Professor

Another vital element in Himbury's preaching in this period was the offering of a historical perspective on his various themes or the situations in which he preached. He also wanted to stress the history of Baptists and its importance for the contemporary life of the denomination.

Preaching for the 160th anniversary of Collins Street Baptist Church in July 2003, he began with a reference to the founding of the church "when John Ham gave a lecture on the nature of a Gospel church" and suggested that it was appropriate to continue from that, with "the characteristics that should be of our church."[17] To do this he would use the discipline in which he was trained, history. But then he remarked, "After all,

---

16. Here Himbury was in fact drawing upon another of Christian growth, with some phrases drawn from Eph 4:15–16.

17. This sermon was titled "The Essentials of a Baptist Church" and was preached at Collins Street Baptist Church on July 20, 2003 (sermon cassette 142).

history is simply the record of the way in which people have experienced life and have tried to express it." In that sermon, Himbury offered a sketch of the emergence of the first Baptists, within the Reformation period. He gave particular attention to the spiritual emphases of various groups, as well as their political and eschatological perspectives, during the time of Cromwell and the Fifth Monarchy Men. He then sought to draw from this story a challenge for the contemporary church to see that loyalty to Jesus Christ is the essential and fundamental concern. The church is a fellowship, of brothers and sisters, who often spend a lot of time quarreling. But if brothers and sisters love their parents that is one thing that holds them together, and so, too, for the church, the love for the Father and the Son "is everything within the church," enabling us to be people who know the truth of God, experiencing the Spirit and living in hope. This, he declared, was how we might make ourselves "worthy of our tradition."[18]

In this remarkable sermon, offering a sweep of historical information most likely entirely new to most of his audience, Himbury nonetheless crystallized the significance of it all for the contemporary church. In his view, it would be tragic for the contemporary church to be unaware of its tradition, but the significance of that history is to focus the challenges of discipleship and community life in the present.

The question of how Christians and their faith in God relates to human society and our life in the world was the central focus of a series of history classes Himbury delivered at Collins Street in 1992.[19] The titles of these lectures were:

- The Church Meets the World
- The Church Compromises with the World
- The Reformation
- The Modern Church's Dilemma.

In the first lecture, Himbury offered the basic thesis that the church's organization grew up because it had to meet real problems, and once these organizations had grown up the people who belonged to them found good theological reasons for why they should exist. In some detail he outlined the change in the role of a bishop, from one who served a local church to a geographically-based role, and the development of an

18. Himbury, "The Essentials of a Baptist Church".

19. These lectures were recorded. Summaries and quotations from the lectures are based on my transcription of those recordings.

administrative structure very similar to that of the Roman Empire. "To meet the problems of the church, the church organizes; and the church always takes the easiest way of doing it. It always takes its pattern from the world around it."

In the broad sweep of the second lecture, Himbury gave particular attention to the work of Augustine, the decline of the Roman Empire, and the later emergence of Charlemagne and a Christian state or civilization.

The third lecture dealt in considerable detail with the Renaissance and the development of modern thought. It described some of the intellectual, political, and economic tensions inherent in this period, and the theological developments broadly referred to as the Reformation.

It was in the final lecture that Himbury offered a particularly insightful presentation of the situation of the church in the modern world, drawing upon the cumulative account of what had gone before. Similar to James McClendon's categorization of styles of church, which he represented by lower-case letters, catholic, protestant, and baptist, Himbury characterized three forms of "churchmanship": the Catholic church, a form also evident in the Orthodox churches; the national churches, in places such as Germany and Britain; and new forms of churches which he called the gathered churches.[20]

This lecture described a series of movements which have shaped and continue to challenge the church in the modern world: Pietism, rationalism (which led to Unitarianism—a movement which included many Baptists), and revivalism—particularly important in the United States of America, but also influencing the Wesleyans and Methodism. He identified a series of more recent movements, beginning with the influence of Darwin, and the historical-critical study of the Bible, and the modern missionary expansion of the church. "The nineteenth century was the greatest era of expansion in the history of the Christian church."[21] On the other hand, Darwin and biblical criticism had led many to a more defensive position, a church seeking its own safety, which Himbury considered a strategy for failure: "the church always fails when it's primarily concerned with its own preservation and its own safety."

---

20. McClendon, *Doctrine*, 332–45.
21. Transcription of lecture.

In conclusion, Himbury said that his hope in these presentations was to help people to see "how God has worked in his church in different periods of the history of the church."[22]

The challenges presented in this final section are particularly informative, in several ways. It is interesting that Himbury made no specific mention of the developing *secularization* in contemporary society. The decline in church attendances and the influence of the churches in society was a phenomenon familiar to him from his life in Wales as well as in Australia. It was not as if he had no interest in those who reflected theologically upon these trends, including, for instance, the Baptist theologian Harvey Cox, in his groundbreaking work *The Secular City*.

In a sense, the issues raised by secularity were fundamental to Himbury's faith and theology. He consistently claimed to be a Calvinist, with a strong emphasis upon the sovereignty of God. It is God who is at work in the world. This meant not only that God is present in the word, written and preached, though that was crucial for Himbury. More than that, he insisted that the preaching of God's word led to experience. Well before the emergence of the contemporary charismatic movement, Himbury drew attention to the spiritual experiences of early Baptists and preached about the essential religious experience, which gives rise to a sense of call upon one's life.

Still, the question must be faced: what does it mean to insist upon the centrality of preaching when people have abandoned church attendance? Was this now an anachronism? Had his life been given over to the wrong emphases or a false hope?

These questions undoubtedly concerned Himbury in these years of both ministry and reflection. It is possible to identify his responses, in several other works and sermons presented within the place where these questions were clearly evident—the pulpit and sparsely populated pews of the Collins Street Baptist Church.

The Theater of the Word

Himbury was commissioned to present a history of the Collins Street Baptist Church for its 150th anniversary in 1993. The work is titled *The Theatre of the Word: Traditions, Ministry, Future of the Collins Street Baptist Church, Melbourne, 1843–1993*.

22. Transcription of lecture.

To understand the approach taken in this work, it is helpful to explain the ways Himbury used the term "ministry." In December 1982, he preached for the induction of Rev. Philip Hughes at Wangaratta Baptist Church. In that sermon he explained that in the church we use the word ministry in two different senses, "and we shouldn't confuse the two." The first use of the word, Himbury explained, relates to those "who have had a special call of God," to a ministry that is set apart, consecrated by prayer and the laying on of hands. In this way people may know "that this one is recognized by the church as having a special service, an ordained ministry."[23]

Then there is a ministry "which belongs to the whole of the body of Christians: the ministry of the whole congregation to the whole world." The church has always been in danger of overemphasizing one ministry or the other, swinging like a pendulum between a clericalism that imagines only certain people can do any great work of God and an anti-clericalism which denies that God calls anyone in particular. Himbury's purpose, however, was to emphasize the relationship between these two forms of ministry: the preaching and nurturing ministry of the pastors, which in turn inspire and guide the ministry of the whole congregation.[24]

Himbury's history of the Collins Street Church is, at first glance, a history of its ministers. It is organized in that way, chapter by chapter. But within each of these sections he shows how the distinctive contribution of each minister called forth the life of the church as ministry in the city, in diverse and changing forms of evangelistic mission and community service—not least those ministries led by several outstanding women.

It is instructive, however, to note how he dealt with the recent decades and ministries, when the church was clearly in decline. In September 1970, Rev. Dr. J. Ithel Jones was inducted as the new minister, having moved from Cardiff where he had been principal of the South Wales Baptist College. With this appointment, Himbury observed, "Collins Street had reverted to its practice of having a distinguished British preacher as its pastor."[25] Soon after, the church also appointed Rev. Dr. Graeme Garrett, newly returned from studies at the Graduate Theological Union, in Berkeley, California. At the beginning of his ministry, Jones made it clear that his first priority was to build up the church. Other matters or

23. I am grateful to Rev Dr Philip Hughes for making available to me a recording of the service of induction held at Wangaratta Baptist Church on December 5, 1982.

24. Sermon at Wangaratta Baptist Church on December 5, 1982

25. Himbury, *Theatre of the Word*, 47.

plans relating to ministry in the wider community would be consequent upon increasing the congregations, with the initial goal of doubling attendances by Easter of the following year, 1971.

Himbury's assessment is quite clear: "The church did not grow."[26] Though the members of the church were quite justified in their belief that they had two of the finest preachers in the country, the reality was that crowds no longer thronged to listen to great preaching. Indeed, during the vibrant, caring ministry of Merlyn Holly (1961–1971) the membership declined from 228 to 191. In Jones's time it further declined to 168. In this period, the Connibere Trust funds, established for evangelistic purposes, were used to invite several other preachers, while substantial funds were raised and expended on a major renovation of the pipe organ.

The final chapter, "Today and Tomorrow," recounts the process leading to new directions, formulated in 1984 and developed in the decade following. Critically, the idea of the church as principally a "preaching station" was now revised. On the one hand, the church would seek to maximize the use of its building and its location in the center of the city, in order to make "a distinctively Christian contribution" to the life of the city.[27] Many different groups have been invited to make use of the church building, for musical and educational activities, for instance. Importantly, these activities are not seen as a means for drawing people into the Sunday services but are an aspect of the church's ministry in the city. On the other hand, the objective of "church growth" is seen, as Himbury put it, as "the task of the traditional ministry of Word and Sacrament, which involves pastoral care."[28] These two aspects of ministry are envisaged as both separate and yet working in harmony, and in his view constituted the best hope for the future.

What is clear from this historical work is that Himbury saw the ministry of this and every Baptist church as grounded in the event of God's word, principally through preaching. But that event is not an end in itself; far from it. The "theater" of the word is not only the church building, nor only the people who gather there to hear it. The word of God is offered to the church *within* and *for* the world, the community of people all around. The ministry of the preacher is to inspire, challenge, and enable the ministry of the whole church in the world.

26. Himbury, *Theatre of the Word*, 47.
27. Himbury, *Theatre of the Word*, 53.
28. Himbury, *Theatre of the Word*, 53.

A Fundamental Conviction: "My Word Shall Not Return to Me Void."

James W. McClendon developed a distinctive approach to theology through the study of biography. Indeed, he proposed biography *as* theology.[29] His methodology was based upon the idea that in every human life there is some fundamental ideal or *conviction* that shaped that person's experience and character. The study of biography as theology involved seeking to identify and learn from those convictions. As a result, McClendon saw theology as the study of character and his own systematic work *began* with ethics, rather than, as many other theological approaches have done, ending with ethics as the "application" or consequence of what has been otherwise established.

In Mervyn Himbury's life and ministry, there are many theological themes and a plethora of images and ways of speaking about God and humanity. It seems to me, however, that his entire approach to ministry was grounded in a conviction about God, expressed in his claim to be a Calvinist, but even more so in his passion for preaching. It is entirely appropriate that this conviction should be expressed through an Old Testament text, Isaiah 55:11, "So shall my word be that goeth forth out of my mouth: it shall not return unto me void, but it shall accomplish that which I please, and it shall prosper *in the thing* whereto I sent it."

The fundamental conviction shaping Mervyn Himbury's life was the belief that God's word could and would sustain itself, moving within the vicissitudes of human life and history, and would fulfill its purpose. It was not the preacher who would achieve this purpose—that was a crucial element in this conviction. No, the preacher was to deliver or offer the word, but the word itself would prosper because it was and is the word of God.

It was out of this conviction, too, that Himbury continually raised, as a theological teacher and denominational leader, questions concerning the kinds of ministers and ministries needed to meet the challenges of the modern era, in a changing society and declining church. What kind of ministers were needed and how should they be educated or trained? Many others offered answers based upon their concern with methods or techniques in ministry, as Himbury called them, models for church growth or other aspects of local church life, worship, pastoral counseling, or Christian education. But Himbury saw all this focus on how things

---

29. McClendon, *Biography as Theology*.

were in the church as secondary to, and in many ways a distraction from, even an avoidance of, the fundamental concern of ministry: to proclaim the word of God as present and active, to fulfill the purpose for which God had sent it forth.

This conviction and its implications are very clear in a sermon Himbury preached at Collins Street Baptist Church in August 1988. The sermon and its themes provide a useful context for reflection upon his life and ministry. Here we see a welding of Himbury's own life story with that of the people to whom he was speaking and the biblical character upon which the sermon was based.[30] The Scripture text was drawn from Judges, chapter 6. Himbury gave the sermon the title, "The Place Called Peace."

He began by describing the desperate situation in which the nation of Israel was placed; so bad, as he put it, that the people did not know what was going to happen. Besieged, they were unable to plant or harvest crops, and so were short of food and all the necessities of life. Then God chose a man called Gideon. As Himbury recounted the story, Gideon did not understand why he has been chosen, because, as he says to the Lord, his family is the least important in the district, and within his family he is the least important member. In spite of this, he accepts that he is the chosen one and declares that the place is to be named Shalom, meaning the Lord is peace (Judg 6:24). This idea becomes the theme and purpose of Himbury's sermon: that people can find peace and the church community can be a place of peace.

Himbury declared that this incongruity in the story struck him as odd: "Here was Gideon, facing a war-like situation, confronted by evil he has to overcome, and by enemies he has to drive out, and he calls the place *Peace!*"

Having introduced the story and his theme, Himbury then offered a reflection, which included his characteristic historical references, providing a wider frame of reference for his audience to consider. What we can learn from history, and from this story, is that "whenever God has to do something about the situation of a people, he calls a man, a person of vision."

Himbury went on to assert that most of the great things that have happened in the world arose because of the vision of a person. "It was the vision of John Smyth, followed by the early Baptists, that saw the acts of

---

30. The content of this sermon was transcribed from Collins Street Baptist Church sermon cassette 410.

Toleration. We take it for granted nowadays that no one should be persecuted for their religious beliefs—too much for granted. But it started with the vision of one man, inspired by God." Similarly, prison reform was brought about by the vision of John Howard and Elizabeth Fry.

In the story of Gideon, Himbury explains, God begins by pointing out that he himself is a God of deliverance, having rescued the nation from slavery in Egypt. Thus, Himbury comments to his audience on the significance of history for faith: "There is always the place for the historian, because we've always got to see our vision in relation to what has been done by God, throughout all the ages past."

The sermon then moved to the question of what kind of leaders are needed to serve and guide the people and the churches today. Gideon is presented as an exemplar of ministry: an ordinary man, who lives with and suffers with his own people—Gideon is the man because of his ordinariness. By contrast, Himbury declared, when we want leaders, we want extraordinary people; but the man chosen to lead Israel to freedom was just an ordinary farmer. He was concerned with the seasons, like everyone else. He knew the problems of the people who rode over the land once it was sown and burned the crops once they appeared.

Gideon was also a frightened man, who shared all the fears of his people. "Why, when God's messenger came to him, what was he doing but hiding from the Midianites the grain he'd brought in? It wasn't the time of the grape harvest, so now he was hiding the wheat in the vats where the wine was stored, trying to keep a little behind from the oppression of the enemy." Yet, in spite of all this, he came to a sense of commitment, expressed in his declaration, "this is the place of peace."

At this point in his sermon, Himbury comments on the significance of this experience, indicating, I think, his own spiritual experience. He reflects on the story with a wider insight about religious experience more generally, which he suggests is often characterized by fear and unease. In this discussion, we see something of Himbury's own assessment of the situation of modern secularity. It is helpful to quote this segment at some length.

> At the very spot where Gideon was commissioned to do God's will, he found peace. He called the place peace because he had experienced the nearness of God.
>
> We are often afraid of religion. I have known men in my family who are terrified of religion, because it speaks of things they don't like. *Sin:* one doesn't want to talk much about sin. It is

not all that pleasant and, in any case, sin ought to belong only to the lower and less pleasant classes of society. "Sin" ought not to be used of us nice middle-classed people—and we're afraid of it.

And we're afraid of the word *judgment*, whether you talk of judgment in this life or in the life to come. We're afraid of the idea that God is righteous, and we may have to face up to him.

We're afraid of *suffering*, because in suffering we are made weak and less heroic in our control of our own destinies.

And we're afraid of *death*: "For in that sleep of death, what dreams may come?" is the fear of Shakespeare, and it is the fear of many people.

All these seem to many people to be the realm of religion and so they've become frightened of religion, of the place of God in life, because God seems to deal with those things.

And yet, the real purpose of religion in the world is to meet the deep need of people who are afraid of these things because they are afraid of living. It is true that we talk of sin, judgment, suffering and death—but with all of them we put God's promise, God's covenant, God's faithfulness, God's peace.

The sermon returned to the idea of the place of peace, linking both the Gideon story and a story of Jesus's appearance to his disciples, with insights leading then to an application for the congregation and Christians in the present era.

Himbury then recounted the situation of Jesus's disciples, following the crucifixion, frightened and hiding in an upper room. "Jesus came and stood in their midst, and his first word to them was, 'Peace be with you.'"

From all of this, Himbury drew his clear affirmation: "A religion of peace, this is the essence of our ministry." We—by which he meant his listeners and the church more broadly—are to be a people who, in the midst of trouble, proclaim the peace of God.

At this point, however, Himbury made a rare application of psychological insight, asserting that it is not possible to be a people of peace unless we overcome fear and tension within ourselves. "If you're going to meet conflict, the way to meet conflict is by first of all finding peace. The first war Gideon had to conquer was the war in his own mind—but it was when he discovered peace, he knew he could overcome."

Himbury then addressed what he saw as an inherent tenseness in the position and faith of Christians in the world today and illustrated his point with an anecdote from an episode he witnessed at the World Conference of Christian Youth, in his student days. Reinhold Niebuhr was one of the keynote speakers, but in a dialogue Niebuhr's brother Richard reproved him. "You are too tense about the future of mankind . . . Every night I get down on my knees and thank my God that he's not half as tense about you as you are about him."

Thus, Himbury made his application and exhortation:

> It is not by being tense about the Gospel that we overcome. It is by discovering its peace. That was the great discovery of Gideon: the place where he is called into conflict is Jehovah Shalom, the peace of God. When we come to worship, we come to find this sense of God's peace. Jehovah Shalom: it is here for all who want it. Let us find it, that we may triumph in the name of God.

In this sermon we see very clearly the character and foundation of Himbury's theology and preaching. It was founded on the conviction that God's word would not fail or return to the Lord empty. The promise of the Gospel was its foundation. In this sermon, he spoke of Jesus overcoming the world and inviting his followers into peace, even in the midst of conflict and concerns.

There were several critical implications of this theological stance. For Himbury, the situation to which Christians may look, the hoped-for reality of God's reign, is not to be identified with the present circumstances of the church. His radical Baptist conviction was that the reign of God is never to be identified with any specific time or place, government, economic arrangement, or ecclesial form. The great mistake of the Cromwellian era was the idea that some specific social or ecclesiastical order would fulfill the Christian hope. The kingdom of God cannot be legislated into reality. The church does not and cannot contain nor enact nor "achieve" the reality of God's kingdom. But that is not to say that this hope rests in some other world or time beyond the present age, as was envisaged by some of the early Puritan groups Himbury had studied. On the contrary, Himbury called women and men of faith, the contemporary church, to participate in the perpetual coming of God's way, with its gifts of peace, forgiveness, hope, and love, and to be continually thankful for God's faithfulness and mercy.

It was on this basis, then, that he urged his hearers, particularly preachers and ministers of the Gospel, not to be nervous or to lose heart. We should expect the surprising presence of God amid our otherwise ordinary, and perhaps unpromising, lives and situations.

Himbury was constantly asking both himself and the Baptist denomination questions about what kind of leaders or ministers were needed to address the challenges of the modern world. We have seen that his answer was profoundly theological and spiritual. It was not essentially a question of the theological curriculum, though of course he was concerned for that. He was convinced that those who thought it was a matter of developing the right techniques for ministry had profoundly missed the central point of ministry: its faithfulness to the sovereignty and grace of God. His conviction was that the kind of ministers needed were people like Gideon. His presentation of this ordinary man from a humble place in society, whose deep encounter with God led him to a sense of peace and a courageous and imaginative approach to battle, also describes his approach to ministerial education and to ministry at large. It was through such people that he believed the life of the church would be served, through the preaching of a Gospel that invited people into the presence and peace of God, and to participate in their own ministries within the world.

It is in these convictions, too, that we can see Himbury's own response to the decline of the churches and the advance of secularism in his lifetime. His understanding of faith and theology did not identify the reign of God with the church, but rather called the church to participate in the presence of God in the world, both within and beyond the church. What that meant in detail was not something he developed in any specific way, as a kind of program for mission. Rather, his constant emphasis was upon the word of God, present and active in the world, through the word of God and the life of the Spirit. These were given realities, the foundations of faith. The place of a minister, and indeed of all Christians, is to serve these realities, trusting in God and bearing witness to the word, in and for the world. Together, the local congregation must discern the implications of God's word for their life and witness, their ministry as a local community of faith.

Preach It Again, and Again.

Very early in his time in Australia, Himbury published an article describing Australian Baptists. The article has a strongly positive and hopeful ring to it. He notes, for instance, that most local churches have some building project, while they are also striving to develop meaningful forms of evangelism in the contemporary world. They are also generous: "No body of Baptists gives more generously to the work of the church than Australians. They too are the most ready contributors to inter-denominational missions and institutions."[31]

The article concludes on what is both a challenging and hopeful note. While there is numerical growth in the churches, it is not keeping pace with the increase in population. This raises for Himbury "the question of the place of the ministry in the work of the church." By "the ministry," he means here the role of pastors. He goes on:

> There is a tendency among some of the churches to regard the pastor as an administrative officer, but there would seem to be at the present time a revival of interest in preaching and worship. Many are asking where lies the best road into the future; in Christian education, in a more active evangelism or in the creation of a better image of the church through a dignified liturgy and effective preaching? There is ample scope for experiment and the future is bright for the young minister who is prepared to tackle the present situation with faith and courage. This is a young country and the possibilities for future service are endless.[32]

We can only speculate what Himbury might have said, had he revisited that subject thirty or forty years later. Many of his observations would still have obtained, though perhaps the focus upon a dignified liturgy would have been replaced by different emphases in worship, especially styles of music. What we do know, however, is that Himbury retained his lifelong conviction about the importance, indeed we might say the centrality, of preaching for the life of the church. This conviction was based upon the imperative suggested in the biblical text, Romans 10:14–15—how are the people to believe if they have not heard the word of God proclaimed, and that, in turn, requires that someone will be sent to preach to them. The challenge, however, as Himbury well knew, is that in most places in the contemporary world, people do not gather to hear the preacher. The "possibilities for future service" he envisaged must now involve finding ways to bring that word to those who do not even imagine there is such a message.

Himbury's own life and ministry may be understood further through another sermon he preached in several places, including at a

---

31. Himbury, "Australian Baptists Today," 10.
32. Himbury, "Australian Baptists Today," 10.

service of induction in November 1983, when I commenced as minister of the Hobart Baptist Church. The title of this sermon was, "Preach it Again."

For this sermon, Himbury took as his text chapter 36 of the book of Jeremiah. There we read a long story about the prophet and relationships with the wider society and the political powers of the day. Jeremiah dictates to Baruch, his scribe, a long message of rebuke and challenge to the nation of Israel. Baruch writes this message upon a scroll. Jeremiah, who has been "prevented from entering the house of the Lord," sends Baruch to read this message to the crowd of people gathered on a fast day. Implicit in this arrangement is the challenge to the people, common to other prophets such as Isaiah and Amos, that God is not deceived by their elaborate displays of piety and temple performance. What is called for is a national repentance, "to turn from their evil ways" so that the Lord may forgive their iniquity (Jer 36:3). The elaborate account explains that when Baruch read this scroll to the community, its content was reported to the palace officials, who summonsed Baruch and asked who had dictated all these words. It was decided that the king must be informed of the content of Jeremiah's prophecy. Meanwhile, Baruch was warned that he and Jeremiah must hide, for their own safety. Then, when the scroll is presented to King Jehoiakim in his winter apartment, where a fire was burning, he took a knife and cut the scroll in pieces before throwing it into the fire. Though his servants urged him not to do so, he persisted in burning the whole thing. After this happened, the word of the Lord came to Jeremiah to take another scroll and to write on it all the words that had been written on the previous scroll—along with an additional rebuke of Jehoiakim and prophecy of the destruction of his kingdom.

What should the prophet or preacher do when the message is not received and even positively resisted? Himbury's answer was simply to preach it again. The message is not to be toned down or adjusted to preserve the preacher's safety or career. Nor is the message to be accommodated to what the public may want to hear. No, the message is to be addressed again and again to those for whom the Lord has intended it. For it is not the preacher's own message, nor is she or he ultimately responsible for its success or failure. The calling of the preacher is to bring the word of the Lord and to trust that in God's own way "it shall not return to [the Lord] void" but will accomplish that for which God has sent it forth (Isa 55:11).

In this story and sermon, we see the fundamental direction of Mervyn Himbury's life and ministry: a preacher of the word of God.[33]

---

33. The catalogue of cassette recordings suggests that Himbury preached a sermon with the title "Preach it Again" at Collins Street Baptist Church in January 1991. Intriguingly, the cassette recording cannot be found. Perhaps that is fitting.

CHAPTER 8

Precious in the Sight of God

MERVYN HIMBURY DIED ON Friday, October 31, 2008. He had been admitted to the Royal Melbourne Hospital the preceding Monday, reportedly lucid and cheerful, but by Wednesday it was clear he would not recover, and he slipped into a coma. Maelor took Marion in to visit him, before he lost consciousness, and they were able to share moments of comfort for one another. He died on Friday evening.

Whitley College placed the following notice in the Melbourne newspaper, *The Age*:

> Himbury, David Mervyn
> Principal Emeritus of Whitley College
> It is with great sadness that we announce the passing of our founding Principal, Mervyn Himbury, on October 31st. His vision for a new theological college within a university setting provided the foundation for Whitley's life as it is today. As a scholar and teacher, pastor and friend, we have loved and admired him. As a preacher, he has been the standard to guide and inspire us. Generations of students are indebted to his care and guidance.
> The Council and Staff of Whitley College: The Baptist College of Victoria, in the University of Melbourne, record our gratitude to God for all that Mervyn has given us. Our deepest sympathy is extended to Marion and to their sons Maelor and Michael.

I wrote an obituary that was published by Whitley College in the *Victorian Baptist Witness* and that provides something of a summary of the story told in the preceding chapters.

Mervyn Himbury, the founding Principal of Whitley College, died on October 31st, 2008, aged 86 years.

When Mervyn Himbury came to Australia from South Wales in 1959, to take up the position of Principal of the Baptist College of Victoria, there was a dream for a new college, to be a university residential college as well as a theological college. Supported by the excellent team of John Hopkins, Geoff Stevens and Olwyn Abbott, Mervyn Himbury's vision and drive made Whitley College a reality. His proudest moment was in February 1965 when Prime Minister Robert Menzies opened the new college.

A graduate of Oxford and Cardiff universities, Himbury was a noted scholar in the radical Reformation. He was a champion of the local church, responsibly seeking God's leading and offering its service in the local community. This was the purpose of theological education: that local churches could be led by a well-trained pastor, "rightly dividing the word of God."

Mervyn was a man of prayer. Most days he would rise very early to spend time praying for his students. To hear Mervyn leading public prayer was to be lifted to new heights.

Mervyn Himbury was a prince of preachers. He loved to take a passage of scripture and to home in on some unusual image or expression, and soar like an eagle, displaying the breadth and depth of God's love.

Himbury saw the university college as a mission, providing quality accommodation and care for all students, regardless of background. Several generations of residents are indebted to him for his pastoral care and support.

Victorian Baptists give thanks to God for Mervyn Himbury's life and ministry and we pray God's comfort and peace to be with Marion and their two sons, Maelor and Michael.

Funeral Service

In keeping with his wishes, a funeral service was held in the Whitley College Chapel, on Friday, November 7. I led the service. Family members and friends, former colleagues and students contributed to the service. Scripture readings were presented by Mrs. Christine Boomsma, the secretary of the Melbourne Welsh Church and Rev. Dr. Tim McGowan, pastor of the Moreland Baptist Church. Emeritus Professor Basil Brown led one of the prayers and another was led by Rev. Alan Marr, director of ministries for the Baptist Union of Victoria.

Dr. Julie Morsillo and Maelor Himbury offered personal and family reflections, and Rev. Milton Warn presented a eulogy, "The Mervyn I Knew." The sermon was preached by Rev. Jim Barr, with the title "Scribe, Priest, Preacher."

Former resident of Whitley College Douglas Lawrence, who had long campaigned for the installation of a pipe organ in the chapel, played the organ. A particularly poignant element in the service was presented by Himbury's sons, Maelor and Michael. In his tribute, Maelor recalled Christmas celebrations as a family, when they would sing together. The sons then sang one of their favorites, "Will the Circle Be Unbroken," with Michael playing guitar, and the congregation invited to join in the refrain.

Following the service, a simple committal took place on the concourse at the front of the college, as another former student, later dean and professor of the college, Rev. Dr. Bruce Rumbold, sang "God Be With You Till We Meet Again."

Extracts from the service are here reproduced, made available by each presenter. Transcripts of each reproduced element are available in the Appendix.

The Mervyn I Knew: Eulogy by Rev. Milton Warn, First Registrar of Whitley College.

Milton Warn spoke of his personal relationship with and appreciation of Mervyn Himbury, under a series of headings:

- The Mervyn I knew was first and foremost a preacher of the Word.
- The Mervyn I knew was a scholar, a tutor and a historian.
- The Mervyn I knew was a family man and a man of prayer.
- The Mervyn I knew was a compassionate counselor.
- The Mervyn I knew held strongly to his Baptist convictions.
- The Mervyn I knew was a builder for the future.

The concluding image of Warn's eulogy was also taken up by Maelor Himbury, in his brief statement:

> Whitley was a huge part of his life but there is one section of Whitley which reflects his character more than any other—this chapel. Here he had a free hand to do whatever he wanted and so it's to this chapel we must turn to get an understanding of the nature of the man.
>
> First you notice the stark simplicity of design—a reminder of the Calvinistic chapels of his youth. You may well now be cursing the fact that those old buildings did not have padded seats. This simplicity mirrors the nature of his faith—despite his considerable learning he never moved far from the basic concept of the wonder and love of God.
>
> Two features draw your attention—the cross of Christ, because that is the central symbol of our faith, and the pulpit—for above all, my father believed in the importance of proclaiming the word. There was no greater privilege or vocation.
>
> The back wall is plain glass and opens up on the rest of the college. The preacher can't help but see that there is a whole world outside the chapel and those outside can see that there are people worshipping within. He was never one to hide his faith away and was always concerned to integrate the Gospel with everyday life.
>
> So I return to my theme, "If you seek his memorial look around you,"—not just at the bricks and mortar but also the people around you. For the measure of a man is not just what he builds, not just what he achieves. The true measure of a man is his impact on those who encounter him as he passes on through.

Michael Himbury introduced the song he and Maelor would then sing, "Will the Circle Be Unbroken?"

> Our father always had a soft spot for country gospel. I think he felt a real connection with the raw heartfelt spirit in the lyrics and the singing. Whenever a country music festival concludes this song is sung and we thought it appropriate to sing it with you today.

Then followed the sermon, preached by Rev. Jim Barr, of Canberra Baptist Church. The following is a summary drawn from Jim Barr's manuscript. The title of the sermon was "Scribe, Preacher, and Priest," and the Scripture text was Nehemiah 8:1–6.

Sermon Preached by Rev. Jim Barr, of Canberra Baptist Church

How shall we select a text to preach on a day like this? For one trained in preaching by Mervyn Himbury the Old Testament glitters like a tray of jewels. So many of his own texts and sermons still ring in our ears:

- Make this valley full of ditches (2 Kgs 3:16)
- The thirty great ones of Israel . . . and Uriah the Hittite! (2 Sam 23)
- Give me this mountain! (Josh 14:12)
- The ax that floated (2 Kgs 6)
- The burden of silence (Isa 21:11)

In the end I have opted for a simple one: "And Ezra the scribe stood upon a pulpit of wood" (Neh 8:4).

The Scribe

In the seventh month the people gathered in the square before the Water Gate and called for Ezra the scribe, a man skilled at the law of Moses, one who had set his heart to study the law of the Lord, and to do it (Ezra 7:6–10).

"Find us a teacher worthy of the task," was their call.

In 1958 the call went out to Mervyn Himbury to be a teacher, a leader of the theological college of the Baptists in this state. He led the college for nearly three decades. He relocated and built the college on this site. He established a relationship with Melbourne University. He laid the foundations, physical and intellectual, for what Whitley College was to become.

Ezra and Nehemiah built walls to defend the city against its enemies. They established ethnic purity to guard against the polluting world. Mervyn Himbury built an open college, dedicated to spiritual and intellectual freedom, a learning community connected to the university and the life of the mind, and to the churches and the life of the faith.

He was a visionary and a builder, but he was also a scribe, a teacher who had set his heart to study the word of the Lord. His lectures could be rambling—I know, I was one of his students—but it was always an interesting ramble. His lectures could be charming and leisurely, but they could also be incisive, analytical, and challenging.

As it was with Martin Luther, his students learned as much from their social times and coffee breaks with him as we did in the lectures. This is an affirmation of a man who shared his life with students, not just his learning. On his retirement one of the gifts his students presented him was Luther's *Table Talk*.

He built this college, defended it against all the ecclesiastical and other inspectors who wanted to narrow its strictures and straighten its ways and control its coffers. He stamped his character on its culture and left an abiding heritage of freedom and faith.

The Preacher

The call went out in Nehemiah 8:1 for Ezra *the scribe*. Who actually showed up, according to verse 2, was Ezra *the priest*.

Having called for a principal, a man of the academy, Victorian Baptists welcomed a *preacher*, a man of the church. Like Ezra, is not every great theological teacher also a man or woman of the church? From his very first sermon the bush burned and we knew we stood on holy ground.

In the Authorized Version it says, "Ezra the scribe stood upon a pulpit of wood," (8:4). If the *genus* Himbury (that strange species) has a natural habitat, there can be no doubt it is the pulpit. Mervyn was a preacher—one of the greatest we have seen in Australia. Anyone here who knew him will have memories of sermons heard, texts glowing, hearts moved, minds crackling with new insights.

He delighted in the unusual or obscure or confronting text. He once preached to a service of bankers to mark some high and holy event of the financial world. His text was Acts 20:8 in the JB Philips translation: "To hell with you and your money! How dare you think you could buy the gift of God!"

It is his preaching that will live long in the minds and hearts of many of us. It was the preaching of a particular style, but it was magnificent preaching. We must not bind him to the styles and oratory of his age. He had an abiding passion for preaching and thought about, and worried for, the future of preaching. The NRSV translates this text "Ezra stood on a wooden platform." He was concerned with the platform, the foundation, on which preaching stood.

Mervyn did not always need a platform—in many ways he was his own platform. Many years ago there was an assembly missionary meeting at the Collins Street Church which clashed with the latest Ingmar Bergman film opening at the Athenaeum just next door. Mervyn and some friends decide to wag the missionary meeting and see the film. His friends arrived early to avoid devout Baptists and loitered at the rear of the foyer. Mervyn wandered up the lane behind the church, went to the vestry, chatted with the guest speaker and the leaders of the denomination and three minutes before the meeting (and the film!) started Mervyn left the vestry and made his royal progress up the aisle of the church, greeting the great and good of the denomination. When he got to the back of the church, he calmly slipped out the door and joined his friends for the movie. Mervyn is one of the few who could make a grand entrance, even when he was making an exit! He was a presence; he was his own platform.

He preached in a world where preachers were taken seriously and the church had significant standing, where the wooden platform did stand higher than ordinary folk.

He lived to see a world where the church and its message were being marginalized. Some years ago, we discussed this, and he wondered where the platform for preaching in the future might come from. Would it be preachers who were bi-vocational, who had standing as lawyers or doctors, or celebrities or scientists and used their social position as the platform for proclamation? Would it come from a church purged of social accommodations until the Gospel burned bright as a holy and countercultural message? These were the questions he engaged in later life: where was the platform for preaching to be found?

The Priest

But Ezra the priest was not just a preacher: "Ezra blessed the Lord, the great God. And all the people answered, Amen, Amen, with lifting up their hands: and they bowed their heads, and worshipped the Lord with their faces to the ground" (Neh 8:6).

Mervyn was a man of prayer, a great man of prayer. I have been with him in prayer as a student as he opened the lecture, as a colleague as we bowed together with Ron Ham in the study at Collins Street, and as a pastor as I visited with him.

Sometimes the eloquence of the preacher overwhelmed the simplicity of the poet, but oftentimes his words resonated with the rhythm of the Welsh bards and the spirit of the Celtic saints. His great gift was the short extempore prayer—the prayer to close a meeting or seal a pastoral conversation. Sometimes when Mervyn prayed everything in the room was lifted up, and all that was within us cried "Amen, Amen!"

You don't learn to pray like that in an armchair or in the soft and comfortable places of life. Often at the Lord's Table Mervyn would quote Psalm 116:12–13: "What shall I render unto the Lord for all his benefits toward me? I will take up the cup of salvation, and call upon the name of the Lord."

Yet the early part of that Psalm makes it clear that the writer has known times of struggle of opposition. Deep experiences of conflict and criticism had gone into that triumphant cry of faith. Mervyn knew such experiences.

Conclusion

A temptation that we all face is that we will see this college—these buildings—as Mervyn's memorial. In one sense that may be so but, in another, Mervyn Himbury was bigger than just a building. His commitment to freedom, his passion for preaching, his voice in prayer—these are his true gifts, the abiding foundation given us through him. More than bricks and mortar, this commitment to the life of the mind, this passion for the Word proclaimed, this powerful, prayerful spirit must be held on to. These must never be thrown off, discarded, let fall into disuse.

We have known among us one of the great ones of Israel: a scribe, and a preacher, and a priest. Let us bless the Lord, the great God, for his ministry and his message, and gratefully receive the legacy he has given us.

Thanksgiving Prayer Offered by Rev. Alan Marr, Director of Ministries, Baptist Union of Victoria

Loving God,

We are grateful for the life and ministry of your servant Mervyn Himbury.

We thank you for those who nurtured his life and faith from the beginning; for the people who invested love and time in him and helped prepare him for the ministry to which he was called.

We thank you that fifty years ago he heard the call from you to come here to Victoria and serve your church here. We thank you for his obedience to that call.

We thank you for the vision and courage he displayed and for the way he helped all of us to think outside the square and to see your creative spirit at work in unusual ways and places.

We thank you for his strong sense of self that enabled him to trust you and see dreams become reality.

We thank you for his determined spirit.

We thank you for his ability to lead us into your presence through his prayers and how your word came to life through his telling of the Gospel story and the preaching of the Good News.

We thank you for his leadership and for the pastoral care he offered to so many of us; thank you for the way he was able to see gifts and aptitudes in us that we were often unable to see in ourselves.

We thank you for Marion, Maelor, and Michael who have so willingly shared him with us.

We who have been his students, his colleagues in ministry, members of congregations in which he served, have been enriched and strengthened by the experiences. We pray that the legacy left to us by your servant Mervyn Himbury will journey with us calling us to be agents of the Gospel of freedom.

He taught us.
He inspired us.
He shocked us.
He entertained us.
He exasperated and frustrated us.
He believed in us.
He forgave us.
He prayed for us.
And we are grateful.

As we leave here today, we ask you to be our first companion. May grace, mercy, and peace from Father, Son, and Holy Spirit be with us all.

Amen.

Ash Placing Service

On February 28, 2009, a brief service was held in the front garden of The Mervyn Himbury Theological Studies Centre of Whitley College, for the placement of Himbury's ashes. Marion, Maelor, and Michael Himbury were present, together with several family friends. I conducted a brief ceremony.

A rose bush was planted and some weeks later a brass plaque was installed, bearing the inscription, together with the Whitley College logo:

> David Mervyn Himbury
> 1922–2008
> Founding Principal
> of Whitley College
> Man of God
> Preacher of the Word

Thanksgiving Service

The following day, Sunday March 1, 2009, St. David's Day, a service of thanksgiving was held at the Collins Street Baptist Church, with many more people in attendance than those able to gather in the college chapel for the funeral service. On this occasion, I was the preacher, and the following excerpts from that sermon provide the concluding elements to this account of Mervyn Himbury's life and ministry. The Scripture readings for that service were Psalm 116:5–19 and 2 Timothy 4:1–5, from the New Revised Standard Version.

> It is a special privilege for me to speak today, in this church where Mervyn Himbury used to preach, and a bunch of us as undergraduate students used to come here on Sunday nights to hear him: and often enough, to cram into his car for the joyride home.
>
> It is a special honor to try to do something Mervyn taught us and modeled for us: to preach from the word of God. I would like to do what he did very often: to take a text from the Old Testament, a text with some little peculiarity in it, and draw people to that strange image, and in doing so allow people to sense in an encouraging and fresh way that their lives, our lives, are with God.
>
> Psalm 116 was a text that Mervyn quoted often, especially at the Lord's Table:
>
> "What shall I render unto the Lord for all his benefits toward me?
>
> I will take up the cup of salvation, and call on the name of the Lord.
>
> I will pay my vows unto the Lord now in the presence of all his people."
>
> Those are verses twelve to fourteen, but the stanza actually goes on with one more verse, which links it back with the earlier verses, where the poet is both anguished, perhaps in some long-term illness or distress, yet is also trusting in God:
>
> This verse adds, "precious in the sight of the Lord is the death of his faithful ones."
>
> It seems a peculiar thing to say, especially after the earlier verses about suffering and anguish. They tell how God has delivered the poet's life from death. It says, "I walk before the Lord in the land of the living": yet now it seems to value the death of God's faithful, as if God wants that. Can we, after these last days of horror and disaster in our state, can we here today live with

the idea that God somehow wants the death of any of us, let alone the faithful ones?[1]

Even more puzzling, if we look to the Hebrew, which offers an alternate translation: Hard, or difficult, in the sight of the Lord, is the death of his faithful ones.

Difficult, and something to be wrestled with—maybe, paradoxically, that sounds a little easier to grasp.

Perhaps the psalmist is saying that if the faithful ones are going to die, God will not leave it at that, but will lift them and will *yet* make something of their lives.

Now that is something to think about!

What shall I render to the Lord for all his bounty to me?

Mervyn used this text often, because he was a gifted person, and he knew it.

He used to say that he marveled that the Almighty took time off from running the universe to call him to the ministry. Such was his intimate relationship with God. He felt that God had given him so many opportunities, and he was grateful.

As I have thought about his life, these days, I recognize in him a rich and deep gratitude. Because he was gifted, he felt obligated: he was given intelligence, a voice—such a voice—and a presence, to use—influence, abilities to lead people, encourage and inspire, even provoke: to stir up something exciting, something hopeful, to make people feel that they had something to give, to do, to venture.

He felt obligated to use his gifts for God and for the good of people, to help them to be who they could be.

My first encounter with him was as a boy from school. He recognized my need, a boy from a coal mining community, an impoverished school, but with the potential to go to university. He made that possible for me.

Within the college, he did this for so many kids from the country, to make sure, for example, that people actually had food to eat, because he had known many who could not do well at their studies because they were simply too hungry.

I remember the day he said to several of us, "I've got to do something about Gill." He was very concerned about the happenings in Queensland, when Athol Gill lost his position teaching at the Baptist college. Mervyn got on a plane and went there, to talk to Athol, to make sure his gift and potential would not be lost; and eventually Athol came to Whitley.

---

1. Just weeks before, there had been horrendous bushfires in Victoria, when 173 people lost their lives, 7500 people lost their homes and 3500 buildings were destroyed.

Mervyn was determined to use his skills, abilities, influence, to lift high the cup of salvation, to open the way of freedom and hope for people.

One of his first students told me that when he came to Melbourne, he sensed that most students and most pastors were in a kind of social straitjacket. It was the era of short back and sides haircuts, and a fairly puritanical ethos among Baptists. Many were aghast at his smoking habit, but more broadly he set about to push back the barriers and conventions.

So he grew his hair long and exaggerated his habits and histrionic style, making fun of himself and of the conventions that bound people: and all the while reminding Baptists that they are the descendants of a radical religious and political freedom.

Generations of students are indebted to him, for his unconventional yet patient commitment to our growth, our freedom, our potential.

Mervyn was a gifted man, grateful and gracious, in giving and living for others.

"What shall I render unto the Lord for all his benefits toward me?

I will take the cup of salvation, and call upon the name of the Lord."

This brings us to our second reading, from 2 Timothy, which calls upon the preacher to be faithful in proclaiming the message, in season and out of season, even when people don't want to hear: and it concludes, "do the work of an evangelist." Preach the Gospel!

In February 1959, two great Baptist preachers came to Melbourne. One of them conducted evangelistic crusades, which were to have a very deep influence on our community and our churches. The other came to head our college, to train pastors and preachers, *and to do the work of an evangelist*.

And with those two great preachers, there came, and there remains, a significant challenge for us: it is one thing to be evangelistic, for a short time, and another thing to be continually evangelical—to preach the Gospel in season and out of season, fully and persistently.

Mervyn Himbury did it.

There is something else fundamental to his life and faith, which is vital for us today. Mervyn, and Marion with him, was an adventurer. He was willing to venture something for God. That, I think, is why the figure of Abraham was one he relished so much.

Roslyn Otzen's history of Whitley College tells about the time when the young Himbury couple went to Switzerland, where Mervyn was teaching at the Ecumenical Institute; and, feeling the strictures of their life in South Wales, they wondered what it might be like to venture somewhere else in the world, to find a future somewhere else. Then came the call to travel twelve thousand miles to Melbourne, to help build a new college. They came, and again and again Mervyn did that—he took a punt, as he used to say—he tried something new, something different, pushing back the barriers of freedom, for people, for the church, for God.

As a good historian, he studied the documents and found that nothing in our procedures limited ordained ministry to men: so he opened the way for women to be ordained in this state, before most other churches could even talk about it. He changed Whitley from an all-male residential college to a coed community, and what a transformation that was, and all the others followed.

Mervyn was an adventurer, willing to have a go: and he encouraged others to do so. Back in the 1960s he encouraged people to develop new forms of church, in a whole range of contexts, some of which are now being re-invented and called "emerging church," or "new missional communities." He saw the need for change and experimentation back then and encouraged students to have a go.

He knew what it is to be gifted, and that it should make us grateful, and stir us to gracious giving, in service for others.

When it was first proposed that I might take up the role of principal of the college, I went to see Mervyn, and he said something to me then which he repeated in what was to be my last real conversation with him.

He said that people imagine that he would be critical of change within the college, but in fact, if anything he would be critical that there has not been more change.

I think we need to take him at his word. We need to consider carefully and courageously what we now do with all that he has given us.

Mervyn Himbury was a man of God, and preacher of the word.

He knew that he was gifted, and for that he was grateful, and obligated: to do all he could, to lift high the cup of salvation, to pay his vows to the Lord, in the presence of *all* God's people.

Now, it is our turn. His life and ministry are a provocation to us.

This is no easy thing.

What shall *we* render to the Lord, for all we have received, through the life of Mervyn Himbury?

Our response calls us to consider how God sees the life of this, one of God's faithful ones.

Precious in the sight of the Lord is the death of his faithful ones: precious, and difficult, hard to take: *unless* God is able to make something of that life and death, to lift up this life, and make yet more of it.

And that means for us to pick up the baton, and to run with this challenge: that we, too, should see how gifted we are, and how we can be people of the word, churches which live and speak the Gospel, not just evangelistic, but evangelical in all we are, and people who push back the boundaries of freedom and hope, for all people:

All this grounded in that one conviction, that God is God, no matter what happens. There is a providence that gives, that graces, that invites and provokes us to new ventures, across the oceans, across the risks and challenges of starting and running a college, leading a people, bringing up a family, nurturing young lives. Have a go, trusting in God.

Mervyn lived his life as a follower of Jesus Christ, who proclaimed and lived and died in this providence of God.

And as Jesus's own life was lifted up by God, so too we believe that Mervyn has been lifted up: precious in the sight of God is the life and death of his faithful ones.

Prayer of Thanksgiving

O Gracious and Loving God, whose heart is always open to our pleadings, we come before you with thanksgiving and humility as you invite us to follow you into the future.

We pray today for all who knowingly or unknowingly are heirs of Mervyn Himbury's rich life and ministry; who have benefited from his rich legacy, his love of the Gospel and preaching, his commitment to prayer and care for his students and the churches of the Baptist union; his valuing of the life of the mind, ideas and learning in the service of others; his love for the world, expressed in his affection for those students to whom he referred with a caring heart as "The Great Unwashed"; his love of the church, particularly its expression in Baptist life and witness in local churches gathered together to discern the mind of Christ.

We pray for all whose lives have been shaped in one way or another by David Mervyn Himbury.

For those who exercise leadership in society: in business, law, politics, science, health, the arts, and the media; may they act with integrity, wisdom, creativity and courage.

For those who have entered the ordained ministry of the church with its preaching, teaching, pastoral care, mission, and prayer; may they hone their crafts; be inspired and inspiring; have insight, faithfulness, compassion, and courage.

For those who use the media to relate faith to life, as Mervyn did in radio and television. Make them responsible. Keep them from compromise and dullness. May their message have substance, relevance, and interest.

For those who take risks and go against the tide of convention to build a dream. Protect them and help them to persevere.

For all who honor the Baptist story and have caught something of Mervyn's love of those early radical Puritans—with their courage, love of Bible, passion for conversion, holiness; belief in the freedom of conscience and the fellowship of believers.

May we live that story and breathe new life into it in our communities of faith. May we keep it alive and write it down for this generation and the generations to come. May the Baptist story live in the broader histories of humankind. Let it not be lost!

We pray for Whitley College—its leadership, staff, and students (present and future). Give its leaders wisdom and sensitivity to make appropriate changes in response to present needs and future directions of church and society. Keep it faithful to its charter of preparing men and women for leadership in church and society. May it find inspiration in Mervyn Himbury's life and ministry, allowing it to plot its future course.

We pray for Mervyn's family—for Marion, Maelor, and Michael. May the memories of their beloved husband and father give them strength and comfort in the present, and guidance for the future.

Finally, our gracious and loving God, we pray for this world that Mervyn loved—for whom he faithfully prayed and led us to pray; for those who suffer because of war, intolerance, famine, natural disasters, illness, dislocation, isolation or addiction—may they receive your help and comfort, hope and healing. Help us to participate in that process through Jesus Christ.

And may the Good News continue to be lived and proclaimed in every corner of the globe.

For we ask this in the name of the Trinity; God our creator, Christ our redeemer, and the Holy Spirit, our sustainer and friend.

Amen.

(Rev. Dr. Marita Munro)[1]

---

1. Adapted from the Prayer of Thanksgiving written and offered by Rev. Dr. Marita Munro at the thanksgiving service at Collins Street Baptist Church, March 1, 2009.

Appendix A

Minute of Appreciation

MINUTE OF APPRECIATION ADOPTED by the 124th Annual Assembly of the Baptist Union of Victoria on the recommendation of the College Council to record the service of Principal Himbury over the last twenty-seven years (October 1986)

Minute of Appreciation: The Rev. Principal D. M. Himbury MA, BD, BLitt.

SINCE HIS APPOINTMENT IN 1959 as principal of the Baptist College of Victoria, now Whitley College: the Baptist College of Victoria, David Mervyn Himbury has given of himself unstintingly in the service of his Lord in the carrying out of that task.

Mervyn Himbury was born in 1922 in Wales. He graduated in arts (with first class honors in history) and divinity at the University College of South Wales (Cardiff), University of Wales. In his postgraduate studies at Regent's Park College, University of Oxford, he took his degree in letters. The degree of master of arts was subsequently conferred on him by the University of Melbourne.

He came to Victoria having been ordained at Chester Street Baptist Church, Wrexham, and having served as professor of church history at the South Wales Baptist College.

He was firstly at Errol Street and was part of the thrust toward the development of the proposed university college on the land that had been purchased in Royal Parade where Whitley College now stands.

He was an energetic and whole-hearted member of the team that traveled throughout the state to raise funds which were essential for the building of the new college. The vision, enhanced by the undoubted capacity and enthusiasm of the new principal, caught the imagination of our people, and the funds raised enabled the project to proceed with the foundation stone unveiled on September 1, 1962.

On February 25, 1965, Whitley College was opened by Sir Robert Menzies and the denomination gave thanks to God for all that had been accomplished.

For Mervyn Himbury, the building of the college has not ceased. He has applied himself and given of himself so that the purposes of the college might be realized in the lives of the men and women who have been its students. For him they have been "my students," and the college has been "my college." As principal, he has evidenced a particular care of the secular students, and has been freely available to them to counsel, assist, and encourage them. Suppers in Helwys House with the principal and his wife have been a feature of college life over the years.

The college has added to its buildings, and has increased the number of students, so that there is now a body of some 140 secular students and around eighty students undertaking theological studies.

During his principalship, special attention has been given by him and the members of the college staff to ensuring that the standards of ministerial training have been raised commensurately with the general academic standards within the community.

In 1979, following earlier sharing on a joint faculty basis, the Evangelical Theological Association was formed in association with the College of the Bible of the Churches of Christ in Australia for the purpose of conducting courses for undergraduate and postgraduate degrees and examining for those degrees.

In the University of Melbourne and its councils, and among his fellow heads of colleges associated with the university, Mervyn Himbury is held in high regard.

In our churches, he has been recognized in our pulpits as a preacher of outstanding merit, one who loves the word of God, and proclaims the Gospel of our Lord Jesus Christ. He has undertaken extensive interim ministries in our churches, and has demonstrated his love for the people of those churches in which he has ministered.

Mervyn Himbury has served our union in many of its councils, and has had a considerable involvement in the work of the executive council of the union over all the years. His particular delight and privilege has been to present the students of the college to the union for ordination, and in doing that he has reminded the union of its responsibilities in the bringing forward and the training of these men and women.

Marion Himbury has been a treasure of love and concern for the well-being of the students and the college. She has entered into the life of the churches, and has been part of the women's work of our union and beyond. She has shared with Mervyn his interest in the worldwide Baptist scene. She is loved by all, and we pay tribute to her.

The successful development of important social traditions at Whitley, and the integration of theological training and the work of the university college, are due in no small measure to the life and work of Mervyn Himbury. At all times he has been diligent in his administration of the college to see that the funds available to the college have the capacity to ensure its future.

The union, the college council, and the members of the teaching staff join in giving thanks to God for all that has been achieved at the college through Mervyn Himbury over the past twenty-seven years.

We pray that God will richly bless him and his wife, Marion, in all the days that follow on from his retirement as principal on December 31, 1986.

We honor you, Mervyn Himbury, for your contribution to the life of our college and of our union.

(signed)
O. C. Abbott
President, Whitley College

Appendix B

Eulogy by Rev. Milton Warn, First Registrar of Whitley College

The Mervyn I Knew

MARION, I WAS VERY CONSCIOUS of the honor you conferred on me when you asked me to deliver the eulogy at today's service of thanksgiving. I am aware that there are some among us who have known Mervyn as long as I, so I decided that I would attempt to recall Mervyn, as I knew him.

The Mervyn I knew was first and foremost a *preacher of the word*. That was what he was doing when, almost fifty years ago, I first saw him. I was thirty-five at the time, pastor of the Traralgon Church, and just starting my exit thesis at the Baptist College of Victoria. I had come to the Collins Street Baptist Church for the induction service of the new principal of the college. Having been inducted, he was called upon to preach. *Never in my life had I heard such preaching*! That night, driving back home, I had but one thought—if only I could preach like that! But from that night on, Mervyn was constantly proclaiming the word to the enrichment of the lives of countless people throughout our state and beyond.

Mervyn loved to preach. The college death notice stressed this aspect of his life—"As a preacher he has been the standard to guide us and inspire us." Mervyn loved to preach, and perhaps never more than in chapel among his students. I will relate one experience. On one occasion, for the regular chapel service, no one turned up to preach. With only a few minutes' notice, Mervyn preached. Afterward, when I expressed my amazement, he said, "I would rather die than say I'm not ready to preach."

The Mervyn I knew was a *scholar, a tutor, and a historian*. He had left his position as tutor of church history at Cardiff Baptist College to come to the Victorian Baptist College. In the first year of his principalship, Carey Press in England asked him to write a Baptist history, mainly for young people. In those hectic years when he was involved in fundraising, he completed it, and it was published as *British Baptists: A Short History* in 1962. So history was his field and I wanted the topic of my thesis to be in the field of church history.

A week or so after that first, if distant, contact with Mervyn, I was actually in his presence to discuss my exit thesis. At first, we talked in general about our personal histories and experiences. We seemed to take to one another, which was not surprising for there was only a difference of two years in our ages. He approved of my suggestion that the topic of the thesis be "The Baptist Doctrine of the Church Prior to 1660," but warned me that the materials for research would be very brief. I should look at the question of Anabaptist influence upon English Baptists. He offered me use of some of his books, arranged for me to meet with him monthly, and sent me on my way with a word I would hear often in the future—"Blessings."

The Mervyn I knew was a *family man and a man of prayer*. In 1963 I joined the college staff as registrar and during that year was also the interim preacher for the Aberdeen Street Baptist Church, Geelong. It had a large manse, partially furnished, and I arranged that the Himbury and Warn families could use it as a base for the Christmas–New Year holiday fortnight. We all got on very well together—the five children played together; Marion and Clare cooked; Mervyn and I cleaned up—I think! A highlight for me were the after-breakfast family prayers led by Mervyn. His daily prayers were an enrichment to my life. It was the same within the college life. Mervyn's prayers in chapel revealed a man who was intimate with God.

The Mervyn I knew was a *compassionate counselor*. He often said that he had gathered around him a college executive of strong, brilliant, capable men, and that he had to be able to convince them of the feasibility of any projects he presented. Sometimes meetings could become battlegrounds! More than once, one member or another would feel that the others were not listening to their contributions. Resignations were offered. I have known Mervyn to spend late night hours or Saturday mornings listening to and helping such members. In my time, he lost none of them. One of them was a person who served the college longer than any other.

Students of the college, university or ministerial, often sought his advice and help.

On a personal note, there was a time after I had left the college when I profited from Mervyn's advice.

The Mervyn I knew held strongly to his Baptist convictions. Mervyn, and his understanding of the Christian faith, were not acceptable to some Victorian Baptists. There were occasions when he was slandered. Very early in his appointment, when the appeal for funds for the new college was in its infancy, he was approached by a well-known Baptist layman who was prepared to make a very large gift for the new college. The man would make the gift on the condition that all who taught in it would sign a faith statement prepared by him. Mervyn explained to him that Baptists held to the principle that each person must be free to interpret and proclaim the Scriptures. Mervyn valued greatly Baptist freedom of belief when interpreting the Scriptures.

The Mervyn I knew was *a builder for the future.* We are met in the chapel of a college that will continue to serve the church and the men and women of Australia for generations only because Mervyn Himbury arrived fifty years ago, saw the possibilities, and dedicated all his energy and ability to turn what was a dream into a reality.

In the crypt of St. Paul's Cathedral, London, where the builder Sir Christopher Wren is buried, there is on his burial slab the words, "Reader, if you seek his memorial, look around you." These words can equally be said of Mervyn Himbury. There were two men responsible for Victorian Baptists building this college–John Hopkins, who originally dreamed up the idea, and Mervyn Himbury who turned the dream into reality. In this college there is a memorial to John Hopkins. Should there not be, perhaps in this chapel, a memorial to the other?

Appendix C

Sermon Preached by Rev. Jim Barr, of Canberra Baptist Church

"Scribe, Preacher, and Priest."

SCRIPTURE TEXT: NEHEMIAH 8:1–6

How shall we select a text to preach on a day like this? For one trained in preaching by Mervyn Himbury the Old Testament glitters like a tray of jewels:

- There were giants in the earth in those days (Gen 6:4).
- Those who lead many to righteousness, shall be like the stars for ever and ever (Dan 12:3).
- The chariots of Israel and its horsemen! (2 Kgs 2:12)

So many of his own texts and sermons still ring in our ears:

- Make this valley full of ditches (2 Kgs 3:16).
- The thirty great ones of Israel . . . and Uriah the Hittite! (2 Sam 23)
- Give me this mountain! (Josh 14:12)
- The ax that floated (2 Kgs 6).
- The burden of silence (Isa 21:11).

In the end I have opted for a simple one: And Ezra the scribe stood upon a pulpit of wood (Neh. 8:4).

The Scribe

In the seventh month the people gathered in the square before the Water Gate and called for Ezra the scribe, a man skilled at the law of Moses, one who had set his heart to study the law of the Lord, and to do it (Ezra 7:6–10).

"Find us a teacher worthy of the task," was their call.

In 1958 the call went out to Mervyn Himbury to be a teacher, a leader of the theological college of the Baptists in this state. He led the college for nearly three decades. He relocated and built the college on this site. He established a relationship with Melbourne University. He laid the foundations, physical and intellectual, for what Whitley College was to become.

During the fundraising for the new college a check was received from a wealthy Christian businessman for the sum of ten pounds. John Hopkins went to him and pointed out that the check had an error in it. The donor took up his pen and perused his check. "I can't see a problem," he said.

"You've left off the three zeros after the ten," replied John.

"Well, I'll consider it," came the reply.

The businessman duly turned up in Mervyn's study and passed across the desk a check for ten thousand pounds, a sum that the new college desperately needed. He also handed across a typed sheet of paper. "I will give you this check," said the businessman, "if you have every professor of this college sign this statement of faith."

Mervyn replied, "Sir, your generosity toward this college gladdens our hearts and we do appreciate it; but I have to inform you that there are some things that are not for sale. Good day to you."

Ezra and Nehemiah built walls to defend the city against its enemies. They established ethnic purity to guard against the polluting world. Mervyn Himbury built an open college, dedicated to spiritual and intellectual freedom, a learning community connected to the university and the life of the mind, and to the churches and the life of the faith.

He was a visionary and a builder, but he was also a scribe, a teacher who had set his heart to study the word of the Lord. His lectures could be rambling—I know, I was one of his students—but it was always an interesting ramble. His lectures could be charming and leisurely, but they could also be incisive, analytical, and challenging.

In these days when everything has to be measured, I can say that there is a robust and accurate measure of Mervyn's teaching. For one whole year I kept count of the *"wassum"*—that evocative and helpful word that sometimes crept into the principal's discourse. The "wassum count" ranged from as many as seventeen per hour to as few as two per hour. The less connected the lecturer was to the lecture, the more wassums would creep in. Any lecture below wassum 3–4 on the scale was wonderful!

As it was with Martin Luther, his students learned as much from their social times and coffee breaks with him as we did in the lectures. This is an affirmation of a man who shared his life with students, not just his learning. On his retirement one of the gifts his students presented him was Luther's *Table Talk*.

He built this college, defended it against all the ecclesiastical and other inspectors who wanted to narrow its strictures and straighten its ways and control its coffers. He stamped his character on its culture and left an abiding heritage of freedom and faith.

The Preacher

The call went out in Nehemiah 8:1 for Ezra *the scribe*. Who actually showed up, according to verse 2, was Ezra *the priest*.

Having called for a principal, a man of the academy, Victorian Baptists welcomed a *preacher*, a man of the church. Like Ezra, is not every great theological teacher also a man or woman of the church? From his very first sermon the bush burned and we knew we stood on holy ground.

In the Authorized Version it says, "Ezra stood upon a pulpit of wood," (Neh 8:4). If the *genus* Himbury (that strange species) has a natural habitat, there can be no doubt it is the pulpit. Mervyn was a preacher—one of the greatest we have seen in Australia. Anyone here who knew him will have memories of sermons heard, texts glowing, hearts moved, minds crackling with new insights.

He delighted in the unusual or obscure or confronting text. He once preached to a service of bankers to mark some high and holy event of the financial world. His text was Acts 20:8 in the JB Philips translation: "To hell with you and your money! How dare you think you could buy the gift of God!"

It is his preaching that will live long in the minds and hearts of many of us. It was the preaching of a particular style, but it was magnificent preaching. We must not bind him to the styles and oratory of his age. He had an abiding passion for preaching and thought about, and worried for, the future of preaching. The NRSV translates this text "Ezra stood on a wooden platform." He was concerned with the platform, the foundation, on which preaching stood.

Mervyn didn't always need a platform—in many ways he was his own platform. Many years ago there was an assembly missionary meeting at the Collins Street Church which clashed with the latest Ingmar Bergman film opening at the Athenaeum just next door. Mervyn and some friends decide to wag the missionary meeting and see the film. His friends arrived early to avoid devout Baptists and loitered at the rear of the foyer. Mervyn wandered up the lane behind the church, went to the vestry, chatted with the guest speaker and the leaders of the denomination and three minutes before the meeting (and the film!) started, Mervyn left the vestry and made his royal progress up the aisle of the church, greeting the great and good of the denomination. When he got to the back of the church, he calmly slipped out the door and joined his friends for the movie. Mervyn is one of the few who could make a grand entrance, even when he was making an exit! He was a presence; he was his own platform.

He preached in a world where preachers were taken seriously and the church had significant standing, where the wooden platform did stand higher than ordinary folk.

He lived to see a world where the church and its message were being marginalized. Some years ago, we discussed this, and he wondered where the platform for preaching in the future might come from. Would it be preachers who were bi-vocational, who had standing as lawyers or doctors, or celebrities or scientists, and used their social position as the platform for proclamation? Would it come from a church purged of social accommodations until the Gospel burned bright as a holy and countercultural message? These were the questions he engaged in later life: where was the platform for preaching to be found? Was it a wooden or an electronic platform? Will it be built in the lofty temple or in the public square before the Water Gate?

The Priest

But Ezra the priest was not just a preacher: "And Ezra blessed the Lord, the great God. And all the people answered, Amen, Amen, with lifting up their hands: and they bowed their heads, and worshipped the Lord with their faces to the ground" (Neh. 8:6).

Mervyn was a man of prayer, a great man of prayer. I have been with him in prayer as a student as he opened the lecture, as a colleague as we bowed together with Ron Ham in the study at Collins Street, and as a pastor as I visited with him.

Sometimes the eloquence of the preacher overwhelmed the simplicity of the poet, but oftentimes his words resonated with the rhythm of the Welsh bards and the spirit of the Celtic saints. His great gift was the short extempore prayer—the prayer to close a meeting or seal a pastoral conversation. Sometimes when Mervyn prayed everything in the room was lifted up, and all that was within us cried "Amen, Amen!"

You don't learn to pray like that in an armchair or in the soft and comfortable places of life. Often at the Lord's Table Mervyn would quote Psalm 116: "What shall I render unto the Lord for all his benefits toward me? I will take the cup of salvation, and call upon the name of the Lord."

Yet the early part of that Psalm makes it clear that the writer has known times of struggle of opposition. Deep experiences of conflict and criticism had gone into that triumphant cry of faith. Mervyn knew such experiences. At one point when the college and its principal in particular were under pressure and being scrutinized by various people, a member of the Students' Association Executive felt he'd like to write to the principal pointing out everything that was wrong with the college and what might be improved. I suggested this might not be a good time, but the Lord had laid it on his heart, and he was not to be dissuaded. The principal summoned him to his study to discuss the letter. Before he had even taken his seat, Mervyn said, "Well, Mr. 'Smith,' I have received your letter of resignation from the Christian ministry and from this college. Is there anything you wish to add before I accept it?"

Conclusion

A temptation that we all face is that we will see this college—these buildings—as Mervyn's memorial. In one sense that may be so but, in another, Mervyn Himbury was bigger than just a building. His commitment to freedom, his passion for preaching, his voice in prayer—these are his true gifts, the abiding foundation given us through him. More than bricks and mortar, this commitment to the life of the mind, this passion for the word proclaimed, this powerful, prayerful spirit must be held on to. These must never be thrown off, discarded, let fall into disuse.

We have known among us one of the great ones of Israel: a scribe, and a preacher, and a priest. Let us bless the Lord, the great God, for his ministry and his message, and gratefully receive the legacy he has given us.

You who teach and study in this place which he built, maintain his commitment to scholarship and freedom.

You who preach, as he labored and cajoled and encouraged a generation to preach, let his love of the Scripture and his passion for the breadth of life inspire and inform you as you climb to those platforms of timber or steel or electronic media or whatever it is that gives the framework for your ministry.

And you who knew and loved him, who glimpsed glory in his preaching and found grace in his friendship, "bless the Lord, the great God," who fashioned him and called him, and gave him to us. Lift up the cup of salvation and call on the name of the Lord. Continue in prayer as he prayed continually. Stand up to preach and bow down to worship. And when the word of the Lord draws near and the presence of God is real, as it happened so often when he led us, may all that is within us rise up and cry out, "Amen! Amen! Amen!"

Appendix D

Thanksgiving Prayer Offered by Rev. Alan Marr, Director of Ministries, Baptist Union of Victoria

Loving God,

We are grateful for the life and ministry of your servant Mervyn Himbury.

We thank you for those who nurtured his life and faith from the beginning; for the people who invested love and time in him and helped prepare him for the ministry to which he was called.

We thank you that fifty years ago he heard the call from you to come here to Victoria and serve your church here. We thank you for his obedience to that call.

We thank you for the vision and courage he displayed and for the way he helped all of us to think outside the square and to see your creative spirit at work in unusual ways and places.

We thank you for his strong sense of self that enabled him to trust you and see dreams become reality.

We thank you for his determined spirit.

We thank you for his ability to lead us into your presence through his prayers and how your word came to life through his telling of the Gospel story and the preaching of the good news.

We thank you for his leadership and for the pastoral care he offered to so many of us; thank you for the way he was able to see gifts and aptitudes in us that we were often unable to see in ourselves.

We thank you for Marion, Maelor, and Michael who have so willingly shared him with us.

We who have been his students, his colleagues in ministry, members of congregations in which he served, have been enriched and strengthened by the experiences. We pray that the legacy left to us by your servant Mervyn Himbury will journey with us calling us to be agents of the Gospel of freedom.

He taught us
He inspired us
He shocked us
He entertained us
He exasperated and frustrated us
He believed in us
He forgave us
He prayed for us
And we are grateful.

As we leave here today, we ask you to be our first companion. May grace, mercy, and peace from Father, Son, and Holy Spirit be with us all.

Amen.

Appendix E

Thanksgiving Service by Rev. Dr. Frank Rees

It is a special privilege for me to speak today, in this church where Mervyn Himbury used to preach, and a bunch of us as undergraduate students used to come here on Sunday nights to hear him: and often enough, to cram into his car for the joyride home.

It is a special honor to try to do something Mervyn taught us and modeled for us: to preach from the word of God. I would like to do what he did very often: to take a text from the Old Testament, a text with some little peculiarity in it, and draw people to that strange image, and in doing so allow people to sense in an encouraging and fresh way that their lives, our lives, are with God.

Mervyn was an encouraging preacher. After he preached at my induction in Hobart, another pastor said to me that Mervyn had made every pastor feel good about their calling: both challenged and honored.

Psalm 116 was a text that Mervyn quoted often, especially at the Lord's Table:

"What shall I render to the Lord for all his bounty to me?

I will lift up the cup of salvation and call upon the name of the Lord.

I will pay my vows to the Lord, in the presence of all his people" (Ps 116:12-14, NRSV)

Those are verses twelve to fourteen, but the stanza actually goes on with one more verse, which links it back with the earlier verses, where the poet is both anguished, perhaps in some long-term illness or distress, yet is also trusting in God:

This verse adds, "*precious* in the sight of the Lord is the death of his faithful ones."

It seems a peculiar thing to say, especially after the earlier verses about suffering and anguish. They tell how God has delivered the poet's life from death. It says, "I walk before the Lord in the land of the living": yet now it seems to value the death of God's faithful, as if God wants that. Can we, after these last days of horror and disaster in our state, can we here today live with the idea that God somehow wants the death of any of us, let alone the faithful ones?[1]

Even more puzzling, if we look to the Hebrew, which offers an alternate translation: Hard, or difficult, in the sight of the Lord, is the death of his faithful ones.

Difficult, and something to be wrestled with—maybe, paradoxically, that sounds a little easier to grasp.

Perhaps the psalmist is saying that if the faithful ones are going to die, God will not leave it at that, but will lift them and will *yet* make something of their lives.

Now that is something to think about!

What shall I render to the Lord for all his bounty to me?

Mervyn used this text often, because he was a gifted person, and he knew it.

He used to say that he marveled that the Almighty took time off from running the universe to call him to the ministry. Such was his intimate relationship with God. He felt that God had given him so many opportunities, and he was grateful.

As I have thought about his life, these days, I recognize in him a rich and deep gratitude. Because he was gifted, he felt obligated: he was given intelligence, a voice—such a voice—and a presence, to use—influence, abilities to lead people, encourage and inspire, even provoke: to stir up something exciting, something hopeful, to make people feel that they had something to give, to do, to venture.

He felt obligated to use his gifts for God and for the good of people, to help them to be who they could be.

My first encounter with him was as a boy from school. He recognized my need, a boy from a coal mining community, an impoverished school, but with the potential to go to university. He made that possible for me.

---

1. Just weeks before, there had been horrendous bushfires in Victoria, when 173 people lost their lives, 7500 people lost their homes and 3500 buildings were destroyed.

I had not done all the right subjects to get into Arts at Melbourne. So Mervyn picked up the phone and he spoke to the registrar at the university, who happened to be a Baptist, to ask him was there a way through the system, how could this happen? And within the college, he did this for so many kids from the country, to make sure, for example, that people actually had food to eat, because he had known many who could not do well at their studies because they were simply too hungry.

I remember the day he said to several of us, "I've got to do something about Gill." He was very concerned about the happenings in Queensland, when Athol Gill lost his position teaching at the Baptist college. Mervyn got on a plane and went there, to talk to Athol, to make sure his gift and potential would not be lost; and eventually Athol came to Whitley. The rest is history.

Mervyn was determined to use his skills, abilities, influence, to lift high the cup of salvation, to open the way of freedom and hope for people.

One of his first students told me that when he came to Melbourne, he sensed that most students and most pastors were in a kind of social straitjacket. It was the era of short back and sides haircuts, and a fairly puritanical ethos among Baptists. Many were aghast at his smoking habit, but more broadly he set about to push back the barriers and conventions.

So he grew his hair long and exaggerated his habits and histrionic style, making fun of himself and of the conventions that bound people: and all the while reminding Baptists that they are the descendants of a radical religious and political freedom.

Generations of students are indebted to him, for his unconventional yet patient commitment to our growth, our freedom, our potential.

Mervyn was a gifted man, grateful and gracious, in giving and living for others.

"What shall I render to the Lord for all his bounty to me?

I will lift up the cup of salvation and call upon the name of the Lord."

This brings us to our second reading, from 2 Timothy, which calls upon the preacher to be faithful in proclaiming the message, in season and out of season, even when people don't want to hear: and it concludes, "do the work of an evangelist." Preach the Gospel!

In February 1959, two great Baptist preachers came to Melbourne. One of them conducted evangelistic crusades, which were to have a very deep influence on our community and our churches. The other came to head our college, to train pastors and preachers, *and* to do the work of an evangelist.

And with those two great preachers, there came, and there remains, a significant challenge for us: it is one thing to be evangelistic, for a short time, and another thing to be continually evangelical—to preach the Gospel in season and out of season, fully and persistently.

Mervyn Himbury did it.

I remember as a student the stir it caused among some churches when Mervyn agreed one Easter to preach at an ecumenical service, to be held in a large suburban carpark. He would take every opportunity to do the work of an evangelist, whether the protectors of Baptist piety approved or not. He refused to accept the idea that he shouldn't preach the Gospel someplace just because there might be some Catholics present.

All that expresses something else fundamental to his life and faith, which is vital for us today. Mervyn, and Marion with him, was an adventurer. He was willing to venture something for God. That, I think, is why the figure of Abraham was one he relished so much.

Roslyn Otzen's history of Whitley College tells about the time when the young Himbury couple went to Switzerland, where Mervyn was teaching at the Ecumenical Institute; and, feeling the strictures of their life in South Wales, they wondered what it might be like to venture somewhere else in the world, to find a future somewhere else. Then came the call to travel twelve thousand miles to Melbourne, to help build a new college. They came, and again and again Mervyn did that—he took a punt, as he used to say—he tried something new, something different, pushing back the barriers of freedom, for people, for the church, for God.

As a good historian, he studied the documents and found that nothing in our procedures limited ordained ministry to men: so he opened the way for women to be ordained in this state, before most other churches could even talk about it. He changed Whitley from an all-male residential college to a coed community, and what a transformation that was, and all the others followed.

Mervyn was an adventurer, willing to have a go: and he encouraged others to do so. Back in the 1960s he encouraged people to develop new forms of church, in a whole range of contexts, some of which are now being re-invented and called "emerging church," or "new missional communities." He saw the need for change and experimentation back then and encouraged students to have a go.

When Merilyn and I were married, he said to us that as we make our lives in ministry, we must not allow ourselves to settle down and get lost somewhere in the suburbs. There is a big world out there, needing our contribution. Don't get lost in your own little world.

A year later, when I completed my BD Honors, Mervyn was, I think, even more delighted than I was with my exam results. He used to trumpet these achievements around the place, but to me he wrote a beautiful card of congratulations. But then, true to his style, he added these words of Jesus: "From everyone to whom much has been given, much will be required" (Luke 12:48).

He knew what it is to be gifted, and that it should make us grateful, and stir us to gracious giving, in service for others.

When it was first proposed that I might take up the role of principal of the college, I went to see Mervyn, and he said something to me then which he repeated in what was to be my last real conversation with him.

He said that people imagine that he would be critical of change within the college, but in fact, if anything he would be critical that there has not been more change.

I think we need to take him at his word. We need to consider carefully and courageously what we now do with all that he has given us.

Mervyn Himbury was a man of God, and preacher of the word.

He knew that he was gifted, and for that he was grateful, and obligated: to do all he could, to lift high the cup of salvation, to pay his vows to the Lord, in the presence of *all* God's people.

Now, it is our turn. His life and ministry are a provocation to us.

This is no easy thing.

What shall *we* render to the Lord, for all we have received, through the life of Mervyn Himbury?

Our response calls us to consider how God sees the life of this, one of God's faithful ones.

Precious in the sight of the Lord is the death of his faithful ones: precious, and difficult, hard to take: *unless* God is able to make something of that life and death, to lift up this life, and make yet more of it.

And that means for us to pick up the baton, and to run with this challenge: that we, too, should see how gifted we are, and how we can be people of the word, churches which live and speak the Gospel, not just evangelistic, but evangelical in all we are, and people who push back the boundaries of freedom and hope, for all people:

All this grounded in that one conviction, that God is God, no matter what happens. There is a providence that gives, that graces, that invites and provokes us to new ventures, across the oceans, across the risks and challenges of starting and running a college, leading a people, bringing up a family, nurturing young lives. Have a go, trusting in God.

Mervyn lived his life as a follower of Jesus Christ, who proclaimed and lived and died in this providence of God.

And as Jesus's own life was lifted up by God, so too we believe that Mervyn has been lifted up: precious in the sight of God is the life and death of his faithful ones.

Bibliography

Adamson, David. "The University of Glamorgan, Social Exclusion and the South Wales Valleys." In *A Community and Its University, Glamorgan 1913–2003*, edited by Dai Smith and Meic Stephens, 127–48. Cardiff: University of Wales Press, 2003.

Allen, Richard C. et al., eds. *The Religious History of Wales: Religious Life and Practice in Wales from the Seventeenth Century to the Present Day*. Cardiff: Welsh Academic, 2014.

Baptist Union of Victoria. The College and the Churches: A Report from the Ministry Consultative Committee on Improving Relationships and Communications Between the Churches, Union Councils and Whitley College. Hawthorn: Baptist Union of Victoria, 1985.

Barth, Karl. *The Word of God and the Word of Man*. Translated by Douglas Horton. London: Hodder and Stoughton, 1928.

Bassett, T. M. *The Welsh Baptists*. Swansea: Ilston House, 1977.

Beasley-Murray, George. "Worship and the Sacraments." *The Second Holdsworth-Grigg Memorial Lecture*. Parkville: Whitley College, 1970.

Bebbington, David. *Baptists Through the Centuries: A History of a Global People*. Waco, TX: Baylor University Press, 2010.

Birch, Ian. *To Follow the Lambe Wheresoever He Goeth: The Ecclesial Polity of the English Calvinist Baptists 1640–1660*. Monographs in Baptist History 5. Eugene, OR: Pickwick, 2017.

Briggs, John. "Memory, Vision and Mission: What Our Yesterdays Have to Say to Our Todays and Tomorrows." In *Baptist Identity Into the 21st Century: Essays in Honour of Ken Manley*, edited by Frank D. Rees, 38–53. Parkville: Whitley College, 2016.

Bustin, Dennis C. *Paradox and Perseverance: Hanserd Knollys, Particular Baptist Pioneer in Seventeenth Century England*. Milton Keynes: Paternoster, 2006.

Child, R. L. "Ernest Alexander Payne, A Brief Memoir." In *Outlook for Christianity: Essays presented to Dr. Ernest A. Payne on the occasion of his retirement from the office of General Secretary of the Baptist Union of Great Britain and Ireland*, edited by L. G. Champion, 1–8. London: Lutterworth Press, 1967.

Clarke, Anthony J. and Paul S. Fiddes. *Dissenting Spirit: A History of Regent's Park College 1752–2017*, Oxford: Regent's Park College, 2017.

Edge, Findley B. *The Greening of the Church*, Waco, TX: Word Books, 1971.

Farrer, K. T. H. and B. M. Spicer. *The Academic Life of Whitley College: An Interim Report to the Council of the College by the Fellows*. N.p.: 1978.

Featley, Daniel. *The Dipper Dipt: or the Anabaptist Duck't and Plunged Over Head and Ears, at a Disputation in Southwark.* N.p.: 1644.

Frame, Tom. *Losing My Religion: Unbelief in Australia.* Sydney: University of New South Wales Press, 2009.

Freeman, Curtis W. "A Confession for Catholic Baptists." In *Ties That Bind: Life Together in the Baptist Vision*, edited by Gary A. Furr and Curtis W. Freeman, 83–97. Macon, GA: Smyth and Helwys, 1994.

———. *Contesting Catholicity: Theology for Other Baptists.* Waco, TX: Baylor University Press, 2014.

Garrett, Graeme. "Where is '… and Earth'? Learning to Preach in the Anthropocene." In *Baptist Identity Into the 21st Century: Essays in Honour of Ken Manley*, edited by Frank D. Rees, 110–23. Parkville: Whitley College, 2016.

Graham, Billy. "The Marks of the Jesus Movement." *Christianity Today,* 16/3 (November 5, 1971), 5.

Harmon, Steven R. *Towards Baptist Catholicity: Essays on Tradition and the Baptist Vision.* Studies in Baptist History and Thought 27. Milton Keynes: Paternoster, 2006.

Haymes, Brian, et. al. *On Being the Church: Revisioning Baptist Identity.* Studies in Baptist History and Thought 21. Milton Keynes: Paternoster, 2008.

Haymes, Brian. "One Church, One Faith, One Lord: Questions of Baptist Identity. In *Baptist Identity Into the 21st Century: Essays in Honour of Ken Manley*, edited by Frank D. Rees, 25–37. Parkville: Whitley College, 2016.

Himbury, D. Mervyn. "Academic Life at Abergavenny." *Magazine of the South Wales Baptist College, Cardiff* 1 (1964) 12–15.

———. "The Aim of Ministerial Training." *The Victorian Baptist Witness,* December 5, 1967, 8.

———. "Australian Baptists Today." *The Fraternal* 128 (1963) 6–10.

———. "Baptismal Controversies, 1640–1900." In *Christian Baptism: A Fresh Attempt to Understand the Rite in Terms of Scripture, History and Theology*, edited by A. Gilmore, 273–305. London: Lutterworth Press, 1959.

———. "Baptist Initiation." In *Initiation in Australian Churches*, edited by William Tabbernee, 49–53. Melbourne: Victorian Council of Churches, 1984.

———. "Baptists and Their Relations with Other Christians in Australasia." *Foundations* 17 (1974) 36–50.

———. "Baptist Spirituality." In Ryan, Noel J. ed. *Christian Spiritualty: An Ecumenical Reflection*, edited by Noel J. Ryan, 281–93. Melbourne: Dove Communications, 1976.

———. "Bequests to Whitley College Open the Way to Additional Work." *The Victorian Baptist Witness*, July 5, 1966, 6.

———. *The Birth of Whitley College.* Parkville: Whitley College, 1967.

———. *British Baptists: A Short History.* London: Carey Kingsgate, 1962.

———. *Centenary History of the Victorian Baptist Fund 1888-1988.* Melbourne: Victorian Baptist Fund, 1988.

———. "The Christian Magistrate as Viewed by the Separatist and Dissenting Groups Before 1660." BLitt diss., University of Oxford, 1950.

———. "Christ's Holy Community." *The Baptist Quarterly* 15/1 (1953) 11–18.

———. *Churches in Fellowship: A Short History of the English Baptist Associations of South Wales.* Cardiff: The Priory, 1960.

———. "Forms of Baptist Ministerial Education." Parkville: Whitley College, 1970.
———. "The Development of Forms of Baptist Preaching,' *Our Yesterdays,* 11 (2003) 49–64.
———. "The Imprisoned Ministry." *To Minister* (1969) 4.
———. "John Bunyan and the Tradition of Baptist Preaching." In *John Bunyan (1628-1688) A Commemorative Symposium*, edited by Ian Breward, 38–43. Melbourne: Uniting Church Historical Society (Victoria), 1988, 38–43.
———. "Preaching in an Age of Uncertainty." *The Fraternal* 150 (1968) 7–13.
———. "The Religious Beliefs of the Levellers." *The Baptist Quarterly* 15/6 (1954) 269–76.
———. "Serving the Undergraduate." *The Victorian Baptist Witness*, June 5, 1968, 1–2.
———. *The South Wales Baptist College (1807-1957)*. Llandysul: Gomerian, 1957.
———. *The Theatre of the Word: Traditions, Ministry, Future of the Collins Street Baptist Church, Melbourne 1843-1993*. Melbourne: Collins Street Baptist Church, 1993.
———. "Thomas Thomas, 1805–1881." *The Baptist Quarterly* 16/4 (1955) 148–56.
———. "Whitley and I." *Monocle: The Magazine of the Students' Club, Whitley College* 1 (1966) 4–5.
Hudson, Winthrop S. "Who Were the Baptists?" *The Baptist Quarterly* 16/7 (1956) 303–12.
Ivanhoe Baptist Church, *1974 Annual Report*, September 1974.
Jenkins, Geraint H. *A Concise History of Wales*. Cambridge: Cambridge University Press, 2007.
Jones, Alex Gruffydd. *Press, Politics and Society: A History of Journalism in Wales*. Cardiff: University of Wales Press, 1993.
Jones, J. Graham. *The History of Wales*, Cardiff: University of Wales Press, 2014.
Lake, Meredith. *The Bible in Australia: A Cultural History*. Sydney: University of New South Wales Press, 2018.
"London Confession, 1644: the Confession of Faith of Those Churches Which Are Commonly (Though Falsely) Called Anabaptists." In *Baptist Confessions of Faith*, rev. ed. W. L. Lumpkin, 153–71. Valley Forge: Judson Press, 1969.
Macy, Paul Griswold, ed. *The Report of the Second World Conference of Christian Youth: Oslo, Norway, July 22 to 31, 1947*. Geneva: Conference Headquarters, 1947.
Manley, Ken. *From Woolloomooloo to "Eternity": A History of Australian Baptists. Volume 2, A National Church in a Global Community (1914-2005)*. Milton Keynes: Paternoster, 2006.
Matthews, D. Hugh. "Baptists." In *The Religious History of Wales: Religious Life and Practice in Wales from the Seventeenth Century to the Present Day*, edited by Richard C. Allen et al., 41–54. Cardiff: Welsh Academic, 2014.
———. *From Abergavenny to Cardiff: History of the South Wales Baptist College (1806-2006)*. Abertawe: Gwasg Ilston, 2007.
Maung-Lat, John. "The Historical Development of Theological Education Among Victorian Baptists (1862–1988)." DTheol diss., Melbourne College of Divinity, 1989.
McClendon, James W. *Biography as Theology: How Life Stories Can Remake Today's Theology*. Nashville: Abingdon, 1974.
———. *Doctrine: Systematic Theology, Vol. 2*. Nashville: Abingdon, 1994.
Morgan, D. Densil. *The Span of the Cross: Christian Religion and Society in Wales 1914-2000*. Cardiff: University of Wales Press, 2011.

———. *Wales and the Word: Historical Perspectives on Welsh Identity and Religion*. Cardiff: University of Wales Press, 2008.

Morgan, Prys. *The History of the University of Wales, Vol. 3, 1939-1993*. Cardiff: University of Wales Press, 1997.

Otzen, Roslyn. *So Great a Cloud of Witnesses: Ashburton Baptist Church 1934-2014*. Ashburton: Mono Unlimited, 2018.

———. *Whitley: The Baptist College of Victoria 1891-1991*. South Yarra: Hyland House, 1991.

Payne, E. A. "Christian Tasks and Prospects in a World of Change." *The Holdsworth-Grigg Memorial Lecture 1967*. Parkville: Whitley College, 1967.

Piggin, Stuart, and Robert D. Linder. *Attending to the National Soul: Evangelical Christians in Australian History 1914-2014*. Clayton, Victoria: Monash University Publishing, 2020.

Phillips, J. B. *The New Testament in Modern English*. London: Bles, 1958.

Randall, Ian. *Communities of Conviction: Baptist Beginnings in Europe*. Schwarzenfeld: Neufeld, 2009.

Rees, Frank D., ed. *Baptist Identity Into the 21st Century: Essays in Honour of Ken Manley*. Parkville: Whitley College, 2016.

———. "Mervyn Himbury: Principal Preacher." *Our Yesterdays* 28 (2020) 4-27.

———. "The Need and Promise of Christian Preaching." *Evangelical Quarterly* 66/2 (1994) 107-21.

Regent's Park Baptist College, *Annual Report 1948-1949*. Regents Park: Regent's Park Baptist College, 1949.

———. *Annual Report 1949-1950*. Regent's Park: Regent's Park Baptist College, 1950.

Regent's Park College Council, *Council Minute Book*. Regent's Park: Regent's Park Baptist College.

Smith, Dai, and Meic Stephens, eds. *A Community and Its University, Glamorgan 1913-2003*. Cardiff: University of Wales Press, 2003.

Smith, Ewart. *Lewis' School, Pengam: A History*. Abertillery, Gwent: Old Bakehouse, 2013.

South Wales Baptist College. *Annual Report 1944-1945*. South Wales: South Wales Baptist College, 1945.

———. *Annual Report 1956-1957*. South Wales: South Wales Baptist College, 1957.

———. *Annual Report 1958-1959*. South Wales: South Wales Baptist College, 1959.

Tolmie, Murray. *The Triumph of the Saints: The Separate Churches of London, 1616-1649*. Cambridge: Cambridge University Press, 1977.

White, Eryn M. "Calvinist Methodism." In *The Religious History of Wales, Religious Life and Practice in Wales from the Seventeenth Century to the Present Day*, edited by Richard C. Allen et al., 79-91. Cardiff: Welsh Academic, 2014.

Whitley, W. T. *A History of British Baptists*. London: Griffin and Company, 1923.

Williams, J. Gwynn. *The University of Wales, Vol. 2, 1893-1939*. Cardiff: University of Wales, 1997.

Wright, Nigel G. "Baptist Christians: Repentant and Unrepentant." In *Beyond 400: Exploring Baptist Futures*, edited by David J. Cohen and Michael Parsons, 1-16. Eugene, OR: Pickwick, 2011.

———. *Free Church, Free State: The Positive Baptist Vision*. Milton Keynes: Paternoster, 2005.

Index

Abbott, Olwyn C., 154–155, 183, 185, 191, 223, 241
Abraham, 56, 258
Adamson, David, 71
Allen, Richard, 24
Amos, 220
Angus, Joseph, 87
Augustine, 209

Ballard, Paul, 61
Barot, Madeline, 85
Barr, Rev. Jim, 224, 225, 226–229
Barth, Karl, 10, 11–12, 12n9, 14
Baruch, 220
Bassett, T. Myrfyn, 67, 98
Batman, John, 139
Bebbington, David, 27, 32–33, 138
Bergman, Ingmar, 227, 250
Bevan, Blodwen, 52–53
Bevin, Aneurin, 25
Bewsher, Ivan, 22
Birch, Ian, 27–28, 29
Blackburn, Rev. Dr. Geoffrey, 6, 203
Boomsma, Mrs. Christine, 223
Booth, Abraham, 117
Boreham, F. W., 119
Briggs, John, 103
Brockington, Rev. Leonard, 93
Broughton, Dr. Peter, 192, 197
Brown, Professor Basil, 73n24, 144, 151, 182, 191, 223–224
Bunyan, John, 28, 116, 126, 127
Bustin, Dennis C., 111n22
Butler, Joseph, 88

Carey, William, 31, 120
Carmichael, Rev. Ian, 6
Chance, T. W., 78–79
Charlemagne, 209
Charles II, 28, 120
Child, R. I., 93n53
Child, Robert, 89–90, 91, 93
Chislett, Philip, 149, 180
Chowm, Herbert, 90, 90n50
Clarke, Anthony J., 87n44, 87n47, 88n48
Clarke, Bill, 94
Clements, Rev. Dr. Keith, 84n42
Cox, Harvey, 210
Crocket, Alexander, 166, 176
Crocket, Margaret, 166, 176
Cromwell, Oliver, 92, 98, 105, 107, 109, 112, 208
Cross, Anthony, 28

Darwin, Charles, 209
Davies, Dafydd, 66
Davies, David, 45
Davies, Dr. Emlyn, 80–81, 90, 99, 161n44
Davies, George, 61
Davis, David, 35
Denne, Henry, 127, 156
Dillon, Rosemary, 190, 193
Dodd, C. H., 71

Edge, Findley, 32
Edmonds, Rev. Bob, 20
Elijah, 201
Queen Elizabeth I, 24

Evans, Christmas, 35–36, 124, 124n49
Evans, D. M., 36n40
Ezra, 226, 227, 228, 248, 249, 250, 251

Farrer, Dr. Keith, 189, 205
Farrer, K. T. H., 190n16
Featley, Daniel, 115–116, 127
Fiddes, Paul S., 87n44, 87n47, 88n48
Frame, Tom, 136, 137
Freman, Curtis, 31
Fry, Elizabeth, 215

Gandhi, Indira, 162
Garrett, Rev. Dr. Graeme, 6, 19, 20, 180, 186, 187, 189, 190, 194, 196, 197, 211
George, Lloyd, 25
George VI, 48
Gibb, M. A., 111
Gideon, 214, 215, 216, 217, 218
Gill, Dr. Athol, 187, 189, 190, 191, 193, 194, 195, 232
Gill, Judith, 187
Gouldbourne, Ruth, 28
Graham, Billy, 1, 13–14, 124, 137, 139
Griffiths, James, 25
Griffiths, John, 79–80, 81
Griffiths, Maelor, 80
Griffiths, Rev. D. R., 81
Grigg, Albert, 143, 144

Hall, Robert, 116
Ham, John, 207
Ham, Rev. Ron, 12, 149, 198, 228, 251
Hand, Dr. William, 192
Harmon, Steven, 31n25
Haymes, Brian, 28, 30, 31
Helwys, Thomas, 27, 29, 105, 106n8, 119, 127, 162
Himbury, Dewi Michael, 148
Himbury, Eleni, 54, 55
Himbury, John Hywel, 42, 46, 48, 50, 53–55, 178
Himbury, Maelor, 42n52, 52n61, 53, 54, 55, 56, 75n27, 129, 131, 222, 223, 224–225, 230, 237, 254
Himbury, Marion, xiv, 46, 53, 54, 55, 56–57, 68, 73n23, 129, 131, 147, 196, 199, 203, 204, 222, 223, 230, 233, 237, 241, 243, 244, 254, 258
Himbury, Michael, 54, 222, 223, 224, 225, 230, 237, 254
Himbury, Mrs. R., 45
Himbury, Philip Maelor, 53
Himbury, Rachel Sophia, 53, 54
Himbury, Reginald Harry, 40, 42, 43, 47, 55, 57, 177
Himbury, Simon John, 53, 54
Himbury, Sita, 55
Himbury, Thomas Stephen, 53
Hinton, Rev. Grenville, 192
Holdsworth, William, 142
Holly, Merlyn, 212
Hopkins, Dorothy, 153
Hopkins, John, 153, 160, 169, 182, 185, 223, 245
Howard, John, 215
Hudson, Winthrop S., 26–27
Hughes, Rev. Philip, 211, 211n23
Humphries, Barry, 162

Iddles, Percy, 154, 160
Ingham, R., 117–118
Isaiah, 220

Jacob, Henry, 28
James I, 33
James II, 28, 120
King Jehoiakim, 220
Jenkins, Dr. Claude, 91–92
Jenkins, Geraint H., 23, 25, 26n11
Jenkins, Roy, 70
Jeremiah, 7, 220
Jesus Christ, 15, 29, 30, 109, 111, 117, 118, 120, 125, 137, 157, 168, 172, 202, 203, 206, 216, 225, 235, 237, 240, 259, 260
John, Professor Mansel, 100
Johnson, Professor Aubrey, 55, 66, 82, 90
Jones, 45
Jones, Alex Gruffydd, 51n60
Jones, Arthur, 149
Jones, David Ceri, 24
Jones, H. G., 50
Jones, J. Graham, 23–24, 25n9

INDEX

Jones, J. Morgan, 69
Jones, Nana, 57, 146, 178
Jones, Rev. Dr. J. Ithel, 12n9, 39, 57, 100, 146, 178, 186, 211, 212
Joseph (son of Jacob), 205
Judson, Adoniram, 31

Keble, John, 117
Kennedy, Rev. Studdert, 47
Kenworthy, Alex, 149
Kiffin, William, 115, 116
Knollys, Hanserd, 110, 111n22, 127, 156

Lake, Meredith, 137–138
Lawrence, Douglas, 224
Lewis, Mrs. Amelia, 131
Lilburne, John, 108, 111
Linder, Robert D., 137n5
Lloyd, Rev. G. R. M., 90
Llwyd, Morgan, 98
Loyn, Henry, 76, 84
Lumpkin, William L., 116n34
Luther, Martin, 102, 226, 227, 249

Macy, Paul Griswold, 84n42
Manley, Rev. Dr. Ken, 139–140, 150n23, 189, 203, 204n12
Manning, Rev. Jack, 140–141
Marr, Rev. Alan, 224, 229–230, 253–254
Marshall, Dr. Dorothy, 75, 75n26
Matthews, D. Hugh, 33–34, 37, 44, 59n4, 66, 72, 80
May, Alan, 6–7
McAdam, Alice, 206
McClendon, James W., xii, 209, 213
McGowan, Rev. Dr. Tim, 223
McKittrick, Rev. Sam, 147
McMahon, William, 135
Menzies, Dame Pattie, 131
Menzies, Sir Robert, 131, 134, 135, 161, 175, 223, 240
Milton, John, 106
Morgan, 45
Morgan, D. Densil, 35–36, 38, 39n48
Morgan, Rev. Haydn, 45, 47
Morsillo, Julie, xiv, 15–16, 224

Morton, John, 106n8
Moses, 248
Munro, Marita, xiv, 56, 73, 147nn20–21, 187, 237
Murton, John, 105, 119
Myles, 156

Nainby, J. L., 97
Nehemiah, 226, 248
Niebuhr, Reinhold, 85, 216–217
Niebuhr, Richard, 217
Niemöller, Pastor Martin, 85
Niles, D. T., 85
Nunn, Alan, 172

Otzen, Roslyn, 5n2, 144, 145, 151n24, 151n26, 159n40, 160n42, 193nn19–20, 194nn21–22, 234, 258
Owen, Annie, 49n58
Owen, John, 106

Paley, William, 88
Apostle Paul, 30, 194, 202, 206, 207
Paxton, Ian, 172
Payne, Ernest, 56, 81, 85, 89, 91, 93–94, 95, 97, 144, 159, 165, 168
Peake, 109
Pell, Rev. Norman, 186
Phillips, Gwladys Marion, 52
Phillips, J. B., 18n7
Phillips, Marion, 100
Phillips, Rev. Thomas, 79
Phillips, William, 52
Piggin, Stuart, 137
Powell, 156
Powell, Ivor, 139

Randall, Ian, 29
Raven, C. E., 71
Rees, 45
Rees, Frank D., xvi, 10n5, 191n17, 204, 220, 222, 231, 234, 255–260
Rees, J. Frederick, 61
Rees, Merilyn, 258
Rees, William, 75
Roberts, 45
Roberts, Edward, 79, 80, 81, 102

Robertson, Rev. Edwin, 165
Robinson, Theodore, 61, 66
Robinson, Wheeler, 89, 93
Rollinson, Rev. F. H., 97
Rowley, Professor, 90
Rowston, Doug, 149, 180
Rumbold, Dr. Bruce, 177n3, 187, 189, 192, 224

Sanham, Charles, 160
Schmidt, Fräulein, 95
Shakespeare, 216
Shakespeare, J. H., 122
Sherry, Brian, 5n1
Smith, Dai, 68n15
Smith, Ewart, 48, 49
Smith, Mr., 251
Smyth, John, 27, 105, 156, 214
Spicer, Professor Brian M., 189, 190n16
Spurgeon, Charles Haddon, 117, 124, 142
St. Catherine of Alexandria, 89
Stephanakis, Charles, 54
Stephanakis, Eleni, 53
Stephanakis, Soula, 54
Stephens, Meic, 68n15
Stevens, Geoffrey, 153–154, 160, 223
Sutton, Rev. Barrie, 21

't Hooft, W. A. Visser, 85
Taylor, Dr. Michael, 177
Taylor, Rev. Gardiner C., 8, 169
Temple, William, 71
Thomas, 45

Thomas, Hywel, 83
Thomas, Idris, 3, 41, 51, 98
Thomas, Maida, 206
Thomas, Olwen (Oliven), 40, 41
Thomas, Rachel, 53, 131
Thomas, Rev. Micah, 37, 59
Thomas, Thomas, 60
Thompson, J. C. (Cliff), 141, 147
Tombes, John, 116
Troeltsch, 119
Tuck, Bernard, 154

Walwyn, William, 111
Warn, Clare, 244
Warn, Rev. Milton, 7, 153, 155, 161, 185, 193, 196, 224–225, 243–245
Watson, Professor John (Jock), 144, 151, 185, 186
Watson, Rev. Barry, 21
Wesley, John, 120
Whale, Dr. Gwen, 75, 75n26
White, Eryn M., 25n7
Whitefield, George, 120
Whiting, Mr., 95
Whitley, W. T., 98, 106n8, 117, 118–119, 142
Williams, J. Gwynn, 67n14, 69, 70n18, 71–72
Williams, Rev. Cheryl, 204
Williams, Vicar, 41
"Woodbine Willy." *See* Kennedy, Rev. Studdert
Wren, Sir Christopher, 245
Wright, Nigel, 29
Wroth, William, 33

www.ingramcontent.com/pod-product-compliance
Lightning Source LLC
Chambersburg PA
CBHW051631230426

43669CB00013B/2254